FOUR SHOTS
IN THE NIGHT

'One of the most compelling books I've read in a very long time. An absolutely extraordinary tale of secret intelligence, infiltration and murder, *Four Shots in the Night* is a brilliantly pieced-together psychological drama that is all the more gripping – and unsettling – for being real rather than fiction. The story is expertly woven together, exploring the characters and motivations of the four main protagonists into a truly page-turning, compulsive and also profoundly moving narrative. Superb.'

James Holland

'Gripping, urgent, superbly reported and brilliantly written. Henry Hemming unfolds a true story of violence, politics and spycraft that sits right at the edge of journalism and history.'

Dan Jones

Also by Henry Hemming

Our Man in New York
M
Churchill's Iceman
Together
In Search of the English Eccentric
Misadventure in the Middle East

HENRY HEMMING

FOUR SHOTS
IN THE
NIGHT

A TRUE STORY OF ESPIONAGE, MURDER
AND JUSTICE IN NORTHERN IRELAND

QUERCUS

First published in Great Britain in 2024 by

QUERCUS

Quercus Editions Ltd
Carmelite House
50 Victoria Embankment
London EC4Y 0DZ

An Hachette UK company

A CIP catalogue record for this book is available from the British Library

HB ISBN 978 1 52942 675 5
TPB ISBN 978 1 52942 676 2
Ebook ISBN 978 1 52942 678 6

Every effort has been made to contact copyright holders. However, the publishers
will be glad to rectify in future editions any inadvertent omissions brought to their attention.

PICTURE CREDITS (in order of appearance): 1 – Kaveh Kazemi/Getty Images; 2 – courtesy of the author;
3 – © Eamon Melaugh (source: CAIN); 4 – Pacemaker Press; 5 – images4media.com;
6 – Independent News And Media/Getty Images; 7 – Douglas Armstrong; 8 – © National Museums
NI Ulster Museum Collection; 9 – Walter Bird/© National Portrait Gallery, London;
10 – Hugh Jordan; 11 – Paul Faith/PA; 12 – April30/Getty; 13 – PA Images/Alamy Stock Photo;
14 – PA Images/Alamy Stock Photo; 15 – Darron Mark/Stockimo/Alamy Stock Photo;
16 – PA Images/Alamy Stock Photo; 17 – *Derry Daily*; 18 – PA Images/Alamy Stock Photo;
19 – Paul Faith/Bloomberg/Getty; 20 – Alamy Stock Photo; 21 – PA Images/Alamy Stock Photo;
22 – PA Images/Alamy Stock Photo

10 9 8 7 6 5 4 3 2 1

Typeset by CC Book Production

Printed and bound in Great Britain by Clays Ltd, Elcograf S.p.A.

Papers used by Quercus Editions Ltd are from well-managed forests and other responsible sources.

For Jonathan Conway

And if the world were black or white entirely
And all the charts were plain
Instead of a mad weir of tigerish waters,
A prism of delight and pain,
We might be surer where we wished to go
Or again we might be merely
Bored but in brute reality there is no
Road that is right entirely.

From 'Entirely' by Louis MacNeice, 1940

Contents

DERRY/
LONDONDERRY

Derry/
Londonderry
Belfast

Dublin

0   ½ mile
0   1 km

Dorothy's home

Grianán of Aileach
(5 km)

River Foyle

Brendan Duddy's
home

Rose Hegarty's
home

St Eugene's
Cathedral

Ebrington
Barracks

Hollyhall
Road

Martin McGuinness's home

Free Derry Corner

Peggy McGuinness's home

Sinn Féin
Cable Street office

Derry City Cemetery

Brandywell
Greyhound track

N

Prologue

In the small hours of 25 May 1986, in a watery, windswept corner of the United Kingdom, a man with tape over his eyes is helped out of a vehicle. On either side of him is a sweep of Neolithic moorland. We will never know exactly what is said to him as he steadies himself in the darkness, the pitch of the words and how they land, but, most likely, he is made to feel safe and is told that everything is going to be okay.

This man is a British agent. A spy. For more than six years, he has had secret meetings with his handlers and passed on details of what he has seen and heard. His information has moved up the intelligence food chain. Some of it has been picked over in the uppermost reaches of Whitehall. After his sudden disappearance several weeks ago, a note was sent to the prime minister, Margaret Thatcher. 'We assess that he is an extremely high-priority target,' she read. 'The relevant agencies at the ports and airports have been alerted.'¹ On seeing this, she underlined the word 'alerted' twice, before smudging the ink.

Now the same agent is walking along a country lane, his cover blown. His eyes are still covered by tape that pulls at the skin on his face. He has spent the last three days in captivity and does not know where he is being taken or what will happen to him. The rain falls easily around him and the night is quiet, almost without sound.

There are several men behind him in the gloom. At least one of them is armed.

The agent knows a little about his captors, but for the most part they have hidden themselves behind a screen of gruff inscrutability. Perhaps as they make their way through the night, he thinks about who they are, if they come from the same part of the country as him, and whether they will be going home later to put their children to bed. It is unlikely that he asks himself if one of them could also be a British spy.

The agent's body was found the next day by a local farmer. No attempt had been made to hide the corpse. It was not that kind of murder. The farmer told the police that he was a heavy sleeper and had not heard the shots in the night.[2]

Word spread, and men from the nearby village began to gather by the police cordon. Occasionally, one would tap the briar of his pipe, tug on his flat cap, or plunge his hands deeper into his coat pockets. Otherwise, they were still and said little. A feathery rain fell as detectives and policemen moved about. Later, a television crew arrived to record a segment for the evening news.

The victim was not from around there, which softened the shock for those who had come up from the village; but at the same time it introduced a note of curiosity. Who was he? Who killed him? Why was there masking tape over his eyes? The police had no forensic leads and very little evidence. There were rumours about who was responsible, as there will be after a crime like this, because the idea of a murder without a solution is a kind of torment, but nobody came forward with incriminating information and the police did not make any arrests.

If every secret has its own weight, some have a way of becoming heavier with time. More than a decade later, a man who thought he knew more than the police about this murder decided to speak out.

He contacted a journalist. Although he did not reveal everything, not at first, he said enough. He explained that one of his reasons for coming forward was that he had known the victim. The other was that he had a pretty good idea of who might have killed him. He believed that the murderer was another British agent: that there had been two spies inside the same extremist organisation, and one had killed the other.

Eighteen years later, in 2016, an English policeman on the brink of retirement began to look into what had happened that night. His name was Jon Boutcher. As he himself put it, he had been around the block a few times. He was measured and tough, a seasoned professional, and ambitious in a way that was not always obvious on first meeting him.

This would be the biggest job that Boutcher had ever taken on – because he was not just looking into this one murder, but a string of killings linked to the same undercover agent: a mysterious figure referred to in the media as 'Stakeknife'. Boutcher's task was to build a criminal case against this individual. What he did not yet know was that this would become the largest murder investigation in British history. At that early stage, he was only interested in finding out what Stakeknife might have done and, if it was anything like what had been alleged in the media, making sure this man spent the rest of his life in jail.

Note to the Reader

Four Shots in the Night is the true story of a murder: the events leading up to it, the act itself, and the kaleidoscopic fallout in the years that followed. It is based on declassified government papers, judicial reviews, police and news reports, academic articles, memoirs, historical accounts, and television documentaries, as well as my own interviews with some of those involved. Most of these conversations took place under the Chatham House Rule, or a version of it, in which interviewees agreed to be quoted or paraphrased on the condition of anonymity. Speech in quotation marks was either passed on to me directly or came from a published source. References are at the back of the book. The conversations I had with former state employees were focused on material already in the public domain, and I have left out anything that might be defamatory, life-threatening, in contempt of court, or damaging to national security.

With most stories, that would be enough. Time to get on with it. But this one has a different profile. Most of the narrative is set in Northern Ireland during a conflict often referred to, with grim understatement, as 'the Troubles'. It began in August 1969 and ended with the Good Friday Agreement in April 1998. 3,720 people were killed, a further 47,541 were injured, and an estimated 10,000 men and women were imprisoned. Many more experienced the Troubles in some other, refracted way. They might have had their homes searched, been pushed up against a wall and frisked, or arrested and held without charge for up to a week. At the very least, they spent a part of their lives carrying within themselves a heavy sense of uncertainty about the future and when this was going to end.

The Troubles is, by a country mile, the least understood conflict in recent British history, as well as the bloodiest and the longest. The scale of it is easy to overlook, as well as the impact. More than a quarter of a million combatants were involved, and almost half of the British military veterans who served in the region have since received counselling or psychotherapy.[1] In a study of mental health in twenty-six countries that had recently experienced conflict, Northern Ireland was shown to have the highest rate of post-traumatic stress disorder.[2] It is a sad fact that during the two decades since the end of the Troubles, more people in Northern Ireland have taken their own lives than were killed in the conflict itself. This period of the past is not yet history, and for many people the memory of what happened is still undigested and raw.

Some of those who lived through the Troubles might ask themselves, on reading that this is a true story, which version of the truth I have in mind and what my link to this is. Put another way – whose side am I on? In those moments when two accounts seem to point in different directions, which way am I more likely to lean?

I have no personal connection to this story. I am not related to anyone involved and have no close family ties to the island of Ireland. I do not belong to a political party, have never served in the armed forces or worked for the British or Irish government. Nor am I Protestant or Catholic. But it is not enough to say I am neutral, because, well, nobody is.

The journalist and author Janet Malcolm once compared writing non-fiction to renting a house. You cannot make structural changes to your temporary home, but you fill it with your possessions. In the same way, the factual architecture of a story does not change, but as a writer, you furnish it with some of your past.[3] In that sense, what have I brought to this narrative? Which cultural belongings do I have boxed up on the pavement, ready to be moved in?

My ancestry is mostly Scottish and Canadian, but I am English. I grew up in and around London during the 1980s and 1990s, at a time when Northern Ireland seemed hard to understand and further away than it really was. As a child, I remember how the mood in the room would change when Gerry Adams appeared on the evening news with his voice dubbed by an actor. At school, I sang Anglican hymns and learned a lot about the Tudors and the Second World War (and almost nothing about the British Empire). At home, I heard about grandparents and ancestors who fought in world wars and others who settled or served in faraway British colonies. Otherwise, I was on a rich diet of books, films, and stories – so many stories, but well-crafted ones with hooks and punchlines often involving British men and women in exotic locations. They were the heroes and were usually made out to be level-headed, compassionate, and fair. Without wading into a judgement on this, that was my starting point.

To anyone from Northern Ireland, this kind of childhood marks me down as pure 'Brit'. Surely it would be hard for me to have any real sympathy in this story beyond the experiences of British officials, soldiers, and spies.

Yes and no, but mainly no. I don't remember this way of seeing the world as one that was ever made to feel imprisoning. It was there to be challenged. Nor was it as narrow as I might have made it sound. Bound up in that tapestry of stories were bright flecks of opposition, tales in which somebody fights for, writes about, or becomes part of a group which is the victim of forces greater than itself. These are the stories I remember being taken in by more than any others. And who wouldn't be? We all love an underdog. I have always been drawn to the opposite point of view, which is why I have spent so much of my life writing about people who were in some way part of the establishment before they turned against an established way of doing things.

In the story that follows, I have tried to look for the strengths in those who were caught up in what happened, as well as the weaknesses, those moments of bravery that stand out against a background of fear, and a capacity for love that is often obscured by a desire to fight. Or, as the writer Michaela Coel put it, in words that became something of a mantra for me when writing this book, 'There's good and bad in everything and everyone. I hope that makes sense.'[4]

PART ONE:

CONTACT

1

Franko

Frank Hegarty is out walking his dog early one day when he notices a figure ahead in the distance. It is a dark, cold morning in February. Winter is tightening its grip on the landscape, and the lane glitters with frost. Frank has just turned onto the Hollyhall Road, an ancient path that meanders along the edge of the city, a place he knows as Derry, although others call it Londonderry. He is used to seeing people out at this early hour, and the person he has spotted is walking a dog, which explains why he is here. But his presence catches in Frank's mind. There is something familiar about him. At the same time, Frank cannot think where this individual has come from and how he has ended up on the Hollyhall Road. Frank did not see him join it, and no lanes feed into this section of the road. Yet there he is, barely a hundred yards away, a man and his dog who seem to have appeared out of nowhere.

Frank and his greyhound make a striking pair. Blue is a triumph of muscular minimalism. She floats along by Frank's side, her paws making only the lightest connection with the ground. Frank has a firmer gait and walks with a mild stagger on account of his bad back. He is neither tall nor overweight, but what locals call 'well made'.

Just a few months shy of his fortieth birthday, Frank has a steady and dependable face, dark hair, and a wolfish grin. A word that will often come up in descriptions of him is 'approachable'. He is the kind of open-faced, affable man who people go to for directions or fall into conversation with if they see him alone in the pub, cigarette in hand, his body angled against the bar. Some will say he's a maverick, others will tell you he is 'dead on', meaning he's decent and good-natured. But nobody will tell you he's perfect. He has made mistakes. And, like all of us, he has his secrets.

The cold fills Frank's lungs and reaches to the back of his throat. He can see his breath making miniature, silent explosions in the air ahead of him as the outlines of familiar trees rear up on either side of him out of the gloom. As he moves further up the lane, through the gothic half-light of the dawn, the figure ahead and his dog seem to be a little closer than before. Perhaps Frank can hear the crackling sound of this other man's feet on the frosty road.

One thing that people who know Frank Hegarty can never agree on is what to call him. His doting mother calls him 'Frankie'. The priest prefers 'Francis'. Almost everyone else knows him as 'Franko' or 'The General', after General Franco, the Spanish military dictator. Most people in Frank's world have a nickname. 'Kinker', 'Smiler', 'Cheeser', 'Weezer', 'Dutchie', 'Hogie', 'Psycho', 'Stud' . . . Your nickname is there to bring you down a peg or two, and is proof that you belong. But a nickname only works if it is in some way funny. The joke here, in calling Frank The General, is in the difference between Spain's Franco – chest out, pompous, medals everywhere – and Derry's own Franko, a man with a less regimented take on life, and just about the last person in Northern Ireland you can imagine taking orders from anyone.

Frank Hegarty's life has taken him all over the island of Ireland. He has friends in the unlikeliest places from his days driving a lorry, or his trips to see the coursing at Clonmel and the racing at

Lifford and Brandywell. Frank has spent many hours on the road, but Derry is his talisman and is where he belongs. This border town at the edge of the United Kingdom – Monaco without the money, as a local journalist will later call it – is the furnace in which he has been forged and he cannot imagine living anywhere else.

By now, Frank and his dog are further up the Hollyhall Road, and so, too, is the person ahead. But he is nearer now. Either Frank is walking faster than usual or the other man is slowing down. Around them, everything remains quiet, which allows the smallest sounds to take on an outsized significance. Frank can hear the bassline thud of his boots and the occasional trill of birdsong. The music of these morning walks is usually shattered by the noise of an approaching car. On hearing it, Frank will bundle up Blue or slip on her lead. But not today. Today the road is empty.

What is in Frank's mind? At some point his thoughts will turn to Blue, the handsome greyhound by his side. Frank has a way with animals. He grew up in a house with dogs, and as a boy he kept pigeons. It was clear from an early age that he had an intuitive sense of how to look after animals, but since he was a teenager the creature he has prized above any other has been the greyhound.

The dog by Frank's side is the finest he has ever owned. Taking Blue for a walk is, for him, like stepping out with a model. He is used to appreciative looks from passers-by, some of them tinged with envy. In greyhound-speak, Blue is 'useful'. She has started to win races and might soon move up a grade. For every greyhound owner, this first rumble of success with a dog will trigger an avalanche of questions. What should Frank be feeding her in the run-up to the next race? Has he cleaned out the kennel, properly washed her feet – as in *properly* washed them, getting the brush right in between the toes – and has he remembered to give her the right medicines and jabs so that she doesn't take sick? Should he be holding her back to get her up to fitness or pushing to have her on the card sooner? Is that the start of a limp, and how are her ears, her teeth, her nails?

Blue stands out for being quick, but she is also unusual for being a 'blue', which is to say she has a grey coat. For most greyhound men, owning a blue is like starting each day by walking under a ladder. It is bad luck, almost like a curse. But Frank does not see it like that. Nor does owning a blue lessen his popularity within the 'doggy' world of local greyhound men: a gnarly, watchful community presided over by men in muddy boots with deep Donegal accents, most of whom think of Frank as 'a good man', 'a man you can trust', 'a kind man'.

Frank Hegarty is good with his hands. He will see to your dog if it is wounded and you cannot afford the services of a vet. He knows how to sew up minor lacerations, the type of injury a dog might pick up after catching itself on barbed wire. Even if he doesn't always get it right, he knows roughly what he's doing. He won't ask for payment, but he's unlikely to be offended if you offer him a few pounds in return for his time.

If Frank can earn a bit on the side, then he will. Like so many Catholic men in Derry – Derrymen, as they like to be known – Frank has recently been out of work. He has clocked some hours as a mechanic, but nothing steady. He is always on the lookout for an inside racing tip, some scrap of intelligence that will set him up for a betting coup. Gambling and greyhounds go hand in hand, and, like most of his fellow enthusiasts, he will place a bet when he can.

The other man is closer still as Frank Hegarty continues up the hill. If Frank was someone who had hung on to the childhood stories he had been told about ghosts, raths, and other strange sightings, tales of the *púca* – the shape-shifting trickster spirits who lurk at the edge of the city, in places like this – he might feel some tug of doubt about this mysterious figure who seems to have appeared out of thin air. Instead, he wants to catch up with him. Frank is gregarious. Anyone who knows him will tell you that he's the kind of person whose reaction on seeing a fellow dog-walker will be to start a conversation.

The distance between the two men becomes smaller. Over to his right, Frank can see broad fields that race away to the horizon in flowing strokes, each one the kind of vivid, iridescent green you rarely see outside of Ireland or the Scottish Lowlands. To his left is the Glenowen estate, a cluster of mean-looking buildings set out over the slope like gravestones. Plumes of peat smoke stream out of the chimneys, close enough to see but not smell. Between the buildings, Frank can glimpse the view out over Derry which comes at him like a stuttering slide show. Over at one end of it, hidden from sight, is the River Foyle, wide as a lake and silvery in the morning light. There are fishing boats and gulls overhead that look like ash above a bonfire. Just below the line of houses are the famous Derry city walls.

Even if he cannot see them, Frank knows that there are British soldiers dotted along these dark stone ramparts. The presence of these troops can sometimes feel like a taunt. The thought of them, with their guns and their gear, immense and unassailable behind their fortifications, is enough to put anyone on edge. As one Derryman said of these troops, 'they were Roman soldiers on Hadrian's Wall and I was one of the savages'.[1] For anyone like Frank, a local Catholic man, one of the hardest parts of living with these soldiers is the feeling they are looking down on you.

Frank and his dog reach the stub of woodland beyond the Glenowen estate, with the other man just a little further on. The vista over Derry disappears and the light shifts. So, too, does the sound. For a moment, it is as if they are enclosed. Rainwater streams past in gullies beneath the road, filling the air with an ethereal shimmering sound. On one side is a wall camouflaged by ivy. On the other, a crumbling barbed-wire fence. For the first time, the city feels distant.

Now that Frank is even closer, he can see that the figure up ahead is smoking a pipe. This detail somehow makes him look more approachable, more knowable. Perhaps Frank thinks about how to start the conversation. A quick – *Morning, how you going, cold today.* Or the other man might begin with a remark about Blue (most people do).

At last, with the distance between them smaller than ever, the man turns around.

Frank can see his face, and he knows at once that they have never met. There might also be something in the way this man turns to him that feels off, some tell that hints at the idea he is about to do more than acknowledge Frank's presence.

The other man opens his mouth to speak, and in an accent that is not from Derry, more like one you might hear in Liverpool, he says:

'Alright, Franko.'

2

Cups of Tea

Eleven years earlier

One day in August 1969, a group of British soldiers fastened their helmets, gathered their gas masks, and checked the safety catches on their 7.62mm self-loading rifles, knowing, as they did this, that they were about to make history. They belonged to the Prince of Wales's Own Regiment of Yorkshire, and had been sent to Derry several weeks earlier, a city marked on their maps as Londonderry. Their orders that day were to relieve the police in the Bogside district of the city, where a riot had been under way for the best part of two days. This was the first time in more than forty years that armed soldiers had been sent out onto British streets. Nobody knew what the reaction would be, least of all them.

The soldiers clambered into a jumble of waiting jeeps and Bedford lorries. It was just after 5 o'clock. The sun was out. The diesel engines made a reassuring growl as the flotilla of khaki-coloured vehicles left the barracks. People stopped to stare as the convoy trundled past. Looking out of the back of their vehicles, the soldiers could see buildings that were still smouldering from the previous night's disturbances and overturned cars on the street, many of them blackened and charred with their windows burned out. Rubble was strewn over the road like crumbs on a table, and ahead of them, the dark star leading them to their destination, they could make out a grey cloud over the Bogside.

Most of these soldiers were used to seeing cities ravaged by fighting like this. The British Army had spent the last two decades either preparing for a Soviet invasion of Europe or attending to the break-up of the British Empire. They had fought against the Stern Gang and Irgun in Mandatory Palestine, the Mau Mau in Kenya, the National Liberation Front and Front for the Liberation of South Yemen, the Ethniki Organosis Kyprion Agoniston in Cyprus, and an array of communist organisations in Oman and Malaya. The troops in those trucks were familiar with the sight of disfigured urban landscapes, but they had never thought they would encounter it here, in their own country.

The British Army had no experience in policing its own streets, which was why the prime minister, Harold Wilson, had been so reluctant to use them in Northern Ireland. But he felt there was no alternative. The violence in Derry as well as Belfast was beginning to spiral, and a failure to act would surely lead to more deaths. Sending in the army appeared to be the least bad option.

The soldiers arrived at the Bogside fifteen minutes after they had left their barracks. Most wore black gas masks over their heads as they jumped out of their vehicles and looked for cover.

No gunfire.

That was the first thing they noticed.

No bricks or petrol bombs arcing through the air towards them either.

Then came a low rumbling sound from the direction of the Bogside, steady at first before growing in intensity. It was hard to read to begin with, before it crossed over into the realm of familiarity, sounding like something you might hear in a football stadium after a goal has been scored. The soldiers were being welcomed as liberators. The roar went up a few decibels as the local police, the 'peelers', staggered off to get some rest. The soldiers removed their gas masks. The adrenaline started to subside.

Then a crowd of Derrymen began to march past. They looked exhausted, sweaty, and jubilant, and they were singing at the tops of their voices. The soldiers might have been expecting to hear an Irish rebel song about rising up to smash the British Army. But instead the protesters sang the American gospel song 'We Shall Overcome', an anthem in the US civil rights movement, and a reminder of why they were here.

Several years earlier, a handful of people had set up Northern Ireland's first civil rights group. Most of them were young, and they included Protestants as well as Catholics. They were inspired by the recent activism of Martin Luther King Junior and others in the United States, but they were also driven by a much deeper feeling of historic injustice which they had carried for most of their lives. Their aim was, simply, to end discrimination against Catholics in the region.

At the time, Catholics in Northern Ireland made up about a third of the population. One of them was Frank Hegarty, then aged twenty-seven and living just up the road from the Bogside. Although Frank had not been persecuted by his Protestant neighbours when growing up in Derry during the 1940s and 1950s – he had not been locked up, attacked, or physically injured because of his religious background – he encountered at different points in his life a fine mesh of prejudice. This affected where he lived, who he spent time with, his political power, and the jobs available to him. At times, the discrimination against Catholics like him was hard to legislate against and winkingly subtle. At others, it was as clear as the sun in the sky.

'People shrugged their shoulders and cracked jokes about it,' one local activist said.[1] Everybody knew what was going on. But it was hard to see how this was ever going to change. 'You are now landing in Northern Ireland,' went the joke, 'put back your watches three hundred years.' This administrative region of the United Kingdom – for that's what it was, not a country, a state, or a province in its own right – could sometimes feel like a Sleepy Hollow in which time stood still. For most of the 1960s, with other parts of the world caught up in post-imperial struggles for nationhood, ideological and cultural revolutions, a nuclear arms race, or plans to put a man on the moon, this corner of the United Kingdom seemed to be stuck. But towards the end of the 1960s, that was no longer true.

Local civil rights activists organised themselves into groups and began to stage protests and marches, including one in Derry, in 1968, calling for 'British rights for British citizens'. Those who took part were attacked by the police, and the footage of this was broadcast all over the world. The international condemnation that followed only added to the feeling among them that this was a battle they were starting to win.

More clashes followed in Northern Ireland between civil rights campaigners and the local police, the Royal Ulster Constabulary, a force dominated by Protestants. As the violence intensified, it became more sectarian. Although Protestants in the region outnumbered Catholics by nearly two to one, if you combined the population for the north and south of Ireland, then Protestants were in a minority. This was the paradox at the heart of their identity. Many of the region's Protestants, referred to in the media as 'Unionists' or 'Loyalists', because they were loyal to the union between Great Britain and Northern Ireland, felt that they were both in charge *and* under siege. They had grown up around the idea that they were locked in an existential struggle for survival, and that ceding ground to their Catholic neighbours was like turning against their own side. 'No surrender!' was as much a battle cry as a manifesto for some diehard Protestants, including many of those serving with the police.

By the summer of 1969, the violence in Northern Ireland was

starting to race away from itself. People all over Northern Ireland were bringing down from the attics of their minds some of their darkest fantasies of purity and sameness. Seven people were killed during two nights of riots in Belfast. In the following weeks, more than 1,800 families, most of them Catholic, were given just hours to clear out of their homes before the buildings were set alight.

A seven-year-old Protestant boy who lived through that summer, and was changed by it, was the actor and director Kenneth Branagh. 'I'd never had to worry before,' he later said of his childhood in Belfast. 'What it signalled for me was this sense that the world could spin out of control very quickly.'[2]

Northern Ireland had gone from being one of the most peaceful places on earth, with an average of just five murders a year, to a land stalked by the spectre of violence.[3] One journalist picked up on a new scent on the streets of Belfast. It was, he wrote, 'the odour of the Blitz, one that the people of London and Dresden had come to know a generation earlier'.[4] Parts of Northern Ireland had begun to look, smell, and sound like a war zone. On 14 August 1969, the local government asked the British prime minister to send in the army. Several hours later, a company of British troops set out for the Bogside, marking the start of 'Operation Banner', the name given to the British Army's deployment to Northern Ireland.

The soldiers who arrived in the Bogside were not really sure what to make of the enthusiastic reception they had received and the sight of protesters singing 'We Shall Overcome'. 'People were waving at us and being very friendly towards us,' one soldier remembered. 'They were even wolf whistling.' He was ordered by his commanding officer to occupy part of Derry's city walls. 'Then they started to shout up the walls, "Are you hungry?" "Yes." So we sent down a rope and they tied baskets onto it and put fish and chips and flasks of coffee in them. It was wonderful.'[5]

Thousands of soldiers arrived in the region over the next few days. All were taken aback by the warmth of the welcome. Many Catholics saw the British Army as a buffer between themselves and the police, and were genuinely pleased to see them patrolling the streets. Troops stationed in an observation post in Belfast, on top of the Divis Tower, were passed entire meals by local residents, including Ulster frys, the gut-busting cooked breakfast of soda bread, potato pancakes, bacon, sausages, black pudding, tomatoes, and eggs. One Catholic woman lent her house keys to soldiers from a nearby army base, saying they could pop in whenever they liked to make themselves tea.[6] Young soldiers all over Northern Ireland enjoyed a similar reception and were greeted with sandwiches, iced buns, and cups of sugary tea. Many of them couldn't help but sympathise with the people who were trying so hard to make them feel at home. 'We all had a feeling there was injustice over housing, jobs, education and even justice,' one soldier remembered. 'I think we certainly felt that we were on the side of the Catholics.'[7]

British troops were soon going out on patrol without either helmets or body armour. They manned roadblocks and checkpoints. They built temporary barbed-wire fences in Belfast that were known as 'peace walls' to separate the warring neighbourhoods. Most of these interventions had a hopeful, *ad hoc* feel to them. 'We were operating blindly,' one army officer admitted. 'The game plan was developing quite literally on a day-to-day basis.'[8] The British were not following some detailed blueprint for peace and had very little sense of what was coming. Intelligence, according to one report, was the army's 'weakest link'.[9]

But whatever it was they were doing, it seemed to be working, and the violence rapidly became less intense. Major political reforms were announced in Westminster, including plans for a new housing authority in Northern Ireland and wholesale reform of the police. The way elections were held would come under review, and the government promised new laws that would tackle discrimination against Catholics.

By the end of 1969, the British Army's peacekeeping mission to Northern Ireland was beginning to look like a success. No soldiers had died, and almost half of the military units which had been rushed out to the region in the summer were being moved on. Newspaper editors recalled their reporters. A sense of hope was reaching out to the horizon, and the British Army's deployment to Northern Ireland felt like a story in search of an ending.

Beneath the surface, though, a different and much darker picture was developing. At the end of 1969, with the army looking to leave, there was a split inside the Irish Republican Army, better known as the IRA. This was the nearly defunct revolutionary group which for years had opposed Britain's presence in Ireland and the existence of the Irish government. The IRA at that time believed mainly in persuasion. Its aim was to start by bringing together working-class Catholics and Protestants, and then begin a military campaign to unite the island.

In December 1969, a faction called the 'Provisional IRA' broke away from the original organisation. This splinter group was younger and angrier, and was shaped around an absolute commitment to violence. Its volunteers agreed to launch a fresh military campaign. There were more bombs than before and the casualty rate began to rise. With every new death, the chances of the British Army leaving the region became smaller, and with each day that the soldiers remained in Northern Ireland, the popularity of this new and deadlier incarnation of the IRA seemed to grow. Known at first as the 'Provisionals', or the 'Provos', this faction of the paramilitary group would soon be referred to in the media simply as the IRA.

3

Quagmire

Two years later

It's a spring day in 1972, and Frank Hegarty is part of an IRA parade that's moving slowly through the streets of Derry. The weather is overcast and uninviting, but the turnout that day is huge and the atmosphere crackles with intent. Frank is near the front of the procession, just ahead of the main body of IRA volunteers in black berets, bright white belts, polished boots, and heavy green jackets. (No balaclavas; they would come later.)

Frank Hegarty is not in uniform. Instead, he is wearing a collarless shirt and fleece-lined anorak. He looks like a man who takes care with his appearance. Frank also gives the impression of being completely relaxed in this setting, like someone who has found a place where he belongs. Some of the people who have come to see the parade recognise him as he marches past. But none can tell just by watching The General what his role in all this could be.

It is hard for any of the spectators to know who is 'involved' in the IRA and who is just tagging along. That's the point. You're not supposed to brag to your neighbours about having been sworn into the IRA. But taking part in this parade, held each year to commemorate the 1916 Easter Rising, when a group of Irish revolutionaries declared independence in Dublin before being overwhelmed by the British, is a way of letting people know that you are, at least, somewhere in the mix.

Another man out on the streets that day is the former butcher's boy who has recently taken control of a local IRA brigade. He is someone Frank has come to know in the previous few months. He has curly red hair and terrible eyesight. He is taller than most of the other men in that parade and, like Frank, you're unlikely to see him in uniform. His name is Martin McGuinness.

Frank Hegarty and Martin McGuinness are both relatively new to this. Both men's parents lived through the partition of Ireland in 1921, which led to the birth of the Irish Free State, containing twenty-six of the island's thirty-two counties, and Northern Ireland, made up of the remaining six, but none of them came to think of themselves as 'republicans'. Neither the McGuinnesses nor the Hegartys believed it was right to use violence in the struggle for a united Ireland. Martin McGuinness had not grown up on stories of relatives planting bombs and risking their lives to force the British government out of Northern Ireland, and nor had Frank Hegarty.

The sight of Frank in the parade comes as a surprise to some people only because it is so completely at odds with his past. After leaving school, Frank became a lorry driver. He spent most of his twenties, which coincided with the 1960s, steering heavy articulated vehicles through the labyrinth of byways, tracks, and A-roads around Derry. His father, Frank Senior, worked for the same company. Often, they were together on the same jobs. Frank was married, and had what appeared to be a steady life.

But by 1972, that has changed. Frank no longer has a job and his marriage is effectively over. He is living with his parents again in the Hegarty family home, a larger-than-average house in Rosemount, a well-to-do area up the hill from the more flyblown neighbourhoods of Creggan and the Bogside. The mood in the city around him is unlike anything he ever experienced as a child. There is anger in the air, a roiling sense of injustice that can be traced back to what happened here, in Derry, just two months ago.

On 30 January 1972, soldiers from the 1st Battalion, Parachute Regiment, known as '1 Para', opened fire on a crowd of mostly Catholic protesters, and in less than half an hour had shot twenty-six people. Fourteen of them would die of their injuries. None had been armed. The casualties on what became known as 'Bloody Sunday' ranged from John Johnston, a fifty-nine-year-old who had not been part of the protest, but was on his way to see a friend, through to the first to be killed, seventeen-year-old John Duddy, shot in the back as he ran away from the soldiers. You would have to go back to 1819, in Manchester, when armed cavalry charged at a crowd of protesters in the Peterloo Massacre, to find a time when more British people were killed by their own armed forces.

Bloody Sunday was enough in itself to turn most Catholics against the soldiers patrolling their streets. But what made this so much more troubling for someone like Frank was that it seemed to be part of a pattern. Troops from the same unit, 1 Para, had been responsible the year before for the deaths of nine people in Belfast, in what was called the 'Ballymurphy Massacre'. One of those killed was Father Hugh Mullan, a much-loved local priest, who was shot as he tried to help an injured man. Another was a forty-four-year-old mother of eight, Joan Connolly, who had once offered sandwiches and tea to passing troops, and whose eldest daughter had recently married a British soldier. Stories were also rippling out across the region about the army's treatment of the 'Hooded Men', a group of fourteen young Catholics who had been taken away with their heads covered, subjected to white noise, stood against a wall, and deprived of sleep and food for long periods.

The army's reaction to each incident usually had the effect of making things worse. A military spokesman would deny any wrongdoing by the soldiers and allege that the victims had been armed. This inflamed the pain felt by those who had just lost a parent, sibling, or child, while also adding to the suspicion many of them had that the British Army was above the law.

Injustice and helplessness are an explosive mix. In the weeks after British soldiers opened fire in Derry, hundreds of young men and women looked for ways to join paramilitary organisations such as the Provisional IRA. Some were driven by a desire for revenge. Others felt this was the only way to protect their community. 'Our motivation had nothing to do with any kind of political ideology,' one of these recruits later said. 'It was instinctive. We had that gut, instinctive feeling that what we were doing was right.'[1] All over the region, ordinary people were being drawn into the vortex of violence, including many who had never before held a gun or so much as dreamed of planting a bomb. One of these was Frank Hegarty.

Even if the nature of Frank's involvement is a mystery to those watching him take part in the IRA parade, shortly after Bloody Sunday, they can see that he is comfortable in this setting. From the shape of his shoulders and the easy expression in his eyes, The General looks as if he is used to this, and that there's nothing unusual about all the paramilitary uniforms, the British soldiers, the massed ranks of police, the more pronounced tribal divisions, the grief, the uncertainty, and the steadily rising death count.

But none of this is normal. Four years earlier, if Frank were to open his window at night, he would have heard little more than the sound of passing cars. By the time of the parade, in 1972, it could be hard to sleep at night for the rumble of passing army helicopters, the roar of distant crowds, the clatter of dustbin lids on pavements as people warned their neighbours of an approaching army patrol, the thump-thump-thump of a Thompson sub-machine gun, or the thunderclap of another IRA bomb. In 1972 alone, IRA volunteers in Northern Ireland detonated more than a thousand explosive devices.

Either they were trying to destroy buildings connected in some way to the British state, or they wanted to kill British soldiers and Protestant civilians. One of their deadliest attacks that year was known as 'Bloody Friday', when a series of IRA bombs in Belfast killed seven civilians and two soldiers and left 130 people injured. This was described in one newspaper as a new nadir in the Troubles, the point at which 'the three-year bloodbath in Ulster reached a new level of savagery'.[2]

The situation in Northern Ireland by the end of 1972 was worse than ever. More people were being killed than at any point in the region's history. The IRA was larger and more active, and the same was true of Protestant paramilitary groups such as the Ulster Defence Association and Ulster Volunteer Force. Both had been responsible for a number of horrific killings. Seventy-two civilians died in the violence that year, as well as 5 policemen, 117 Protestant paramilitaries, and 229 IRA volunteers.[3]

Eighty-one British soldiers were also killed in 1972, and senior army officers were starting to run out of ideas for how to end the bloodshed. Some were struggling to adjust to this strange and hostile environment. 'Soldiers were burned by petrol bombs, hurt in riots or shot at by snipers,' one army officer recalled. 'There would be riots every night and you had bricks and bottles raining down on you.' It was, he said, 'complete chaos', adding ruefully, of the contrast to the start of the Troubles, 'there were no cups of tea this time'.[4]

British soldiers had been sent over to Northern Ireland to restore peace. Three years later, they were up against a full-blown insurgency. For many of them, it was if they had been ordered into a quagmire, and the harder they tried to get out, the deeper they sank. It was a Catch-22. They could only leave Northern Ireland once peace was restored, and for that to happen they needed to leave. The problem was not just their presence but the way they reacted to some of the attacks. Most soldiers were being told to use tactics that had last been tried during the break-up of the British Empire in countries such as Kenya, Malaya, and Cyprus. Often, the troops were 'too indiscriminate and vigorous', one officer wrote, 'too many citizens had been unnecessarily inconvenienced and alienated, too many random arrests had been made, and some wholly unjustifiable incidents had occurred'.[5]

If the British Army was going to find a way out of Northern Ireland, it needed a new approach. The situation was so bad that ordinary people like Frank Hegarty, with no history of violence, were becoming involved. But some army officers saw in this an opportunity. It meant that more individuals than ever were carrying around knowledge that could be turned into intelligence and then used to prevent future attacks. One question was how to get at this information and find out what people like Frank knew. Another was whether this was really going to make a difference.

4

Fishers of Men

Six years later

Brigadier James Glover, Jimmy to his friends, spoke with the kind of precision that came from having spent most of his life telling soldiers what to do. By November 1978, he seemed to be in the home stretch of his military career. He was working at a desk in Whitehall, and was attached to the Ministry of Defence with the rank of brigadier-general. Glover was the army's most senior officer working on intelligence from Northern Ireland. His job was to read reports from the region and work out what was most likely to happen next.

Six years on from Bloody Sunday, Glover could see that the number of IRA attacks had fallen dramatically. Fewer people were being killed, and the army's presence in the region was smaller and less abrasive. Senior army officers had grasped the importance of public relations – and no longer thought of this as something that had to be done for the sake of it, but as a tactic that could improve the military situation. They seemed to have acquired a better understanding of themselves and were no longer using the past as their playbook.

By 1977, Northern Ireland was even considered safe enough for a visit from the Queen, as part of her Silver Jubilee celebrations. Due to security concerns, she was only there for one day and spent the night at sea. But this felt like a turning point. The outlook for Northern Ireland was tantalisingly good. In private, the army's commanding officer in the region said that the IRA insurgency was about to 'peter out'.[1] One Northern Ireland secretary thought 'the tide has turned'; his successor announced that the region was 'almost permanently free' from 'terrorism'.[2] Most British newspaper editors agreed and had all but lost interest in the conflict. In Cabinet, the Troubles was barely discussed, with one senior government advisor admitting that it would not even make it onto a list of their top thirty priorities.[3]

Each day, Jimmy Glover walked into an office in Whitehall, where he was surrounded by people who thought the conflict in Northern Ireland was essentially over. His worry, in 1978, was that it had only just begun. Even if the security forces had contained one version of the IRA, he thought they were about to be up against a very different one and that the IRA had undergone a silent metamorphosis. Its leadership was preparing a new armed campaign, Glover explained in a classified report, 'Future Terrorist Trends'. A core of dedicated volunteers such as Martin McGuinness was turning the IRA into a more disciplined organisation – one that was harder, younger, and leaner, and almost impossible to penetrate. It would have 'the sinews of war', Glover wrote, to keep the British Army pinned down in the region for many years.[4] He also warned that this new version of the IRA was preparing a series of sensational attacks he called 'spectaculars'.

Jimmy Glover's report 'didn't find all that much favour', he said, because 'it wasn't a message that British government really wanted to hear'.[5] Some civil servants thought he was doing what soldiers like him always did in moments like this, which was to give a pessimistic assessment of what was going on in the hope of being given more resources and then 'let off the leash'.[6] Others wondered how Glover had arrived at his Eeyorish conclusion. Elaborate hunch, educated guess, or did the British Army have a well-placed source inside the IRA?

Glover's forecast turned out to be little short of clairvoyant. On one day, in late November 1978, with his classified paper still being chewed over in Whitehall like a piece of gristle, the IRA detonated bombs in sixteen towns across Northern Ireland. Next, they moved on to targets in England, adding more misery to the 'Winter of Discontent'. The IRA attacked diplomats overseas, murdering the British ambassador to the Hague and his valet. In the same month, the IRA's rival paramilitary group, the Irish National Liberation Army (INLA), killed the Conservative politician Airey Neave. In Northern Ireland, the IRA attacked military bases and soldiers out on patrol, and at around the same time the British Army learned that this paramilitary organisation had tapped some of their telephone lines and was listening in to calls made by their most senior officer in the region.

With the outlook suddenly so much worse, Jimmy Glover was sent out to Northern Ireland. He arrived in February 1979 as the new 'Commander Land Forces (Northern Ireland)', which meant he was in charge of the army's day-to-day operations in the region. Glover understood the main problem his soldiers were facing. Most people recognised that. But he also had an idea of how to solve it.

Jimmy Glover was convinced that the best way to contain this new version of the IRA was with more intelligence, better intelligence, and improved analysis and coordination of intelligence. He wanted intelligence to become the priority for the security forces in Northern Ireland. As he loved to say: 'intelligence is the key'.[7]

Glover began by changing the way soldiers in Northern Ireland recruited and ran agents. He set up a new centralised unit dedicated to agent-running. Until then, this work had been parcelled out to the army's three brigades in the region, each of which had its own unloved 'Research Office'. Now there was a single military unit referred to in army paperwork as 'the Forward Research Offices', or 'the FRO'. It was later renamed the Force Research Unit, or 'the FRU', a label that stuck.[8]

This elite new agent-running outfit was cloaked in mystery. The FRU had its own identity, its soldiers wore civilian clothes and grew beards, and there was a rigorous selection procedure for those who wanted to join. Its insignia was a figure with a trident and net, and its motto was 'Fishers of Men'. It reported indirectly to Glover, who was adamant that intelligence was going to be decisive in Northern Ireland and that the FRU would play a central part in this.

Most of his colleagues disagreed. Some objected to what Glover was doing on principle, believing it was unconstitutional for soldiers to be running spies inside the United Kingdom. Others worried about the legal side of what was going on. Northern Ireland had not been declared a war zone. For the most part, ordinary British law applied. Was it lawful to have soldiers running agents who might commit criminal acts? Then there were those who knew that the army had tried this in the past, and it had ended in disaster. A secretive military unit called the MRF had been set up earlier in the Troubles. It had begun by running agents, but ended up carrying out random attacks on civilians in Belfast, and was disbanded after one of its soldiers was charged with attempted murder.

Ordinary soldiers also objected to intelligence work, usually because they thought it was a waste of time. Many struggled, one paratrooper recalled, to 'take any of this intelligence nonsense seriously'.[9] They disliked the idea of paying an IRA volunteer to let them in on the secret of where he had planted a bomb. They could not see how running agents was going to play a part in ending the Troubles.

History was on their side. There was no conflict in world history that had been decided by intelligence work. Even in the Second World War, with Bletchley Park and secretive organisations like the Special Operations Executive, intelligence had only played a peripheral role in the Allied victory. Conflicts were decided by soldiers with guns, not spies. It was hard to see why Northern Ireland was going to be different.

Jimmy Glover was travelling by helicopter across Northern Ireland when he heard on his radio headset something about an IRA attack south of the border in County Sligo. It was 27 August 1979, a Bank Holiday Monday. Two teenagers had been killed, as well as an eighty-three-year-old woman, and the former first sea lord, viceroy and governor-general of India, and prominent member of the British royal family, Lord Louis Mountbatten.

Several hours later came a second IRA attack. An army convoy at Warrenpoint, County Down, was struck by two enormous bombs. 'I don't remember a sound as such. It's a sensation,' one of the survivors said. 'I can remember my legs being moved and then "bang". For I think about seven days, I had no recollection of anything.'[10] Eighteen soldiers from '2 Para' were killed, ranging from a twenty-two-year-old from Stockton-on-Tees, Corporal John Giles, a father of two young children, through to thirty-four-year-old Major Peter Fursman, from Northamptonshire.

The IRA took responsibility for both 'spectaculars', and in a triumphant communiqué they threatened more, saying, of the British Army, 'We will tear out their sentimental imperialist hearts'.[11] The window of doubt had closed. The conflict in Northern Ireland was not about to 'peter out', and the recent surge of IRA activity could not be dismissed as some kind of dead-cat bounce. Jimmy Glover was right. The IRA had been born again, and the British were facing a new and altogether different enemy.

Several days after the Warrenpoint attack, the new prime minister, Margaret Thatcher, swept through the region like a 'blue torna-do'.[12] Her visit included set-piece meetings with some of the soldiers who had survived, many of whom were struck by her intensity and conviction, both qualities that were rarely seen in visiting politicians. When Thatcher was shown the epaulette worn by the most senior officer killed at Warrenpoint – 'this, Prime Minister, is all that is left of Colonel Blair' – she began to cry.[13]

On the same day, Thatcher was introduced to Jimmy Glover.

It is worth pausing here for a moment, with Glover standing before Thatcher and both poised on the threshold of their conversation. Her attention was on him, brows knitted together, blue eyes flintier and sharper than they looked on television. Glover might have just picked up a trace of her perfume, Penhaligon's Bluebell, a woozy citrus scent that would have been dazzling in that military setting.

Glover knew that this was his chance to tell the prime minister about what needed to change in Northern Ireland, and that he would never have an opportunity like this again. He understood that Thatcher wanted to act, but she was not yet sure how. He could have told her that now was the time to send in more troops, or, the opposite, that she needed to reduce force levels. He might have said that the army was not cut out for this kind of work and that it was a policing job. Instead, Jimmy Glover told Margaret Thatcher that if she wanted to end the Troubles, she had to make intelligence the priority.

Margaret Thatcher left Northern Ireland convinced, she wrote, 'that a lot needs to be done and we cannot delay much longer'.[14] Over the next few weeks, she oversaw a carnival of restructuring and bureaucratic change. Most of this was designed to increase the scale and intensity of secret work in the region. Intelligence was going to be key. Undercover operations in Northern Ireland were about to become so large, and so complex, that Margaret Thatcher decided to send over one of the country's most experienced spymasters to help.

Sir Maurice Oldfield was a former chief of Britain's Secret Intelligence Service (SIS), sometimes called 'C'. He was also the inspiration for Alec Guinness when playing George Smiley in the television adaptations of John Le Carré's novels. In the weeks after the IRA's Warrenpoint attack, this Smiley-esque figure was either wheeled, dragged, or lured out of his retirement at All Souls College, Oxford – accounts vary – and flown over to Northern Ireland to become 'Security Co-ordinator', a new post.

On the day before Oldfield's appointment was announced, British embassies around the world received a guidance telegram. 'If asked if this means an increase in intelligence effort you should say [. . .] unattributably that the Security Forces in Northern Ireland naturally depend heavily on intelligence in dealing with terrorism. The more they have the better.' The telegram then finished with a line that might have been written for Francis Urquhart in the television drama *House of Cards*: 'But this is not the reason for Sir Maurice's appointment.'[15]

It was precisely the reason for his appointment.

'James Bond's "M" New Head of North Security' was the headline in the *Irish Press* on the day that Oldfield began to be briefed on the intelligence situation in Northern Ireland. Clearly, he was impressed. The beady-eyed Cold War veteran told colleagues in London that 'intelligence will be the match-winner'.[16] But he warned that this was going to take time and stressed to Margaret Thatcher that information 'from the heart of the Catholic community', in particular, 'was very difficult to obtain'.[17]

In the following days, Jimmy Glover's experimental new agent-running unit, the FRU, went on a recruitment drive. They began to take on more personnel and look for larger offices. They also drew up lists of men and women who could be taken on as agents. One of the names that was handed to them, by someone outside the FRU, was that of Frank Hegarty.

It was early 1980. The stage was set.

In the world of intelligence, sometimes the grandest and most elaborate strategies will depend on a series of actions that sound almost banal when you write them down. *Take a photograph. Listen to a conversation. Leave a piece of paper somewhere. Befriend a stranger.*

So it was that on a wintry morning in 1980, as part of the British response to the latest incarnation of the IRA, following bomb attacks, multiple deaths, a state funeral, and high-level discussions between generals, politicians, and senior intelligence officials, a pipe-smoking British soldier turned to an unemployed man on the outskirts of Derry and said:

'Alright, Franko.'

5

'Jack'

'Alright, Franko.'

Frank Hegarty has no idea what is happening. How can he? His expectations have been perfectly eclipsed. He is still scrabbling to make sense of what's going on as the stranger in front of him continues to talk. He compliments Frank on his dog and makes a point of calling her by her name, Blue, to show that he knows this. The stranger says he was impressed with how well she did in her last race, and asks if anyone had good money on her. He wants to know how everything is going at home, and if Dorothy is well.

The confusion Frank feels at first gives way to a more frazzled sense of uncertainty. This stranger, whoever he is, knows a lot about him – more than he'd thought possible only seconds ago, and Frank has no way of guessing where his knowledge ends. He might be worried about where all this is going, but he also wants to know more. Anyone in his position is bound to feel some mixture of fear and curiosity. Frank is wary of this pipe-smoking stranger who sounds like he grew up in Liverpool, but he is also intrigued. There is something oddly flattering about this man having taken the time to find out so much about him. Perhaps he sees qualities in Frank which other people don't, a thought which is like a sugar rush for the soul.

Frank is soon back into his stride, and so is the stranger beside him. They walk together along the Hollyhall Road, two men with their dogs. The road is flatter up here, and although the morning is still cold and they can see their breath in front of them, it is becoming brighter.

Frank's mind is less of a whir as he begins to make sense of what's going on. In some ways, this bizarre situation is familiar to him, only because he has been warned about it so many times. In Frank's world, almost nothing is worse than passing on information to the British and becoming an informer. 'Better by far to be a rapist, a murderer,' wrote one spy, 'anything but an informer.'[1] Or in the more chilling words of IRA volunteer Dolours Price, someone personally involved in the punishment of suspected informers: 'death was too good for them'.[2]

For a Derryman like Frank, a Catholic who has lived through more than a decade of the Troubles, having a mysterious Englishman sidle up to you like this will set alarm bells ringing. He knows how he is supposed to react. He understands what he should be doing, or what he should *not* be doing. But Frank is going off script. He has not walked away in the opposite direction. Either the alarm has failed to sound, or, for reasons that are not yet clear, he has chosen to ignore it.

The informer has a very specific place in Irish culture, one that only makes sense in the history of Britain's involvement in Ireland. Not so much the months leading up to Frank's encounter on the Hollyhall Road, but the centuries before that.

During the Viking settlement of Ireland, from the ninth century onwards, there may have been informers dotted around the island: local men and women who passed on information to the newcomers in return for mercy, money, or some other reward. But they left little trace on Irish history. The same goes for those who supplied intelligence in the wake of the Norman invasions during the twelfth century.

In the sixteenth century, though, the picture changed. The trigger was King Henry VIII's break from Rome. The young king worried that a European army might use Ireland as a staging post before invading England. He sent men across the Irish Sea to establish English law and enforce it. English, Scottish, and Welsh soldiers were dispatched to put down rebellions in Ireland and extend the Crown's authority (which was non-existent in most parts of the island). But the change that trumped all others in terms of its impact on Ireland at the time, and in the years ahead, was the introduction of 'plantations'. Not plantations of sugar or cotton, but plantations of people.

Visit Derry today, and one of the first things you see will be the city walls. This crenelated caterpillar of limestone, earth, and cement was built early in the seventeenth century. Its purpose was to protect some of the thousands of Protestant and Presbyterian immigrants who had recently arrived in the area from the north of England and the Scottish Lowlands, and who called themselves 'planters'. During the first half of the seventeenth century, as many as 100,000 of these planters arrived in Ireland. Most were skilled and impoverished, and had come to Ireland to start a new life and escape the sectarian violence in England. They moved to places like Derry, hoping to find peace and leave behind the troubles of their past. Some saw themselves as part of a utopian project. One enthusiastic English politician described Ireland as 'our new worlde'.[3]

Most of the planters made their homes inside new plantations like the one in Derry. These offered security and community, and soon plantations were popping up all over Ireland, from Limerick in the south to what would later be Offaly and Laois, Leitrim, and Cavan. Other plantations were being built at exactly the same time on the east coast of America, in places like Virginia, and often with very similar layouts and inhabitants. Many of the same entrepreneurs, such as Sir Humphrey Gilbert and Sir Walter Raleigh, were involved

in the Irish and American plantation projects. But the greatest concentration of English plantations in the world by the start of the
seventeenth century was not in America but in the north of Ireland,
in the province of Ulster.

Although many of these new Irish plantations were private enter-
prises, they were strongly encouraged by the Crown. They seemed
to be bringing in to Ireland loyal, English-speaking citizens who
would defend the island against European invaders. The plantations
were also generating income for the Crown in the form of tax. But
what really fuelled the spread of plantations across Ireland was the
Tudor innovation of the joint-stock company. This allowed any private individual to buy or sell shares in something like a plantation
without having to live in or even visit it. The new age of financial
investment in London had begun to transform Irish society. Nowhere
was this more obvious than in Derry, later renamed Londonderry in
recognition of the huge financial investment from several guilds in
the capital, which was soon being talked about as a model example
of what an Irish plantation could be, like a show home on a new
housing development.

But for many Irish men and women these new plantations resulted
in a loss of income or led to them being forced off the land they had
always thought of as theirs. Each new settlement was like a grappling
hook of empire, and soon people began to fight back. Attacks on the
English were led by aristocrats such as Hugh O'Neill, Earl of Tyrone,
Sir Cahir O'Doherty, or Patrick Sarsfield, the original Lord Lucan,
and others who became known as the 'kerne', 'wood kerne', 'tories',
'raparees', or just rebels.

European commentators at the time sometimes referred to England
as a failed state, and the English king as 'Rex Diablorum', the king of
devils, by reason of their many rebellions'.[4] The Crown was used to
this kind of thing. Its response to each of these uprisings in Ireland
was the same as when similar disturbances occurred elsewhere in

the British Isles, which was to send over more soldiers, build more walls, and take on more spies.

There was a story about an Irish informer that Frank Hegarty knew better than most, as it involved his namesake.

Father James Hegarty was a Catholic priest who lived outside Derry in the early eighteenth century, at a time when the first of the 'Penal Laws' were introduced. These draconian regulations made it illegal for Catholics to take on certain jobs, marry Protestants, have the same political power as their Protestant neighbours, or serve their communities as priests. This left Father Hegarty with a choice. He could move overseas to a European country to practise his faith in peace (and where Protestants were persecuted instead), or he could remain in Ireland and continue his holy work in secret, knowing that if he was caught, he might be killed.

Father Hegarty decided to stay. For the next seven years, he and his congregation celebrated the Eucharist and other liturgical rites in a cave outside Buncrana, near Derry, which had glorious views out over Lough Swilly, the glacial fjord known as the Lake of Shadows, or the Lake of One Thousand Eyes.

One day in 1711, Father Hegarty was betrayed. He was leading a Mass in the cave when the Redcoats burst in. They had been tipped off by Hegarty's brother-in-law, who had passed on his whereabouts in return for £5. Somehow the priest escaped, and galloped off on a horse lent to him by local people. He was chased to the shores of Lough Swilly, where he ran into the sea and began to swim to the other side. As the priest powered through the icy water, the Redcoats called out from the shore. They promised that if he turned back, he would come to no harm.

Perhaps Father Hegarty was tiring and had realised that he was never going to make it to the other side. Either that, or he felt that these men could be trusted. Whatever it was, he swam back to the shore. He pulled himself out of the water, his wet clothes pulling down on his body, before staggering up to the Redcoats.

It was a trap. The soldiers cut off the priest's head. The place where this is said to have happened is known today as Father Hegarty's Rock. No vegetation grows on the rocks which are thought to have been touched by his severed head as it bounced down to the sea.

Most people come away from this narrative with a powerful sense of Father Hegarty's bravery and devotion, his support among local people, and, of course, the duplicity of the English. But what makes the story unusual is how little it says about his brother-in-law, the man who betrayed him. Other Irish tales focus much more on the informer, to the point of fascination. This figure is often described as being different to everyone else, a misfit who has stood out since the day they were born. Passing information to the authorities becomes less of a decision than the result of a personality trait. In other words, if you consider yourself normal, you would never do something like this. What's also striking about these stories is how rarely the informer is an outsider, a visitor, or a stranger. Usually, they are so close that you would never think to suspect them. Father Hegarty was not betrayed by some distant parishioner he had fallen out with long before, but by his own brother-in-law.

Another theme of many Irish stories about informers is that once someone has passed on information, it is as if they have chosen to remove themselves from their community and can no longer rely on its protection. Most of these tales finish on the same brutal note. The informer enjoys a temporary reward, usually money, but they pay for it with their lives. Their murderers go free.

There is both a seriousness and a sense of tragedy that seams through these stories. In 1641, the Irish Rebels were said to have been brought down by an informer. In 1798, the United Irishmen rebellion, led by Wolfe Tone, was crushed 'thanks to the saturation of the rebel movement at all levels by government spies'.[5] In 1867, the

Fenian Rising was believed to have failed because the body behind it was 'plagued with spies, informers, government agents and agent-provocateurs'.[6] Even the failure of the 1916 Easter Rising was later blamed on Irishmen supplying information to the British. In one reading of Irish history, every uprising against English or British rule has been undone by spies. Without them, according to a 1974 piece in *An Phoblacht*, the IRA newspaper, 'it is possible that the people of Ireland would have had full control over their country a long time ago'.[7]

This is how Frank Hegarty has learned to think of informers. It hardly matters that in the cold, historical light of day secret agents have never been as influential as these stories make out, and many were scapegoats for other failures. Nor were the British as cunning as the storytellers like to say. What matters here is that in 1980 the informer is seen by most ordinary Derrymen as some kind of folk devil, and it is this, more than anything else, makes Frank's decision to keep listening to the English stranger so striking.

'Jack', as we shall call him – which is neither his actual name nor the name he has given to Frank – is the army corporal from the FRU who's been chosen to make the approach. He shares Frank's love of animals and is a keen bird-watcher. When looking out onto the Derry skyline, Jack can pick out the different silhouettes of pale-bellied brent geese, whooper swans, golden plovers, or great northern divers, as well as the more familiar movements of the dunlin, knots, oystercatchers, and pintails, which he has known since he was a boy. He is friendly without being an extrovert and he speaks to Frank as an equal.

Jack is also English. He comes from across the water, not from across the road. It is obvious to Frank, just by listening to this man's voice, that he is unlikely to be close to any of his friends in Derry, and this makes the idea of speaking to him feel less dangerous. But perhaps more than anything else, the way that Jack speaks to Frank contains a level of respect – and respect is something that Frank has not always felt since the start of the violence and the arrival of the British Army on the streets of Derry.

None of this is coincidental. The team in the nearby FRU office, a dingy Portakabin in the army's Ebrington barracks, chose Jack for this task because they thought he might have a rapport with Frank, and that in the ground between them a seed of friendship could grow.

Jack mentions to Frank that the road is surprisingly quiet. The reason for this, he goes on, is that his unit has blocked off the lane at either end. Any vehicle that tries to drive up the Hollyhall Road will find a minivan parked across the road with a plainclothes soldier next to it holding a sub-machine gun. Jack wants to impress Frank, which is part of the reason for telling him this. We are an elite organisation is the message he wants to convey. We will look after you better than the police can. But Jack also understands that he must appeal to something deeper within Frank. At one point in their conversation, he tells Frank that the unit he works for is dedicated to saving lives and preventing IRA attacks. They are the good guys. They want to bring peace to the region, and to end the senseless attacks.

This part of Jack's patter might have reminded Frank of the recent IRA bomb at La Mon Hotel, outside Belfast, in which a group of off-duty policemen was targeted but instead twelve members of the Irish Collie Club were killed, with many more suffering horrific, life-changing injuries. Frank does not need to hear Jack make the case against IRA violence. He has already made his mind up about this, and the feelings he had about the organisation at the time of Bloody Sunday have changed.

Perhaps Jack also brings up a bomb attack that took place at the nearby British Army barracks in the early 1970s, in which two local people were killed. His reason for doing so would have been straightforward. There is a rumour that Frank might have been involved in preparing this attack. Just by mentioning this to Frank, Jack is able to hint at the idea that he has some kind of leverage over him – even if, in reality, he does not. Frank was never charged, and there is nothing to suggest that the police have a case against him. But in the way a conversation like this will work, it can be enough for Jack to gesture at the possibility that he might have something on him.

In a different sense, if Frank was involved in this attack, perhaps his memory of what happened has left him with a sense of guilt for which he needs to atone. Frank does not yet know what Jack wants, but if he can help to prevent more unnecessary deaths, then it makes sense to listen. This is how ordinary people like him can make a difference.

Frank has heard about what happens to informers. He knows that some are given twenty-four hours by the IRA to leave their homes, and others are kneecapped, tarred and feathered, or humiliated in another way. He also understands that a small number are murdered. But Frank's understanding of the local IRA is different to many other people's. This is because he knows some of the local volunteers, and will have a friend in common with the others. It is harder for him to think of the IRA as some mysterious and faceless organisation because it is made up of people like him.

Frank is also acquainted with the figure at the very top of the local IRA hierarchy, the local kingpin, a man whose 'identity can be conjured up in any conversation,' the journalist Kevin Toolis wrote, 'distinguished from the mass of ordinary everyday Martins who fill the Catholic city, with a tiny shift in tone – "Did *Martin* say that?"'[8]

6

Martin

'He was a very nice young fellow like a thousand other young fel-
lows,' the Nobel-Peace-Prize-winner John Hume said of Martin
McGuinness. 'The difference with him was he had a good face.'[1]
Always well turned out and focused, Martin McGuinness bore a
strong resemblance at the time to the American folk singer Art
Garfunkel. He was also, he once said, 'blind as a bat', and tended
to keep his gaze fixed on the pavement as he moved around Derry,
which sometimes made him look like an absent-minded student.[2]

By 1980, Martin McGuinness was the IRA's chief of staff – arguably
the most powerful figure in this illegal paramilitary organisation –
and in Derry he was worshipped by the IRA rank and file. 'It's hard
to explain,' one local man said. 'These guys loved McGuinness. They
knew he had power. They knew he wouldn't let them down.'[3] 'There
was a body language of respect,' said another. 'You could tell it was
a case of, "Whatever Martin says, goes".[4]

'Cold Martin' was how some people knew him.[5] If he felt that you
had made a mistake, according to the Sinn Féin politician Mary Lou
McDonald, 'McGuinness didn't have to raise his voice, he would
simply have to give you "The Look"'.[6] He was someone who understood how to weaponise the gaps in a conversation. But the respect
that IRA volunteers had for him was about more than this. As

historian and journalist Ed Moloney put it, 'Nothing mattered more in the IRA than a person's military record'.[7] McGuinness was revered in Derry because of the number of attacks he had taken part in, usually helping to plan, organise, or authorise the operation. He was part of the IRA leadership team which had, according to one intelligence report, 'carefully considered and approved' the Warrenpoint attack, the assassination of Lord Mountbatten, and many, many others.[8] All this before he had turned thirty.

But Martin McGuinness also carried inside himself the renegade sense of being an outsider. Unlike Gerry Adams, widely believed to have been his predecessor as chief of staff, McGuinness did not come from IRA royalty. His parents were not republicans, and his mother was shocked when she learned he had joined the organisation. Family mattered within the IRA almost as much as a volunteer's military record. This left McGuinness at a disadvantage – a situation only made worse by his poor eyesight, which meant he could never be a frontline operator. He compensated for this with the zeal he put into planning attacks, the energy he gave to the cause, and the brutality with which he responded to anyone who crossed him. When asked how informers should be punished, Martin McGuinness was unequivocal: 'Death, certainly'.[9]

This was how Martin McGuinness had won over the IRA hardliners, most of whom came from republican families – he made himself terrifying. Arguments on the streets of Derry at that time might end with one person screaming at the other either, 'I'll get yee kneecapped!' or, 'I'll see McGuinness about yee!'[10] His name had become shorthand for extreme punishment. He was renowned for being ruthless, because it was all he had. His greatest fear was that one day his comrades in the IRA might think he was not really one of them, he had gone soft, or, worse – so much worse – they might wonder to themselves if he had a secret relationship with the enemy.

*

One of the first times Martin McGuinness came to the attention of British intelligence was in 1972. He was twenty-two years old, and had been selected to join the IRA team flown over to London for a meeting with Willie Whitelaw, the Northern Ireland secretary. Their conversation was a failure. 'Awful,' Whitelaw recalled.[11] But it allowed both sides to take a closer look at each other.

Martin McGuinness and Gerry Adams were accompanied on this trip by Frank Steele, a pipe-smoking Arabist who worked for Britain's Secret Intelligence Service, or SIS, also known as MI6. Steele observed both men with his usual hawk-like intensity. He wanted to gain a sense of who they were, who they might become, and whether it would ever be possible to develop a relationship with either one. The SIS officer described Gerry Adams as 'very personable, intelligent, articulate, and self-disciplined', and wondered if, deep down, he yearned for a ceasefire. He came away from this trip thinking that both Adams and McGuinness had the potential for leadership.[12]

Martin McGuinness always remembered that trip to London, how he and the other IRA men were taken by helicopter to a military airport outside Belfast before being flown across the Irish Sea, and the way they were greeted on arrival by an RAF officer who stood to attention as they stepped off the plane. It must have been intoxicating. A butcher's boy from Derry who had left school at fifteen seemed to have the attention of high-powered British government officials. 'I couldn't be anything but impressed by the paraphernalia surrounding that whole business,' McGuinness later said, especially, he added, 'the cloak-and-dagger stuff of how we were transported from Derry to London.'[13]

But Martin McGuinness also came away from that trip with a better understanding of the people he was dealing with – one that stayed with him for the rest of his life. 'I had learned in two hours', he said of his meeting with Willie Whitelaw, 'what Irish politicians still haven't learned: that the British don't give in easily.'[14]

This was the man that Frank had most reason to be wary of in Derry. But he did not seem to think of him in the way that other people did. Frank Hegarty was not exactly close to Martin McGuinness; few people were. But they knew each other and had overlapping histories. Both were Catholic Derrymen who came from large families. They were devoted to their mothers and had grown up within a mile of each other. Each had roots over the border in Donegal. One of Frank's grandparents was a McGinniss. This similarity in their stories begins to explain why Frank Hegarty never seemed to be scared of Martin McGuinness in the way that other people were. The parallels between them made it harder for him to feel the fear that otherwise attaches itself to the unknown.

7

Decision

Frank is still on the Hollyhall Road next to Jack, the army corporal who has just approached him. They hear a vehicle coming. A van pulls up next to them and several men get out.

These are soldiers from Jack's unit. They are disguised as civilians, but the look is probably not quite right. Another Derryman who was picked up by the same team remembered seeing them with their bright trainers, white socks, and leather jackets, and thinking to himself straight away: 'Fucking Brits'.[1]

The soldiers are friendly, but they hold back. Jack is in control here. Birdwatching Jack. Thoughtful, pipe-smoking Jack, who decides, at last, to ask the question he has been building up to since the start of this encounter. He wants Frank to come with him in the van. There is more that he wants to say, but not here.

The General has a decision to make. His greyhound, Blue, is by his side. The van's engine putters merrily in the background. A patch of woodland stretches out along one side of the road and, overhead, the leafless branches of oak trees form a latticed ceiling. Frank's future stretches out ahead of him, until it is lost in the glare of the moment. He understands the stigma of being an informer and the danger he could face if he says yes. But he also knows that stepping into that van with Jack might help in some way to bring the violence to an end, and at this point in his life, unbeknown to the soldiers, he is starting to think about the future in a different way.

Frank met his new partner, Dorothy, several years ago in a pub. One visitor remembered this place as 'an absolute hell-hole'. Dorothy was a barmaid, married with children. Frank was a regular. She had a steady, no-nonsense manner, and was streetwise. She stood out in that pub, as she did on her road, where she was one of the only Protestants in a mainly Catholic neighbourhood.

Soon Frank and Dorothy had moved in together. Although it was now unusual to hear about a Protestant and a Catholic living under the same roof in this part of Derry, that hadn't always been true. When Frank was growing up in Rosemount, families from different backgrounds often mixed and there was less stigma attached to relationships like this. Frank's mother, Rose, liked to tell the story of the rival Protestant and Catholic bands in their area who got on so well that they would borrow each other's drums during marching season over the summer.

Things have changed since then, and Frank knows some people do not approve of him living with Dorothy. But they are both ready to weather that. If this has placed more pressure on their relationship, there is no outward sign of it, certainly not after their recent news.

Dorothy is now expecting their first child together. By the time Jack approaches Frank on the Hollyhall Road, Dorothy is three months pregnant. Frank is set to become a father for the second time. (He briefly reunited with his wife and they had a daughter before he moved out again.) Hearing about Dorothy's pregnancy, only a few years after his own father's death, must have felt like the start of a second act. Some of Frank's friends might have reacted to the news with a blokey kind of dread, but he doesn't. He's an optimist. For as long as he can remember, he has had a gambler's faith in the future. Frank's response to uncertainty is often to tell himself things are going to work out, even when the odds suggest otherwise.

One soldier familiar with this encounter on the Hollyhall Road remembered how Frank was 'motivated in a very much more idealistic way' than any of them had anticipated. 'He had genuinely grown to hate the violence that was wrecking his beloved home town and country.'[2]

The idea of bringing a child into the world seemed to have sharpened Frank's focus on the future. But it will take more than this to persuade him to climb into the back of the van. At the heart of his decision is the impression he has formed of Jack, the soldier standing before him. The best handlers are interested and interesting. They are able to make their recruits feel special and understood, and they carry inside themselves a sense of their agent's vulnerability. They also have a way of inspiring trust. Frank will only get into that van if, on some level, he feels that one day he might be willing to put his life in Jack's hands.

Frank makes his decision. He moves towards the vehicle and clambers in. His back is so stiff that sometimes he struggles to tie the laces on his boots, so he needs a little help. Blue and the other dog leap up next to him. The door closes with a clunk, and the vehicle sets off down the Hollyhall Road.

Irish storytellers, or *seanchaidhthe*, will occasionally talk about the in-between places you find beyond the edge of a city, just before the start of the countryside: the wastelands that open up after the last of the houses on lanes like the Hollyhall Road. These areas are where unsuspecting travellers might experience visions or feel a new sense of clarity and understanding. In a more prosaic sense, these are the places where people find it easier to see things in a different way. We may never know what was in Frank's mind on the Hollyhall Road that morning, only that his decision to step into the van will catapult him into a new world. He has not yet agreed to become an agent and still has a lot of questions.[3] But entering that vehicle marks a point of departure. It is a rupture with the rest of his life. He wants to push back against the darkness and do more than endure the chaos.

Frank Hegarty has placed many bets in his life, but this is the biggest one yet.

Next to Frank in the back of the van is Jack, whose mind will soon be streaking ahead. Once he gets back to base, Jack needs to write up an account of what has happened. This document will be passed up the reporting chain, rewritten, added to and shortened, until it reaches those with an overview of British intelligence activity in Northern Ireland. For these people, Frank Hegarty is a single feature on a vast and increasingly detailed map. In the same topography they can see a different agent who has already infiltrated the IRA. This other man's intelligence is so valuable, his potential so great, that the army has recently set up a specialist unit to look after him.

Frank is unaware of this other agent. But their paths have already begun to veer towards each other. Events have now been set in motion that will lead to the discovery, six years on, of a corpse by the side of a road with masking tape over the eyes.

PART TWO:

INFILTRATION

8

'Stakeknife'

One morning in 2016, George Hamilton, a middle-aged man with a hangdog expression, sat down at a table that looked too small for him in front of a pack of journalists. Hamilton was Chief Constable of the Police Service of Northern Ireland. Most of the journalists knew him fairly well, but none was familiar with the man who had just followed him into the room and quietly sat down beside him.

This press conference, Hamilton began, was to mark the launch of 'Operation Kenova', a police investigation into the activities of – and he was careful with his words here – an alleged army agent known as 'Stakeknife'. This person was thought to have been involved in murders, attempted murders, and unlawful imprisonments previously attributed to the IRA. One of his victims was believed to be the British agent whose body was found by the side of a country lane in 1986 with masking tape over its eyes. But the most shocking part of this story was the scale of it. Stakeknife was believed to have been involved in dozens of killings. Operation Kenova was shaping up to be the largest murder investigation in British history.

Originally, the police in Northern Ireland had been asked to investigate Stakeknife's activities, but Hamilton felt this should be handled by someone from outside the region, which explained the presence of the Englishman sitting next to him.

'I have every confidence in Chief Constable Boutcher,' Hamilton went on, in his rattling Belfast accent, 'and I have no doubt his previous experience when it comes to dealing with highly complex and sensitive investigations will be of great benefit to him as this investigation progresses.'[1]

The room's focus turned to Jon Boutcher, a weathered middle-aged man with a buzz cut. He was chief constable for Bedfordshire Police, which had recently been ranked as one of the worst in the country. But that had nothing to do with him. He had only joined the year before and was there to turn things around. So far, this had not happened, but most people agreed that it was going to take time. A different type of policeman might have turned down Operation Kenova, so that they could concentrate on the task in hand, but Boutcher liked to be busy, and he had arranged to divide his time between the two jobs.

'I do not underestimate the huge task,' Jon Boutcher began, face flickering in a burst of camera flashes, reading glasses halfway down his nose. 'With both the passage of time and the very nature of these crimes, the truth will be a difficult and elusive prey.'[2] His priority, he explained, was to work with the families who believed that their relative had been killed by Stakeknife. 'It is them who we should be thinking of throughout,' he continued, speaking with the cushioned cadence of a grief counsellor. 'It must be extremely hard to have listened to various commentaries within the community and the media about how and why your loved one died,' he went on. 'I hope this investigation ultimately addresses the uncertainties and rumours. All I can promise is an absolute commitment to trying to find the truth.'[3]

Jon Boutcher had spent most of his career investigating serious crimes, including many murders. The price for this, you felt, watching him in this press conference, could be seen in the look of quiet melancholy that sometimes washed over his face. Ask him a question, and he had a way of pausing for a moment before answering, as if, having scanned through the possible answers, this was the only one suitable for you. 'My wife tells me I have no emotion,' Boutcher later said, adding, 'I put all my emotion into the work.[4] Everyone agreed that he loved his job. Colleagues described Jon Boutcher as 'a typical 'Old Bill'', or 'a real old-school copper', hinting at a livelier and more colourful past. In private, he was quick with his deadpan asides and could put himself down easily. But in front of the cameras that day in Belfast, his performance was exact and polished.

Operation Kenova sounded impressive and serious. Jon Boutcher came across as sincere, considerate, and committed. He clearly had a lot of support. Boutcher revealed that he had a budget of £35 million, he was planning to take on as many as seventy detectives, and the time frame he had been given was five years. But as far as some people in Northern Ireland were concerned, even if Jon Boutcher had all the detectives in the world working for him, he was never going to get Stakeknife to appear in court.

One of the problems Boutcher faced was that the standard of evidence required in any murder prosecution in the United Kingdom is extremely high. Even if his detectives managed to find historic intelligence reports indicating that Stakeknife had been involved in a particular murder, these documents would not be admissible in court. His team would need to track down the author of each report and have them read out the text while under police caution. This was not going to be easy.

Others saw Operation Kenova in a more cynical light. 'I don't think the British state have any inclination to seriously investigate their own police services,' one former IRA volunteer said at the time.[5] For some people, this investigation was a performance being staged for the benefit of the victims' families. The British government did not have a good track record of holding its intelligence agencies to account. National security usually took precedence over criminal justice. It was hard to see why this would be any different.

But the argument against that, and the reason why anyone who saw this press conference might have come away with a sense of hope, was Boutcher himself. He would not stop, he said, his voice hardening, until he found out 'how and why these murders occurred during those dark days'. He was determined to 'bring those responsible for these awful crimes, in whatever capacity they were involved, to justice'.[6] There was a chance that he was being set up to fail. But something about his performance in Belfast that day suggested that part of him was already invested in this and he was not just going through the motions.

In the months before that press conference, as he weighed up whether to take on this job, Jon Boutcher had spoken to a number of different people. One of these was John Stevens, or Lord Stevens of Kirkwhelpington, a former commissioner of the Metropolitan Police. Stevens was one of the country's most decorated ex-policemen, and seemed to spend most of his life being awarded honorary fellowships, doctorates, degrees, medals, and tough-sounding military ranks. He had reached the pinnacle of his career and was enjoying his time in the House of Lords. But one subject still had a way of unsettling him.

Long ago, in 1989, Stevens had led a police investigation in Northern Ireland, in which he looked into whether army agents had been involved in any serious crimes. Stevens was told at first that the army did not run agents in the region. He learned that this was a lie, and built a criminal case against a key army agent.

Stevens's team was about to have this man arrested when a fire broke out in his office. His investigation room was left looking 'like a Salvador Dali painting,' one policeman remembered, 'only lacking in colour, with melted computer screens and furniture, everything having been burned or soot-stained to a black monochrome'.[7] Stevens was convinced that this was an arson attack. He blamed the FRU, which ran the agent his team had been about to arrest. 'In almost thirty years as a policeman,' Stevens said of his time investigating the

FRU, 'I had never found myself caught up in such an entanglement of lies and treachery.'[8]

Stevens later got his man, and the FRU agent ended up in jail. At around the same time, Stevens heard rumours about another FRU agent known as Stakeknife. Several decades later, when Jon Boutcher told him that he had been asked to investigate the same figure, Stevens might have warned him off. After all, that's what everyone else seemed to be doing. One colleague told Boutcher he would be 'bonkers' to take on the job. Northern Ireland was a graveyard for reputations, they said, and Stakeknife might be what was known in the secret world as a 'protected species'. There was no way of knowing how far the people looking after him would go to keep him out of jail. Others reminded Boutcher of what had happened to John Stevens and to John Stalker before him – another English policeman sent over to Northern Ireland to investigate alleged wrongdoing by the security forces, who became the subject of a smear campaign that effectively ended his career in the police.

But Stevens did not tell Boutcher to walk away. Investigating Stakeknife would be, he said, 'the ultimate test of detective work'.[9] Perhaps he knew the effect this would have. 'If anyone tells me I can't do something,' Boutcher said, 'it makes me want it more.'[10] Maybe he could go further than John Stevens. Do this well, and without ruffling too many feathers, and there was no knowing where it might take him. The top job in policing, the commissioner of the Metropolitan Police, might soon be in his sights. But if he failed, given how close he was to retirement, this was likely to be his last job in policing.

Jon Boutcher left the press conference and walked out into the crisp Belfast sunshine. He had more to do than most people realised. He still had no members of staff, no premises, no evidence, and no model for how to run an investigation like this. Even the scale of his task was unclear. At one point, Hamilton had suggested that Stakeknife could have been involved in over fifty murders. Boutcher jumped in to correct him, saying, 'I don't want to talk about numbers'. This was because he still did not know how many murders could be linked to this agent. Nobody did, other than Stakeknife himself.

In Belfast, the reaction from senior government ministers to the launch of Operation Kenova was surprisingly muted. One of those who remained silent in the days that followed was the deputy first minister of Northern Ireland, Martin McGuinness.

His mind may have been on other things. There was the looming 'Brexit' vote, less than a fortnight away. He also had a royal visit in his diary.

Later that month, Queen Elizabeth II arrived in Belfast. One of Martin McGuinness's official responsibilities as deputy first minister was to greet visiting heads of state, and that day he was on hand to meet her.

'Hello, are you well?' McGuinness began as the Queen came into sight.

'Thank you, yes,' she replied. 'Well, I'm still alive,' she went on, smiling back at the former IRA man.

Thirty-seven years earlier, the Queen's cousin Lord Louis Mountbatten, also her husband's uncle, had been killed by the IRA. At the time, Martin McGuinness was on the IRA Army Council and would have been one of those who approved and authorised this attack.

After their brief exchange in front of the cameras, Martin McGuinness and the Queen walked into a large room. The door closed, and for the next hour they spoke in private.

The following day, CNN anchor Christiane Amanpour quizzed McGuinness in a live interview about their conversation. She asked if they had discussed the recent Brexit vote. There were fears that Britain's departure from the European Union could trigger violence in Northern Ireland, and Amanpour wanted to know the Queen's thoughts on this.

McGuinness's response was both unexpected and stern. Rather than hint at what the Queen might have said, he invoked royal etiquette, under which you must not disclose details of a private conversation with the monarch. 'I wouldn't want to,' he said, 'under any circumstances, break that protocol.'[11]

The CNN anchor looked bemused. She asked McGuinness if he thought the Queen's reply to his greeting – 'Well, I'm still alive' – was an 'indirect dig', given that she 'was on the list of targets during the Troubles'.

'I don't think that for one minute,' McGuinness replied testily. 'She had many reasons not to meet me in the first instance,' he said of the Queen. 'I had many reasons also not to meet with her.' He then stuck out his tongue for a split second, an involuntary *so there*. 'No, I don't think for one minute that she was in any way attempting a dig. That's not the sort of person that she is.'

Martin McGuinness's handling of this question was statesmanlike, and he came across in that interview as thoughtful and conciliatory. It was a different Martin McGuinness to the one who had first appeared in the British media forty years earlier as the IRA 'boy general' who would pose for photographs while brandishing weapons. A lot had changed since then, but one part of Martin McGuinness's personality remained the same. This was his ability to keep a secret. He did not reveal the details of his conversation with the Queen, just as he did not react in public to the launch of Operation Kenova. It would have been interesting if he had, because he possessed a much better understanding than Jon Boutcher of who Stakeknife was, the world in which he operated, and the crimes he was accused of carrying out.

In the days after speaking to CNN, McGuinness returned to his job of helping to run Northern Ireland. In an office close to

Westminster, Jon Boutcher began to recruit his team of detectives. Not far away, in Parliament, the repercussions of the Brexit vote were starting to play out. Elsewhere, speculation grew about who Stakeknife really was and what might happen to him. There were different theories as to who he could have been. Some wondered if Stakeknife was actually a project, and whether the word referred to more than one person. But one of the most persistent rumours was that Stakeknife had been connected in some way to an IRA unit known across Northern Ireland as the 'Nutting Squad'.

9

The Nutting Squad

Thirty-nine years earlier

In 1977, a young Martin McGuinness set out on a series of walks with Gerry Adams. 'We went away up the lanes,' Adams said of these excursions. 'Just dandering. Just the two of us.' He made it sound like two friends off for a carefree stroll. But McGuinness remembered these walks differently, and how they involved some 'very, very serious conversations about the future of this country'.[1]

Martin McGuinness and Gerry Adams had a complex and absorbing relationship with each other, one that changed over time. They were entirely different and perfectly matched. Adams was more talkative and intellectual, but harder to read. McGuinness was quieter, and at the same time easier to warm to. Their relationship was defined both by the contrast between them and the lack of friction. They could disagree – and frequently did – but neither came to see the other as a threat. After spending hundreds of hours in each other's company, they became more like brothers than rivals, sometimes sharing a bed when necessary.

'No, he didn't snore,' Adams said. 'But I did.'[2]

The purpose of Martin McGuinness and Gerry Adams's walks in 1977 was to thrash out the future of the IRA. At the time,

McGuinness ran the IRA brigade in Derry. Adams, who had just been released from Long Kesh, the British internment camp south of Belfast, was seen as one of the leading figures in the IRA – an organisation he would always deny having joined. Morale inside the IRA was at a historic low. Victory seemed to be out of reach. McGuinness and Adams needed to agree on what had gone wrong and how to fix it. Speaking indoors was risky because any room they were in might have been bugged by the British, so they set out into the countryside.

On most days, the two men began their walks in Derry at the home of McGuinness's mother, Peggy, later described by Adams as 'a great woman'.³ From there, they struck out for the border, tramping past the Hollyhall Road before crossing over into the Republic. The country was damp and open, a world away from the more shuttered atmosphere of the city they had left. Their destination, most times, was the ancient hilltop fort outside Derry called the Grianán of Aileach, or sun temple of Aileach – a circular and spare structure with an elemental kind of beauty. Standing on its high stone walls, the two IRA men could see majestic views that reached to the horizon in every direction. The Ancient Greek scholar Ptolemy had once included the Grianán of Aileach in his map of the world. The building was said to have been built by the Uí Néill, a local clan, who used it for difficult or drawn-out discussions, like the one that McGuinness and Adams had begun to have.

Part of the IRA's problem was to do with expectations. Most senior IRA figures talked about victory as if it were just around the corner. They declared each January that *this* was the year they were going to drive the enemy out of Ireland. The British government was casting off other imperial possessions, so why not this one? But Martin McGuinness and Gerry Adams understood that British politicians did not think of Northern Ireland as a colony and were not about to cut ties with the region, because most of the people living there wanted to remain within the United Kingdom. Nor was the British Army on the brink of defeat. Rather than have the IRA push for an unlikely victory in the next twelve months, they wondered if their emphasis should be on avoiding defeat. Rather than go all out for a win, it might be wiser to play for a draw.

The two men wanted the IRA to wage what they called a 'Long War' – one that could last another decade or more. But for this to work, the organisation needed to change. It would have to become smaller and more professional, with better training and more forensic awareness. Some of the older IRA men, the middle-management, were probably not up to this and might need to be eased out of the way. McGuinness and Adams also wanted to replace the quasi-regimental structure of battalions and companies with a more cellular system centred on Active Service Units, each a self-contained section that was sealed off from the others. That way, if one were compromised, the others would not be affected.

They also talked on these long walks out of Derry about the need to change their political stance. Adams wanted the IRA to move to the Left and be seen as an 'anti-capitalist' organisation. Both men recognised that if the IRA was to keep going for another decade, they needed to do more to win over the ordinary Catholics they claimed to be representing and for whom they were fighting. The IRA had to funnel more resources into its political wing, Provisional Sinn Féin, usually referred to as Sinn Féin.[4]

They even discussed the idea of putting up Sinn Féin candidates for election. For most IRA hardliners, the so-called 'military' or 'army' men, taking part in an election was out of the question. As far as they were concerned, the subject was not even up for debate. One of the reasons they had broken away from the original IRA, at the start of the Troubles, was that they wanted absolutely nothing to do with the democratic process. The IRA often encouraged its supporters to burn their polling cards or start riots outside polling stations.[5] But out here in the open air, Martin McGuinness and Gerry Adams flirted with the idea of breaking this taboo.

Most of this 'Long War' strategy had already been discussed inside Long Kesh by prominent IRA men like Ivor Bell and Brendan Hughes, but this was the first time two figures with the combined standing of McGuinness and Adams, who were in a position to act, had brought these ideas together into a coherent plan. The new strategy sounded smart. It was radical, far-sighted, and bold. But it had a flaw. In becoming tighter, smaller, and more professional, the IRA was going to rely on a smaller pool of people for a longer period of time. Suppose the enemy – the British – could find a way to work agents, or informers, into the senior ranks of the IRA. If they could do that, there was a danger that they would have enough information to bring parts of the organisation to a standstill.

McGuinness and Adams had an inkling of this. They understood that to make the Long War strategy work, they needed to purge the IRA of spies.

But how?

There's a story about Martin McGuinness from later in his life that begins with him being shown for the first time into the Cabinet Room at No. 10 Downing Street. 'So,' he says, looking around, 'this is where the damage was done.' His hosts are taken aback. That's because an IRA mortar recently exploded on the lawn outside the window, and it sounds as if this is what he's talking about.

But he's not.

'I meant', McGuinness explains, 'this is where Michael Collins signed the treaty in 1921.'[6]

The Anglo–Irish Treaty of 1921 was a central event in Martin McGuinness's life, even if it came into being many years before he was born. This treaty marked the end of the Irish War of Independence (also known as the Anglo–Irish War), and led to the partition of

Ireland, while also setting the stage for the Irish Civil War that followed. McGuinness had a bottomless interest in this period of the past. But of all the different personalities he learned about, the figure that always drew him in more than any other was the senior IRA man Michael Collins, one of the five Irishmen who signed the treaty.

In the years leading up to the signing of this treaty, Michael Collins played a starring role in the IRA's campaign against the British. With very little training and few resources, his men pinned down a much larger force. The IRA volunteers fought with courage, resilience, and skill, giving a masterclass in guerrilla warfare. Military tacticians would later pore over the details of what they had done in the hope of imitating their success. During the 1940s, a senior Sternist fighting the British in Mandatory Palestine used the codename 'Michael' in honour of Collins. The IRA's performance also had a profound effect on their opponents – the British. During the Second World War, when Winston Churchill was thinking about how to wage a guerrilla war in Nazi-occupied Europe, he looked to this legendary IRA campaign for inspiration.

But the IRA's record against the British was about much more than battlefield tactics or the weapons they used. It was also about the way they were seen by the local population, and their ability to stop people passing on information to the enemy. Michael Collins, the IRA's director of intelligence, had been clear from the start of this conflict that to avoid defeat they had to win the intelligence war. Collins wanted to 'put out the eyes of the British', because 'without her spies, England was helpless'. As far as he was concerned, intelligence was key. Rather than just expose British agents and force them to leave the island, he gave the order that each one should be killed.

In July 1919, Michael Collins set up a new IRA spy-hunting unit called 'The Squad'. Its job was to track down and kill anyone believed to be a British spy. The following year, members of this unit, assisted by more than a hundred IRA volunteers, attacked the homes of

British intelligence officers and soldiers, as well as Irish policemen and one secret agent. They killed fifteen people in the space of a few hours. Later that day, British soldiers and the local police retaliated by opening fire on the crowd at a Gaelic football match in Dublin's Croke Park, killing fourteen people.

What became known as the first 'Bloody Sunday' was seen as a success for the IRA. The British lost experienced intelligence officers and found it hard in the following months to recruit new agents. The brutality of the IRA meant that few people wanted to risk their lives by working for the British.[7] By the time Michael Collins walked into the Cabinet Room at No. 10 Downing Street, his men had murdered as many as 200 people believed to have been British spies – many more than were actually being run as agents. Some of the victims were 'disappeared', which meant their bodies were buried in unmarked graves so their families could not find them.

Martin McGuinness and Gerry Adams knew about Michael Collins's spy-hunting unit and his merciless attitude towards spies. The question for them, more than fifty years later, was whether they were prepared to go to the same lengths. Gerry Adams may not have needed much persuading on this. In the early 1970s, he is alleged (but has always denied the allegations) to have helped set up a new version of the Squad called the Unknowns, an IRA group that also 'disappeared' suspected informers, murdering them, and burying the corpses where they could not be found.[8]

Even so, Adams and McGuinness both recognised the moral challenge they faced. Neither man was a sadist who appeared to take pleasure in death. Adams attended Mass and always seemed alive to the possibility of divine judgement. McGuinness's religiosity was more overt. His uncle was the Bishop of Nottingham, and he presented himself as a devout, churchgoing Catholic. 'Not the sort you'd tell a dirty joke to.'[9] Setting up a modern-day version of the Squad required each man to square with himself the idea of ending a life for no other reason than this person *might* have been passing on information to the British.

Gerry Adams was later alleged to have said that 'anyone living in west Belfast knows that the consequence for informing is death'[10] (a claim he later denied), while McGuinness, at around the same time, went on the record to say that 'if republican activists who know what the repercussions are for going over to the other side, in fact go over to the other side, then they, more than anyone else, are totally and absolutely aware of what the penalty for doing that is'.[11]

The logic in both statements had the same twisted finality. If enough people knew that the punishment for spying was death, then anyone who became a spy was essentially taking their own life. McGuinness and Adams wanted to shift the blame for these murders away from the perpetrators and onto the victims.

The IRA's new spy-hunting unit came into being soon after Martin McGuinness and Gerry Adams stopped taking their long walks through the grassy grandeur of the Northern Irish countryside. It was a blend of the Unknowns and the Squad, but more disciplined, and was bound by its own macabre set of rules. This new 'Internal Security Unit' would be responsible for vetting new IRA recruits, interrogating volunteers who had been held in police custody, and dealing with those accused of being informers. Suspects were to be taken to a safe house for questioning. Anyone who confessed to being a spy was told to produce a written statement, for confession was at the heart of this enterprise. They would be recorded as they read it out, and the tape had to be listened to by at least one member of the all-powerful IRA Army Council, who would decide whether the suspect should be killed. If the victim was sentenced to death, they were allowed to write a final goodbye letter. This was either posted to their family or delivered by hand. After that, they were taken away and murdered, usually by the same people who had carried out the interrogation.

In Northern Ireland, 'nut' was another way of saying 'head'. 'To nut' someone meant shooting them in the head. It would not be long before the IRA's new spy-hunting team became known as the 'Nutting Squad'.

Scap-a-fuckin-tichi

One day in 1977, at around the time that McGuinness and Adams began their long walks, a man called Freddie Scappaticci was led into a police station in Belfast. It was not the first time this had happened. Thickset and short, with dark, lustrous eyes, Scappaticci had been 'lifted' earlier that day from his home. He lived in the Markets area of Belfast, known as 'Little Italy', after the rush of Italian immigrants that began to arrive there in the late nineteenth century. One of these was Daniel Scappaticci, who went on to set up a successful ice-cream business. Now his son, Freddie, was sitting in the local police station with a scrum of other young men.

This was a 'screening', a hangover from the early days of the Troubles. A group of people would be rounded up by the police or the army and interrogated individually for about an hour. They were asked everything from the names of local IRA commanders to the colour of the wallpaper in their neighbours' living room. No detail seemed to be too trivial. But the police used these screenings for more than gathering information. Each one was an opportunity to speak in private to their agents, who would be included in the round-up.

Freddie Scappaticci was proud to call himself a 'Belfast Sixty-niner', which was a way of saying he had been involved in the violence from as early as 1969. Even if he had not inherited a centuries-old grievance against his Protestant neighbours, on account of his Italian ancestry, Scappaticci was a practising Catholic, his community had been under attack, and he passionately believed that the best response to the situation was taking up arms and joining the IRA.

Two years later, Scappaticci was interned in Long Kesh. Although he was not one of the top players in the IRA's Belfast brigade, he became close to a man reputed to be one of them: Gerry Adams. Scappaticci came to be seen as one of Adams's enforcers. He had an obviously physical presence. He was good in a fight as well as loyal. Shortly after his release, 'Scap' was interned again. Not many people had been interned twice, and this, for him, became a badge of honour.

Scappaticci left Long Kesh for the last time in 1975. After returning to his life as a bricklayer, he heard about a tax scam going on in the building trade. It involved the 715 tax booklet that needed to be filled out at the end of a job. There was a way of fiddling the forms. As far as he could tell, most of the people he knew were doing it, and he decided to have a go himself. But he was found out, arrested, and taken to a police station in Belfast where a clever, fast-talking detective from London told him he was going to jail.

Once this idea had settled in Freddie Scappaticci's mind, the detective offered him a way out. Perhaps Scappaticci was expecting him to ask for information about the IRA. But he did not. The detective only wanted the names of other builders who might have been involved in the same tax scam. If Scap agreed to work for him as a police informer, then he would not be charged, and he could even earn a little on the side.[1]

Freddie Scappaticci had spent most of the last four years away from his wife and young family. He did not want to be behind bars again. Agreeing to help the police on this one thing might not make him a traitor in the eyes of the IRA. It was also a way for him to get back at anyone in the trade he had fallen out with. Knowing him, there would have been a few.

Anyone who lived in the Markets area could tell you that Freddie Scappaticci had a quick temper, as well as a heavy punch and what one journalist called 'a deep, unwavering, Manson-like stare'.[2] This was someone who understood the pathology of power and cared deeply about status. Some of this could be traced back to growing up in Belfast with a surname that people liked to get wrong because they knew it would wind him up.

'It's Scap-a-tichi,' he would roar. 'Scap-a-fuckin-tichi!'[3]

Scap's response to most attacks was full-throttled and fast. This had always been his survival strategy. Now the friendly detective seemed to be offering him a cleaner way to get back at those who had crossed him. It was like throwing meat to a tiger. He said yes.

More than a year later, in 1977, Freddie Scappaticci was again in a police interview room for what he imagined would be a routine conversation with his police handler. Except it was not, because they were joined by someone else.

The third man in the room that day was called Peter. Friends of his would say that he spoke with a lovely West Country burr, one that sounded like a car being driven over freshly laid gravel. He had longish dark hair, was taller than most, twinkly-eyed and sturdily built. Peter was one of those people who could charm the birds out of the trees, someone who seemed to live for the thrill of throwing himself into a conversation without knowing where it was going to end. Though he was not from Northern Ireland, he had an affinity for the region. Before the start of the Troubles, he had spent time in Belfast, married a model, and become friends with a local singer-songwriter called George Morrison, later known by his stage name Van Morrison. Peter was lively, unpredictable, and warm, and he had a way of drawing people in and making them feel wanted.

Peter was also a soldier: a staff sergeant in the British Army on his fourth emergency tour of Northern Ireland with the Devonshire and Dorset Regiment. He had recently joined his battalion intelligence cell, which meant he was on the lookout for potential agents. This was something he had mentioned in passing to the detective running Scappaticci. He may not have thought anything would come of it, as the local police rarely shared their agents with the army. But this detective liked Peter and his unsoldierly manner and decided to make an exception.

Peter began to talk to Freddie Scappaticci in the police station that day, and the two men hit it off. It would be wrong to say that the plan was working, because there was no plan. But a relationship had started, and it would go on to change the history of the Troubles.

Peter did not force his relationship with Freddie Scappaticci in the days that followed. But he made sure to bump into him again, and suggested that the two of them go for a drink.

This took courage. At almost exactly the same time, a different British soldier called Robert Nairac, a captain in the Grenadier Guards and a liaison officer attached to the SAS, went to a pub in South Armagh to recruit a new source. Like Peter, Nairac had an affinity for Northern Ireland. He felt at home there, and that night he decided to go to the pub without any back-up or indeed a clear sense of who he might meet. He also decided to spend the evening speaking in a fake Belfast accent.

Robert Nairac was bold and fond of risk. He was also a romantic with an old-fashioned approach to agent-running. He liked disguise and was well-versed in the Middle Eastern adventures of T. E. Lawrence and the Victorian explorer Richard Burton, who had once smuggled himself into Mecca disguised as a woman. Growing up, he had read books like Rudyard Kipling's *Kim* and John Buchan's *Greenmantle*, and loved the idea of being an Englishman abroad who could 'go native'.

One of the men in the pub realised that Nairac's accent was wrong and that he was not who he claimed to be. At around closing time, a group of men followed the soldier outside, bundled him into the back of a car, drove him away, tortured him, and killed him. His body has never been found. It was buried, according to one rumour, in a peat bog. Either that or it was taken to a nearby meat-processing factory. 'They put him through the mincer,' one IRA man said. 'They scalped him, cut out his innards and turned him into meat and meal.'[4] But at no point in this ordeal did he break. 'Nairac was the bravest man I ever met,' one of the IRA volunteers convicted of his murder would say. 'He told us nothing.'[5]

Peter was taking a considerable risk by going for a drink with Freddie Scappaticci, a well-known IRA man. But he had a different approach to Nairac, and he took precautions. He made sure to meet in a place where neither man was likely to be recognised, and he did not try to pass himself off as being from Northern Ireland. Peter also put together a plan for what to do if it turned out that this was a trap.

During the meeting itself, Peter did not rush. He kept the conversation to what they had in common, such as music, women, and football. Scappaticci had once been a talented footballer, going on trial with Nottingham Forest as a teenager, but it came to nothing. Slowly, the two men developed a bond. 'The relationship between agent and handler is a marriage,' Peter later said, 'but, a one-sided one. The handler must know everything about his agent: his fears, his personal problems, his concerns about money, how often he has sex, and with whom; his relationship with his wife; and, who he hates within the IRA, and who he likes.'[6]

This last point was crucial. Freddie Scappaticci had recently become disillusioned with the state of the IRA. After sounding off about some of the senior figures in his area, he had been taken outside, beaten up, and told that he no longer belonged to the organisation. Scappaticci was physically hurt, but the psychological wound was deeper. The IRA had taken away the status he had enjoyed in this part of Belfast, and in its place came an almost insatiable need for revenge.

Peter realised that this was his way in. He recognised in Freddie Scappaticci the urge to get back at those who had hurt him. He also thought his new friend was someone who might enjoy espionage, 'the buzz and the deceit', as he put it, 'the intrigue, the thought of knowing something that no one else knew'.[7] Scappaticci was a child of the Markets area. 'The people there are dealers,' the Irish commentator Kevin Myers later wrote, 'whose slyly intrusive fingers are adept at rigging the scales, hiding the bad apples at the bottom of the bag and miscounting your change.'[8] Scappaticci had an eye for a deal. He was someone who loved to be a step ahead of everyone else, which made him perfectly suited to life as an agent.

The bond between handler and agent often flourishes in the uncertainty surrounding what they are doing. Peter never propositioned Scappaticci, sometimes known as Fred, Freddie, or Alfredo – never asked him outright if he was willing to risk his life to become a British spy in return for cash. 'You even don't want them to say, "I want to work for you",' Peter would explain to an army officer. 'You don't want to remind them what they are doing.'[9] Instead, he crossed the line slowly, keeping his language loose and suggestive. It was the recruitment equivalent of grandmother's footsteps. He did not suddenly put his new friend in a situation where he was forced to decide, until the distance between them had all but gone and there seemed to be no way back.

Now they could get down to brass tacks. Payment. The type of information Peter wanted. How to meet. Scappaticci's conversations with Peter would usually take place at night in a vehicle fitted with hidden microphones. They developed a system for working out where to meet, when, and what to do if either man was late. During each meet, they would drive around Belfast chatting about the political situation and the IRA, as well as their own lives and any other gossip they had heard.

Their relationship was rooted in a friendship, and this made it unusual. In the past, when a British soldier took on a source in Northern Ireland, they sometimes thought of this person as being nothing more than an 'informer' – a derogatory word for an army agent – and often saw the bond between them as purely transactional. Peter had a different approach. Both men were soon opening up to each other about things they kept hidden from others. Scappaticci came to trust Peter, and in the early days, he was said to call him up to ask his advice on everything. He rang at any time of day, which must have been tiring for those running him. But it was also encouraging. It showed that Scappaticci understood the seriousness of what he was doing, and that he had the chess-playing nous to keep himself a few moves ahead of everyone else.

The army officers monitoring this situation could have responded to Freddie Scappaticci's need for round-the-clock advice by saying he wasn't worth it, letting him go, or rationing the time he spent with his handler. Instead, they set up a boutique agent-running unit exclusively to look after him. Nothing like this had been done before. This tiny office consisted at first of just Peter and one other soldier, a talented field intelligence non-commissioned officer, or FINCO, with a photographic memory and an ear for accents. Their office became known as the 'Rathole', partly because of its location in a dingy Portakabin room directly below the office of the man running army operations in the region, Jimmy Glover.

The intelligence that came out of the Rathole was useful in a tactical sense, because Scappaticci would sometimes pass on what he had heard about a forthcoming IRA attack. Although he had been forced out of the IRA, he was still in touch with volunteers and often picked up scraps about what was about to happen. But his information also had considerable strategic value, in that it gave his handlers a better understanding of the broader shifts inside the IRA. Without this intelligence, Jimmy Glover's controversial 1978 report about the IRA's metamorphosis would have read very differently. Scappaticci had become, as one senior army officer put it, a 'priceless asset', and already his recruitment was being talked about as a 'breakthrough'.[10]

But Scappaticci was still on the outside of the IRA, looking in. Those running him began to wonder how much better his intelligence could be if he was ever able to find a way back inside the organisation.

According to the ancient Chinese military general and historian Sun Tzu, there are five types of spy. The first is what he called an 'expendable agent', or, as it appears in the gloomier translation from the original Chinese, the 'doomed spy'. This agent is dispatched to the enemy camp to spread false ideas but is not expected to come back. Next comes the 'living agent', or 'surviving spy', who sneaks into the enemy camp and returns to report on what they have seen. Then comes the 'double agent' who collects intelligence for one side while secretly working for the other. Sun Tzu also mentioned 'local spies': casual informants who live in enemy territory and provide low-grade intelligence at little risk to themselves.

But for Sun Tzu, the most sought-after spy was the 'inside agent', or 'inward spy'. This is an enemy official who agrees to pass on information to one side while continuing to work for the other. Frederick of Prussia, in the eighteenth century, called this kind of operative a 'spy of consequence'.[11] These will always be the most valuable spies, the ones who can make a difference. An inside agent can do more than steal secrets or share their thoughts on what an enemy leader *might be* thinking. They can also affect *what* that leader is thinking. They are passive as well as active; one moment observing, the next exerting a gentle kind of influence. While a double agent works for the other side as a spy, and is only really concerned with espionage and intelligence, the inside agent will be closer to the heart of the organisation you're interested in and more likely to know what it is going to do next.

From Ancient China to Northern Ireland in the 1980s, agent handlers have always valued 'inside agents' over any other type of spy and thought of them as the ultimate prize. Agents like these are both precious and rare. After the Irish War of Independence, a classified British analysis of the conflict concluded that the British had found it 'practically impossible to place a man in any inner circle' because, 'for Irishmen, the risks of discovery and of its consequent results were too great'.[12] Inside agents are hard to come by for one simple reason. For most of human history the punishment for this kind of activity, in Ireland or anywhere else, has been death.

Freddie Scappaticci understood the danger of trying to get back into the IRA. He knew that if he slipped up, the new Nutting Squad could be onto him. But he agreed to have a go.

Very soon after, Scappaticci told his handler that he had succeeded. He had become an IRA volunteer again. For those running him, this was a stunning development. There was no way to know how far he might rise inside the organisation, or the quality of information he could one day access. But that sense of excitement and opportunity was framed at first by doubt. Scappaticci might not last. He could be expelled again, or interrogated by the Nutting Squad and killed. There was also a small danger that the army's new inside agent had never really left the IRA and might actually be a double agent working for the enemy. This had happened before, earlier in the Troubles.

Only after Scappaticci began to supply intelligence from inside the IRA did his handlers realise that he was working exclusively for them. His information allowed them to foil attacks and save lives. It was consistently excellent – much too good to be the kind of 'chickenfeed' the IRA would willingly pass on to the British. Scappaticci even revealed on one occasion that the IRA had been going through some of the rubbish coming out of the British Army's barracks in Lisburn, outside Belfast, and discovered the name of his handler. Scappaticci did not quite save his life, but close enough.

Scap, as he was often known, was the real thing. By the start of the 1980s, he was supplying as much information as he could get his hands on. All the team tasked with running him needed to do, it seemed, was keep him alive.

London Calling

When Frank Hegarty met Jack on the Hollyhall Road, in 1980, it was not the first time he had been approached by a stranger while out walking his dog. Only a few weeks earlier, Frank had been on the same lane when he noticed two men hiding in the undergrowth. His greyhound, Blue, was probably the first to become aware of them. Frank could see that they were soldiers and they were trying to hide. But from who or what, he had no idea.

He kept walking. You can imagine the fear rippling through his body. Something was about to happen. Then he saw a figure ahead. Once he was within earshot, this other man started to speak.

'Englishmen', John le Carré once wrote, 'are branded on the tongue.' The individual who tried to draw Frank into a conversation that day was a former officer in the British Army, and had a voice that sounded perfectly normal to him, his wife, his family, and to his colleagues. But to Frank, this man would have come across as clipped and a little grand, a *sassenach* – the less-than-flattering Irish term for an Englishman. Frank wanted nothing to do with him and walked on in silence. The stranger eventually gave up, and that seemed to be the end of it. But it was not.

The soldiers Frank had seen by the side of the road belonged to the army's elite surveillance unit, 14 Intelligence Company, known as 'the Det'. Their job that morning had been to provide cover for the man trying to engage Frank in conversation, who was legally unable to carry a firearm because he was not a soldier. He was a case officer for MI5.

At the start of the Troubles, the Security Service, Britain's domestic intelligence agency, better known as MI5, had just two officers working on Northern Ireland. One was a newcomer called Stella Rimington, who would go on to be the first female director-general of MI5. She remembered having a 'tottering pile' of reports on her desk which, she said, sadly, 'did not at that stage contain much in the way of real intelligence'.[2] When it came to Northern Ireland, as far as she could tell, 'MI5 had practically no sources of information'. Most of her superiors saw this conflict as something that should be dealt with by the army and the local police. They were more interested in hunting down Soviet spies. In 1970, when asked by the prime minister about what the service could do to help, the MI5 director-general waved the question away, saying, 'No amount of intelligence could cure Northern Ireland's ills'.[3]

Fast forward ten years, and this attitude had been turned upside down. By 1980, MI5 was run by Howard Smith, a career diplomat from the Foreign Office and a former Bletchley Park codebreaker, who had a very different perspective on Northern Ireland to most senior MI5 officers – which was the point, and part of the reason why he had been given the job, much to the annoyance of his new colleagues. Smith believed that MI5 could play a part in ending the violence.[4] At the same time, a new generation of young officers were moving up through the ranks of MI5, including newcomers like Stella Rimington, who remembered there being at this time a 'huge change in the way we worked and in the whole culture of the Service'.[5] Another recent addition to MI5 was the historian Stephen Lander, also a future director-general, who echoed what Rimington said about the gap opening up between those at the top of MI5, many of them middle-aged, right-wing, and military-minded, and beneath them a new breed of 'able, ambitious, proactive young Security Service officers'.[6]

Lander was also struck by how many of the fresh recruits to MI5 wanted, like him, to serve in Northern Ireland. Ten years earlier, at the start of the Troubles, MI5 officers would do almost everything they could to avoid being sent there. Now the opposite was true. Some went out to join the MI5 surveillance section in Belfast, which specialised in planting bugs and an array of increasingly ingenious recording devices. Others worked in the office of the director and coordinator of intelligence (DCI), where they received information, assessed it, and produced reports for customers in Whitehall. The DCI's office would also draw up a list of intelligence requirements at the start of each reporting cycle that was passed on to the other MI5 offices in Northern Ireland. Finally, there were those like Stephen Lander who became part of the 'Irish Joint Section' in Belfast, later known as 'Joint Section'. Their job was to recruit and run agents.

Joint Section was unusual in that it contained officers from both MI5 and SIS, giving it a distinctive, offbeat character. Even if they were operating on British soil, the atmosphere inside Joint Section was similar to what you might find in an overseas SIS station. They were working in an environment that felt like a war zone. There was said to be an IRA unit devoted to identifying, capturing, interrogating, and executing people like them who were working for British intelligence. This could come as a shock for some MI5 case officers posted to Joint Section for the first time, whose experience of field-work before coming out to Northern Ireland might have involved nothing more dangerous than sitting in the back of a Left-wing political meeting or shadowing a Soviet diplomat around London. Few had operated in an environment like this. They began to live with the idea that when they left their compound each day, there could be someone beyond the gate waiting to kill them. The fear this produced could press against the edge of their senses, making everything around them feel sharper and more alive, in a way that sometimes only became clear after they had left the region and noticed its absence.

Following the IRA's 'spectacular' at Warrenpoint several months earlier, MI5 began to have a much larger presence in the region. More MI5 officers than ever before were arriving in Belfast. There were soon so many of them that the local police had a nickname for the newcomers. They were the 'London Calling' boys, after the new single from The Clash, and many of them were ambitious and eager, and wanted to make their mark.[7]

In late 1979, one of these London Calling men set out to recruit Frank Hegarty as an MI5 agent. His approach did not work. There was nothing unusual about this. As a general rule in the world of intelligence, the first attempt to recruit an agent usually ends in failure. The MI5 officer could have moved on to another target, and Frank's life would have been very different if he had. Instead, he decided to try again. He spoke to his counterparts in the police and was soon in touch with the FRU office in Derry.

Although the FRU and MI5 were not rival organisations, and they had separate priorities and areas of expertise, both were in the business of trying to take on agents, and it was inevitable that they would compare themselves to each other. Soldiers in the FRU often thought of themselves as more practical and direct than the university-educated, middle-class officers over at MI5, who they would sometimes resent because they appeared to have more power and greater resources. But MI5 did not control the FRU or have authority over it. As one MI5 officer put it, he and his colleagues could *advise* their counterparts in the FRU, but 'in no way' could they 'dictate to them how they ran their agents'.[8] Both organisations were in the region to help the local police, and most of their communications were with them. But there were times when they found themselves working together, and one of these was the attempt in early 1980 to recruit Frank Hegarty.

Jack's team in the FRU office in Derry agreed to take on the job of approaching Frank. If they were successful, the deal between them was that Frank would be run jointly by the FRU and MI5. The soldiers began by looking for ways to improve on the original MI5 recruitment plan. They liked the idea of making contact with Frank while he was walking his dog on the Hollyhall Road, but thought that their man, Jack, should also have a dog because this would make him more approachable. They soon found someone who could lend Jack a dog for his attempt to take on Frank.

The FRU also wanted their target, Frank, to be familiar with the sight of Jack before they actually met. In the weeks leading up to the 'point' (army-speak for the first contact between a handler and their potential agent), Jack walked the dog he had been lent along this lane at a time when they knew Frank was going to be out there with Blue. His instructions on those first few walks were to remain near enough to Frank that he could be seen, but not so close that the target could catch up with him.

The team in the local FRU office also thought it was a mistake to have men hiding by the side of the Hollyhall Road. It was winter, and there was little cover in that pocket of woodland. A better plan was to wait for Frank to get onto the lane before blocking it off at either end. This also had the advantage of giving Jack more time to make his pitch without worrying about being disturbed by passing vehicles.

Jack's colleagues then carried out more research into Frank's life. They picked up extra details about his greyhound, his partner, and his family, and they chose Jack as his potential handler, rather than one of his commanding officers. They wanted to use someone from a similar background to Frank, who might have a better chance of getting on with him. They also felt it would help from a psychological point of view if, on the day of the meet, Frank was trying to catch up with Jack, rather than the other way around. That way, he would have decided already that he wanted to talk to this stranger, before finding out who he really was.

In this, and so many other ways, the FRU's approach to taking on Frank Hegarty was a subtle improvement on the earlier attempt by MI5. It was also informed by the fundamental lesson that the army had learned from taking on Freddie Scappaticci. What had happened over in Belfast with Peter and the former IRA man underlined to them the importance of friendship when trying to recruit a new agent.

The plan worked. Frank agreed to get in the back of the van with Jack, and they drove to a well-known hotel outside Derry called the White Horse Inn, a place that was popular with Protestant families and just about the last place you would expect to bump into anyone with links to the IRA. The White Horse also had two entrances, meaning Jack and Frank could enter separately. In the privacy of a hotel room, Jack explained to Frank roughly what he wanted him to do. He stressed that they were not asking him to join the IRA, only to pass on gossip he heard around town. Very little in Frank's life would have to change. If Jack's team found out that Frank was in danger, they would intervene to keep him safe and, if necessary, take him out of the region.

Frank Hegarty had a lot of questions for Jack as they sat together in the hotel room. He wanted to be sure that he was doing the right thing. Eventually, he agreed to help.

'Agent 3018', as Frank would appear in most army reports, began to meet up with Jack about once every fortnight. Their conversations always finished with an agreement about where and when the next pick-up was going to take place. Between them, they had a roster of about five or six locations that they referred to with letters of the alphabet. So Jack might end a meeting by saying something like: *Next meet is Tuesday week, 19.30, D.*

'D' could refer to a stretch of oak woodland outside Derry, or the car park of a Protestant golf club – anywhere Frank was unlikely to be recognised. Handlers sometimes referred to these areas where an agent was unlikely to be noticed as 'dead ground'. Jack changed the locations as often as possible. Like every soldier in Northern Ireland, he was familiar with the shouty poster pinned to the walls of his barracks that said: 'STAY ALIVE. BREAK YOUR ROUTINE'.[9] The IRA was good at spotting patterns.

In spy thrillers, agents tend to meet their handlers on street corners, cafés, or park benches. The FRU preferred 'moving meets'. Jack would give Frank a short route to walk rather than a fixed location. Once Frank was into his stride, an unmarked army van would approach from the opposite direction. Two soldiers in a separate vehicle were on hand to provide 'close cover' in case Frank had been compromised. If either party was late, both knew to rendezvous at the same place sixty minutes later – a system called the 'second hour'.

Once the soldier driving the van had spotted Frank and was closing in on him, he would slow down. Meanwhile, a man in the back rolled open the back door. Frank clambered in as the van came up next to him, before the vehicle set off again. Like birds mating on the wing, nobody was ever still and the whole thing was over in a few seconds. Even if someone had looked over at the precise moment that Frank got into the van, public transport in Northern Ireland was patchy and there was nothing strange about seeing a man accept a lift from a passing vehicle.

With Frank in the back of the van, the soldier at the wheel would carry out some basic anti-surveillance drills to make sure they weren't being followed. This involved cutting back on himself and speeding up or slowing down to let other vehicles pass. This might have looked random, but it was not. Owing to the geography of Northern Ireland, in which one wrong turn could take you into a hostile area, these routes were always planned in advance. Once the driver was sure he had nobody on his tail, he would deliver Frank to his handler.

Jack might be waiting for Frank in a nearby caravan, the White Horse Inn, or in a safe house with a connecting garage which would allow him to walk from the van to the house without being seen. But on most occasions, Jack was waiting for his agent back in Ebrington Barracks, the army's sprawling base close to the heart of Derry.

Some Special Branch detectives were bemused by the lengths that the FRU went to when picking up agents, calling these operations 'Spielberg productions'.[10] But the soldiers understood how important they were. Most agents in Northern Ireland were not at their most vulnerable when gathering intelligence, but when they tried to pass it on. Each handler had a duty of care to their agents. During the days between meets, it was often too dangerous to make contact, so the few hours in which the handlers met up with their agents were usually the only ones in which they were in complete control of the relationship. It made sense to take every possible precaution. By putting so much effort into these pick-ups, Jack and his colleagues also showed Frank that he mattered to them and they took his safety seriously, which helped to strengthen the trust between them.

Jack did not at first tell Frank Hegarty that he was being run by the FRU as well as MI5. Instead, he wrote up his conversations with Frank and passed these reports on to his MI5 counterpart in Joint Section. Later, he would receive a reply from Belfast with questions to ask Frank at their next meeting.

This arrangement appeared to be working well. Frank's information was adding to the overall intelligence picture coming out of Derry, and Jack had no complaints with his new agent. But six months into the new relationship, the MI5 officer who had first tried to recruit Frank had an idea. He wanted to run Frank himself. Within some intelligence agencies, an agent is not thought of as being under control until he has been run by more than one handler or case officer. Sometimes an agent's loyalty is not to the organisation for which they work, but only to the person who recruited them.

When Jack told Frank about this new arrangement, he simply refused to go along with it. He would only work with Jack. That was it. The bond between them was still too important, and so the idea was put to one side.

In the following weeks, Frank Hegarty began to settle into more of a routine. Like Freddie Scappaticci on the other side of the region, he continued to supply his army handler with information that could help break up IRA attacks or improve the government's understanding of what was happening inside this organisation. Both men were becoming more familiar with the strange, tectonic pressure of life as a spy. Each one had a young family and doted on their children. Hegarty and Scappaticci were attentive to their partners and conspiratorial with their handlers. They enjoyed having extra cash in their pockets and took comfort in knowing that they might be helping to end the violence. They were both still adjusting to their new reality and the feeling that they belonged to two very different worlds at the same time, when everything around them changed.

The Link

One of the other IRA volunteers held in Long Kesh at the same time as Freddie Scappaticci was a man called Bobby. He was younger than most prisoners, had long, wavy hair, loved to play the guitar, and was released at around the same time as him in the mid-1970s. After that, the course of their lives branched off in opposite directions. Scappaticci was soon kicked out of the IRA and became an army agent, while Bobby Sands was involved in a gunfight with the police, arrested and sent to jail.

Almost five years later, on 1 March 1981, Bobby Sands told the prison authorities that he had begun a hunger strike. Aged just twenty-six, he was the most senior IRA man in the prison complex once called Long Kesh but recently renamed HM Prison Maze, and known to most people as 'the Maze'. Bobby Sands was refusing to eat unless Margaret Thatcher reversed the previous government's decision to end 'special category' status for paramilitary prisoners like him. He wanted to be treated as a prisoner of war, not a criminal, and was willing to die for this. 'I am standing on the threshold of another trembling world', he wrote, later that day. 'May God have mercy on my soul.'[1]

The first IRA hunger strike in the Maze had been called off several months earlier without loss of life, after the British government made several concessions. But only some of the original IRA demands had been met. Now Bobby Sands and nine other hunger strikers wanted to finish the job off. Rather than refuse food *en masse*, they had agreed to join the strike at staggered intervals as a way of exerting more pressure on the government.

Bobby Sands had gone five days without food when a by-election was called in the Northern Irish constituency of Fermanagh and South Tyrone. Ordinarily, this would have been of no interest to the IRA, as they did not get involved in elections as a matter of principle. But on this occasion, one IRA man wondered to himself what would happen if they put up Bobby Sands as a candidate in the by-election. He suggested this to Gerry Adams, who began to think it through. The obvious danger was that they might not get enough votes. Bobby Sands's hunger strike had attracted little media attention until then, and his candidacy might be dismissed as nothing more than a stunt. Then again, it could raise the profile of what he was doing, and if he won, Thatcher would come under huge pressure to give in.

Several days later, Bobby Sands was announced as a candidate in the by-election. But he was not standing for Sinn Féin. Instead, he ran under the 'Anti H-Block' banner (the Maze was often called H-Block). Gerry Adams and Martin McGuinness could still look anyone in the eye and tell them that they had not entered politics, and yet, as everyone knew, Sinn Féin officials were campaigning hard on Sands's behalf and nobody made any attempt to hide the fact that the man they wanted everyone to vote for was a member of the IRA.

Bobby Sands won 30,492 votes in the by-election, 1,446 more than anyone else and enough to secure victory. His fellow prisoners banged their pipes and danced in their cells. As one SIS officer put it, the IRA had 'pulled a joker out of a pack'.[2] It was a publicity masterstroke. Margaret Thatcher was under more pressure than ever to meet the hunger strikers' demands. But she refused. Thatcher's argument was that if a convicted IRA volunteer like Bobby Sands was treated like a prisoner of war, other paramilitaries would think they could launch fresh attacks with impunity. It might give them what she called 'a licence to kill', and it was clear from the way she phrased this that she did not think anybody should have that.[3]

After sixty-six days without food, Bobby Sands died. The reaction to his agonising death was furious and global. The Queen was attacked with ketchup-filled balloons on her state visit to Norway. British businesses in Europe were firebombed. Streets in Paris and Tehran were renamed in honour of Bobby Sands. The Libyan leader Colonel Muammar Gaddafi hailed him as a martyr who had died 'fighting for a just and sacred cause'.[4] In the United States, the long-shoremen's labour union refused to unload cargo from British ships, and more money than ever poured into the coffers of the pro-IRA group NORAID.[5]

The reaction in Northern Ireland was more visceral. The region was buffeted by waves of disbelief and rage. There were massed peaceful marches as well as sudden outbreaks of violence. But the depth of feeling here, and across the island of Ireland, was about more than the death of Bobby Sands, and could be traced back to a deeper historical wound.

During the Great Hunger in the nineteenth century, *an Gorta Mór*, the Famine, or, for English schoolchildren, the Irish Potato Famine, as many as 1 million people in Ireland died from starvation and malnutrition, and twice as many moved overseas. The potato crops in Ireland had failed because of a blight that had swept across Europe, but the extent of the famine was the result of decisions made by the British. In the years leading up to this, the government had failed to reform land ownership in Ireland or reduce the dependency across the island on a single crop. Nor was it willing, in the face of mass starvation, to set aside its attachment to the idea of free trade and intervene to stop the export of food from Ireland. The British appeared to have turned a blind eye then to Irish suffering. Now, in

1981, a miniature version of the same thing seemed to be happening again. The unlaid ghost of the past had come to haunt the present, not only in Ireland, but in the United States, where millions of Irish–Americans had ancestors who left the country during the famine. Many of them experienced this episode as part of an inherited trauma that had been passed down through the generations.

Bobby Sands was dead, and the IRA's popularity was at an all-time high. Margaret Thatcher's was plummeting to a new low, and nine more hunger strikers were ready to follow in Sands's footsteps. It was at this point in the second hunger strike that the IRA and the British government began to negotiate in secret.

Michael Oatley was impressive-looking and tall, and worked for SIS, Britain's overseas intelligence service. He was also a good listener. In the early 1970s, Mike, as he was known in the office, was posted to Northern Ireland on behalf of SIS where one of the first people he met in Derry was a fish-and-chip-shop owner called Brendan Duddy.

Oatley's new friend appeared to know everyone, from the local police chief to Martin McGuinness. Brendan Duddy was a Catholic, a pacifist, and a cross-country runner for whom no distance seemed to be too far. Each day, he went for a run up to the Grianán of Aileach. Duddy enjoyed being around Michael Oatley, the handsome British intelligence officer. 'He was like a film star,' Duddy later said. 'A very articulate British diplomat who knew everything.' The attraction was mutual, and they became fast friends. The Englishman and the Northern Irishman both seemed to recognise in the other something they saw in themselves. Not just a desire for peace but a certain maverick quality, a willingness to see things in a different light and to start a sentence with the words: *What if* . . . They also understood at an early stage in their friendship – and this was the point on which everything turned – that they could help each other.

What made the growing British intelligence operation in Northern

Ireland so distinctive, even at this early stage, was the number of different agencies at work, and how they all wanted slightly different things. Michael Oatley had no desire to take on Brendan Duddy as an agent and to run him in the way that the FRU looked after someone like Frank Hegarty. He saw Duddy instead as a conduit to the IRA. While the police, the army, and MI5 were busy gathering tactical and strategic intelligence, Michael Oatley was more interested in finding ways to send messages to the IRA leadership, and engage in what was called 'covert diplomacy'.

SIS had a long history of speaking in the shadows with Britain's enemies. Oatley wanted to do the same thing in Northern Ireland. He hoped that by getting to know Brendan Duddy he could set up talks with the IRA, because he was convinced that this was the first step towards ending the violence. Eventually, the two men made a breakthrough.

In 1975, Michael Oatley and Brendan Duddy engineered peace talks between the British government and the IRA. Duddy's code-name was 'The Link', while Oatley was known within the IRA by an array of colourful monikers that sounded like the titles of spy thrillers including 'The Man from Jerusalem', 'The Donkey Rider' (another nod to Jerusalem), or, the one that stuck, 'The Mountain Climber'. The peace talks they set up did not take place in a luxurious hotel compound in a neutral country, but in Brendan Duddy's front parlour, with security provided by a British colonel sitting outside in a Ford Granada.

At last, peace in Northern Ireland seemed to be within reach. The British even went to the trouble of purchasing a yacht, moored on a lake in Fermanagh, on which they hoped the final peace accords would be signed.[6] But the talks broke down on account of disagreements on both sides, and Oatley was posted away from the region.

Before he left, however, Michael Oatley made an unusual arrangement with Brendan Duddy. The new line from the British government was that there was to be no further contact between British officials and the IRA or intermediaries like Duddy. Oatley ignored this, because he felt his relationship with Brendan Duddy was too valuable. Rather than break off their friendship, he left Duddy instructions for how he could be reached wherever he was in the world. Like some latter-day King Arthur, the SIS man would reappear in a time of need. All Duddy had to do was make the call.

Five years later, during the first hunger strike, Brendan Duddy picked up the phone and told Michael Oatley that Martin McGuinness and Gerry Adams wanted to end the strike, but needed a way to do so without losing face. Oatley went straight to SIS Headquarters in London where he composed a draft agreement between the British government and the hunger strikers. Soon a version of this was being read by Margaret Thatcher in No. 10 Downing Street, while Oatley sat in a car outside, waiting for her response. The black door opened. A civil servant hurried over. The prime minister had approved the proposal. Oatley's instructions were to deliver it to the IRA immediately. He raced to Heathrow Airport and was soon on a plane to Belfast with the document in his briefcase.

Michael Oatley had been told to wait in the Arrivals lounge of Belfast Airport with a newspaper under one arm and a red carnation in his suit buttonhole. The British spy was eventually met by a local priest, a go-between with the IRA known as 'the Angel'. Oatley handed over the thirty-four-page government proposal that allowed paramilitary prisoners to wear different clothing. Once those in jail heard that this document was on its way – but before they had actually gone through the text – they called off the hunger strike. One of their men had been hours away from death and nobody wanted him to die in vain. Lives were saved, but it was obvious once they read the proposal that some of the prisoners' demands had not been met, which was why Bobby Sands decided, several months later, to launch a second strike.

Brendan Duddy and Michael Oatley went to work again, pushing in secret for a deal between the IRA and the government. They relayed messages between representatives on both sides. Bobby Sands would write to Duddy shortly before his death to thank him for his efforts. At one point, Thatcher passed a message to McGuinness and Adams saying that if 'there is subsequently any public reference to this exchange we shall deny it took place'.[7] As she requested, the talks remained secret. Both sides had a lot to lose from news of the negotiations ever leaking out. At an early stage, a deal appeared to be close. One of the offers from Thatcher's government had been accepted by the prisoners, according to the author and former IRA volunteer Richard O'Rawe. But the hunger strikers were overruled by senior IRA figures on the outside including – allegedly – Gerry Adams, who wanted the strike to keep going because of the positive impact it was having on the popularity of the IRA.[8]

All ten hunger strikers died, and Michael Oatley and Brendan Duddy's efforts went down as a noble failure. Margaret Thatcher vowed never again to negotiate with McGuinness and Adams. The IRA, meanwhile, made plans to have the prime minister killed. The door to a negotiated peace appeared to have been slammed shut.

But the secret talks were useful in other ways. If nothing else, the British came away with a much sharper sense of who Martin McGuinness was and what his role within the IRA had become. They realised for the first time that this senior IRA figure had the respect of not only Gerry Adams and his more politically minded followers, but the hardliners as well – the absolutists who were likely to be the hardest to win over to a political compromise. Adams was the face of the movement; McGuinness was the heart. The British also understood that they now had a way of contacting him.

In the long night of the Troubles, trust was the light with which people found their way. Michael Oatley had become by this stage a good friend of Brendan Duddy's – 'closer than brothers,' he later said.

But so was Martin McGuinness, whose wife, Bernie, knew Brendan Duddy's wife, and who had himself delivered burger meat to Duddy's fish-and-chip shop in the days before the Troubles.[9] Duddy remembered McGuinness from those days as a teenager with 'absolutely no interest in politics'.[10]

Brendan Duddy had played host at different times to the IRA leader and the SIS officer. Both McGuinness and Oatley trusted him, and having a friend in common changed the way these two felt about each other. Could Oatley and McGuinness have spoken in person at around this time? It is possible. They might have met in Duddy's home or in the nearby SIS safe house near Limavady codenamed 'Coffee House'. Brendan Duddy could easily have set this up.

At the very least, Michael Oatley and Martin McGuinness each had a sense of who the other was, and how they might, one day, be useful. This relationship was in its infancy. The British also came away from the secret talks with the realisation that there were men at the top of the IRA with the 'persuasion, education, and knowledge' to lead the organisation towards a political compromise and peace.[11]

The most senior MI5 officer in the region had already hinted at what this could mean in a message to Margaret Thatcher. 'From time to time,' he wrote to her in 1981, 'we have considered whether and under what circumstances the Provisionals [IRA] might switch the focus of their efforts to the political front.' The likes of McGuinness and Adams pushing for a political solution could be, he said, 'a development to be encouraged'.[12]

To be encouraged. These last three words are at once coy and revealing. It is as if by using the passive infinitive this encouraging would happen by itself, without anyone having to do anything. Or, perhaps more accurately, if someone were to do something, it could never be traced back to them. The first part of the message is simply an observation, a musing out loud, but those last words – *to be encouraged* – hint at the possibility of covert action.

A radical idea had washed up on the shores of MI5. Some of the intelligence officers working on Northern Ireland had begun to wonder if it might be in Britain's interests for Martin McGuinness and Gerry Adams to remain in control of the IRA, and whether they could ever 'encourage' them to move towards a political solution.

Others were not so sure. Although it is tempting to think of MI5 as a single cohesive unit, and to imagine that what one member of staff might have been thinking will reflect what their colleagues believed as well, the reality is different. The region's most senior MI5 officer could be writing one thing to civil servants in the Northern Ireland Office, while officers in Joint Section were saying something else entirely to their agents in the field. There was often a gap within MI5 between what was happening at a political level and an operational level. Separate parts of the service tended to move in the same direction but at different speeds.

But by 1981, for the first time, *some* MI5 officers had begun to imagine an alternative ending to the Troubles. At the time, Martin McGuinness and Gerry Adams were routinely portrayed in the British media as mass murderers, criminals, and terrorists. The idea of the British government doing anything to protect them, or in any way help them to achieve political power, was an outrageous one. But the logic behind it was by no means new.

There was a time in the 1940s, in Mandated Palestine, when the British government would refer to Menachem Begin, then leader of the Zionist military group Irgun, as a terrorist and an insurgent, only later to embrace him as a political ally and respected statesman. In Cyprus, soon after, the British had Archbishop Makarios exiled from the island because of his links to the insurgency against their rule, before bringing him back and having him elected as the first Cypriot president. In Kenya, the activist Jomo Kenyatta was detained and imprisoned by the British, before being befriended by an SIS officer and later welcomed as the first leader of a newly independent

Kenya. The SIS officer who forged such a close relationship with Kenyatta was Frank Steele, the same man who accompanied Martin McGuinness and Gerry Adams on their 1972 trip to London.

In the years after the Second World War, both SIS and MI5 devoted many of their resources to managing the break-up of the British Empire, often doing so on a shoestring budget. One of the tactics honed by SIS during this period was the art of singling out an enemy insurgent with the potential for political leadership, winning them over quietly and out of sight, and helping to set them on the path to power. The aim was to bring not only peace and stability to the territory in question, but to have it run by a leader who was sympathetic to Britain. It would have been strange in Northern Ireland if those working for SIS and MI5 had not thought about trying something similar.

But the idea in itself was not enough. By the end of the hunger strikes, in the summer of 1981, there was little that anyone from MI5 could actually do to 'encourage' Martin McGuinness and Gerry Adams to turn their attention to a political solution. The British intelligence operation was still not big enough, and they had no levers to pull. They needed the IRA to take the first step towards politics, and after that they might be able to act as a catalyst. It was only possible to 'encourage' something once it had begun. Until that happened, they would have to be patient.

They did not have to wait long.

The Ballot Box and the ArmaLite

Danny Morrison looked out at his audience, took a breath, and began to speak. The room was packed, and Martin McGuinness was sitting by his side. It was October 1981, only two months after the end of the second hunger strike, and Morrison had begun to address the Sinn Féin Ard Fheis, or annual conference, in the capital's Mansion House, the same building in which Sinn Féin politicians had once set up their own Irish Parliament, in 1918, in defiance of Westminster. As the party's director of publicity, Danny Morrison knew that sympathy for the IRA was at an all-time high. He also appreciated that the organisation's hardliners wanted a new military campaign.[1] They imagined that those who had marched in support of the hunger strikers also wanted the IRA to launch a fresh offensive, and that each vote for Bobby Sands was a call to arms. Morrison saw things differently.

'Who here really believes we can win the war through the ballot box?' he asked, knowing that few of them did, especially when he phrased it like that. 'But will anyone here object if, with a ballot paper in one hand and the ArmaLite in the other, we take power in Ireland?'[2]

'What the fuck's going on?' McGuinness hissed up at him.[3]

Danny Morrison seemed to have got in a muddle. The ArmaLite

was the IRA weapon of choice. How could they take power using guns *and* votes? Surely, it was one or the other? But all he had done was move too soon. The idea of Sinn Féin taking part in British elections while the IRA continued its military campaign was, Gerry Adams later confirmed, one that 'we have been coming to terms with over the last three or four years'.[4] Danny Morrison had just decided to bring things forward.

Call it a landmark, a milestone, a turning point – there could be no way back. Sinn Féin would be putting up candidates in the next Northern Irish elections. A priest who had known Gerry Adams in the 1970s, Father Denis Faul – known as 'Denis the Menace' within the IRA, because of his opposition to violence – said that if he had been told that Adams and those around him would ever end up in politics, 'I would have laughed at them, I would have said that's insane, they're just physical-force men'.[5] For most IRA hardliners, the idea of taking part in an election was still a heresy. They were purists. They wanted what the Irish revolutionary Patrick Pearse called 'the peace of mind of those who never compromise'.[6] Even if the original Sinn Féin had played a vital part in the 1918 struggle for Irish independence, winning 73 of the 105 parliamentary seats covering Ireland, the modern-day hardliners tended to see Sinn Féin as something of an indulgence and a waste of resources. 'They couldn't get it,' one Sinn Féin official said of the IRA. 'They just wanted to kill Brits.'[7]

Martin McGuinness and Gerry Adams knew that putting up Sinn Féin candidates in the next election was a gamble of the highest order. There were people inside their movement who wanted them to fail, as well as all those on the outside. In private, though, McGuinness was beginning to wonder if the IRA might soon run out of road. He later explained this with a reference to the Grianán of Aileach, the circular hilltop fort outside Derry where he and Adams had debated the move into politics.

'You walk round it,' McGuinness said, 'hitting the wall with your head. It's not moving and you're not moving. But then you come to a door and the question is, if I open that door and go in, am I in more danger than out here? But if I go in there, I might make a change. We'd tried the other one and after a lot of discussion we decided we'd go for this option.'[8]

Martin McGuinness was going to try the political door, but that did not mean he was about to abandon his military past. He would try to pass himself off as a politician, and along the way he might experience some kind of personal redemption, but he still hoped to stay close to the IRA hardliners whose respect and support he had always prized. He would try the political door, and if it worked, his plan was to wait in the doorway and encourage others to follow him in.

The following year, in 1982, on the terraced streets of Derry, Martin McGuinness began his career as a politician. It was a bizarre sight. This IRA chieftain, one of the most feared men in Derry, was politely asking passers-by if he could count on their vote in the forthcoming elections to the Northern Ireland Assembly. He did his best to project certainty and confidence, like any would-be politician, and had dressed up for the occasion in a tweed jacket with leather-patched elbows. He looked as if he was off to church. But behind the smart outfit and the rictus grin were flickers of doubt. Martin McGuinness was still not entirely sure that he was doing the right thing.

'Martin's arm had to be twisted to stand in these elections,' Danny Morrison remembered. 'He realised, I think, that there would be considerable concentration on him. And on his family,' he added. 'He also probably thought at the time that his role lay in areas other than politics.'[9] McGuinness had always seen himself as a hardliner, and someone who was likely to choose the ArmaLite over the ballot box. Putting himself up for election was a huge step away from this. It would also place him in the spotlight like never before. McGuinness remained an intensely private, inward-looking person, and, as one local activist put it, 'something of a home bird'.[10]

The other fear for McGuinness was that he might not get the votes. Perhaps he was less popular than he had always thought. There was no way for him to know how ordinary people in Derry were going to react in the privacy of the voting booth to his reinvention as a politician. Nor did he know what the IRA hardliners would say if he was defeated and this political experiment ended in humiliation. It was also unlikely that Martin McGuinness had a sense of the reaction to all this within MI5.

14

Whatever It Takes

One day in 1982, shortly before the elections in which Martin McGuinness was taking part for the first time, a British agent contacted his handler to pass on important information. The agent's name was Willie Carlin. He had the wiry build of a jockey, bright eyes, and a dazzling memory. He was a former British soldier, a Catholic, and a Derryman. He had volunteered to work for the British only the year before, after the death of Joanne Mathers, a young mother who had been going door to door to collect information for the British census when she was murdered by an IRA gunman. The order for her killing was said to have come from McGuinness.[1] Working for the census was seen by some hardliners as collaborating with the enemy. Willie Carlin was among the last people to have seen Joanne Mathers alive.

'It had a profound effect on me,' Carlin said of her death. 'Somewhere, somehow, the animals were back. The IRA hadn't gone away at all.'[2] Offering to help the British was, for him, a way to end the violence.

In the weeks leading up to the 1982 elections, Willie Carlin was working for Sinn Féin. He had become a trusted figure in the party's Bogside office, where everyone was going flat out to get Martin McGuinness elected. They were either on the phone encouraging supporters to vote, handing out leaflets, putting up posters, or arranging transport to the polling stations. But that was not all they were doing.

As Carlin explained to his MI5 case officer, Sinn Féin was planning to rig the election. On polling day, they would carry out widespread voter fraud and personation, or 'plugging', as it was known locally, to make sure Martin McGuinness was elected.

Voter personation had been going on in Northern Ireland for years. 'It was regarded as a sort of honest crime,' one local journalist wrote. 'Both sides knew it was going on, it usually worked out about even, and nobody got hurt.'³ People would laugh about it. 'What do you mean he's been taken off the register?' Went the joke – 'he's only been dead three years.' But this was different, as Carlin told the MI5 man. The voter personation that Sinn Féin was about to carry out was on a completely different scale: they were not just adding one or two votes to the final count, but hundreds – possibly thousands.

Willie Carlin would always remember the response from his MI5 case officer. Carlin was expecting him to say that he would take steps to stop the voter fraud. But he did not.

'It's imperative that you do what you can to get McGuinness elected,' he said.⁴

'Even if it means breaking the law through vote stealing?' Carlin asked.

The MI5 officer 'just smiled'. 'Whatever it takes, Willie, whatever it takes.' As if the message was not clear, he added: 'It's important that by next week Martin McGuinness is an elected representative of Sinn Féin.'⁵ 'There's a view amongst Unionists,' he also said, 'that your man' – McGuinness – 'speaks for nobody. He's a terrorist and he holds the people of Derry to ransom, and they're afraid. Now we need to change that.'⁶

Willie Carlin became intrigued by MI5's relationship with Martin McGuinness. On one trip to London, he was debriefed by MI5 officer

Stella Rimington and remembered how McGuinness was the person she wanted to hear about more than any other. Back in Derry, Carlin's handler often grilled him about the same man, until Carlin started to refer to this part of their conversations as 'The McGuinness Half Hour'. On the face of it, MI5's curiosity made sense. Martin McGuinness was a senior IRA figure, and it was natural that they should want to know more about him. But Carlin began to wonder if something else was going on, and if the British might have a closer connection to this man.

Shortly before Martin McGuinness stood for election, Willie Carlin had been on his way to see his MI5 case officer outside Derry when something very unusual happened. Carlin had been told to go to a local safe house – probably the same place beyond Limavady used by Brendan Duddy and Michael Oatley for some of their meetings. As Carlin was about to turn into the drive which led up to the house, he noticed a car pulling away from the same building. He looked at it more closely, and saw Martin McGuinness sitting in the passenger seat.

'I could feel my right foot shaking on the accelerator and sweat running down the back of my shirt,' he later wrote. 'What the hell was Martin McGuinness doing coming out of an MI5 house?'[7] Perhaps Carlin had mistaken someone else for him, or McGuinness had taken a wrong turn. Maybe the IRA man had gone to see the people living in this house about something else, unaware that their home was also used by the British as a meeting place. But it was at least possible that Martin McGuinness had gone to this house for a clandestine meeting with a British official, and due to a monumental error – the kind of thing that could have ended the careers of those involved – Carlin was scheduled to be there at around the same time.

On polling day in 1982, Willie Carlin voted fourteen times for Martin McGuinness. One of his colleagues in Sinn Féin outdid that, casting sixty-seven votes. Carlin stole polling cards meant for 'doctors, nurses and other medical staff from the local hospital', even 'the votes of the nuns from the Good Shepherd Convent'.[8] 'I hear Unionists complaining about it all the time,' one IRA volunteer said of his personation work for Sinn Féin. 'They're right, it was massive. I had loads of dead people, I had babies' names. I had babies who weren't born, babies who were in the graveyard; they all voted.'[9] By Carlin's reckoning, he and the rest of the Sinn Féin team took or personated more than 800 votes. A report by the Northern Ireland Office later put the figure in Derry at more than 2,000 personated votes.[10]

Martin McGuinness and Sinn Féin performed better than expected in the 1982 Northern Ireland Assembly Elections. McGuinness was formally elected to the assembly, and his party received more than 64,000 votes. This put them in fourth place overall, with more than 10 per cent of the vote. Almost twice as many people voted for the nationalist alternative, the Social Democratic and Labour Party (SDLP), led by John Hume, a Catholic Derryman resolutely opposed to violence, who comfortably outperformed McGuinness in Derry. Here was a reminder that the IRA did not have anything like a popular mandate from the local Catholic population, and that most of the people they claimed to represent did not support their military campaign.

But for McGuinness and Adams, fourth place felt like a victory. Danny Morrison's line about the ballot paper and the ArmaLite was starting to make sense. The IRA's move into electoral politics had not ended in all-out defeat. McGuinness was now an elected politician. Sinn Féin had a foothold from which they could start to climb.

The same was true, in a way, of MI5. Conversations which, until then, had been peppered with words like 'might', 'if', and 'could' now became more fluent and expansive. The case officers in Joint Section, and their colleagues in the MI5 parent section in London, started to adjust their projections of the future. The IRA's move into electoral politics was under way, and this gave them something with which to work.

Eight months later, Gerry Adams was elected as the new MP for Belfast West, a result described by the Northern Ireland secretary as 'a tragedy'. Several hours before the announcement, a British soldier had been killed by the IRA in Ballymurphy, where Adams was said to have once run the local IRA battalion. Adams left the count to cries of 'murderer'. For the IRA hardliners, taking this soldier's life was a way of reminding Gerry Adams, and the rest of the world, that success for Sinn Féin at the ballot box did not mean they were about to lay down their ArmaLites. The 'armed struggle' was still on.

The Sinn Féin performance several miles away in Belfast East received much less media coverage. This was a mainly Protestant constituency, and the Sinn Féin candidate, Denis Donaldson, won less than 2 per cent of the vote. Donaldson was a stout, energetic figure with a dark moustache and a brush of thick hair, and was known to be one of Gerry Adams's most trusted aides and strategists. Within the IRA, 'Wee Denis' had an unimpeachable pedigree.[11] Like so many senior republicans, he was a graduate of the 'University of Long Kesh' where he had been close to Bobby Sands, and was respected within the organisation as a physical-force man. Recently, Donaldson had been arrested on his way back from a Lebanese training camp and was judged by the British to be so dangerous that he – as well as McGuinness, Adams, and Morrison – had been banned from entering Great Britain.

If it was a surprise to see a hardliner like Donaldson taking part in elections, his defeat was more predictable. Nobody imagined that Denis Donaldson was going to be elected in Belfast East, and his failure to win was barely mentioned in the news. But the response would have been different if it had leaked out at the time that this Sinn Féin candidate was also an MI5 agent.

'I was recruited', Denis Donaldson later explained, 'after compromising myself during a vulnerable time in my life', something he never expanded upon in public.[12] The people who recruited him may have found some detail in his private life, such as an affair with the wife of another IRA man, which they could use in their approach. Better to take your chances with us as a spy, they might have said, than answer to a cuckolded paramilitary. Nor did Donaldson reveal exactly when he became a British agent. But it is telling that the exclusion order banning him from visiting Great Britain was quietly lifted between the middle of 1981 and late 1982, which was probably around the time he was taken on. Donaldson was recruited by Special Branch, but MI5 soon became involved and he began to be run by both organisations.

Denis Donaldson became a prized agent, given the access he had to senior IRA figures. But he never found a way to reconcile himself to what he was doing. He had not volunteered for this undercover work, and that changed the way he felt about it. The nature of his recruitment shaped the character of his secret life. After his exposure, it is telling that he did not ask to be resettled thousands of miles away but instead chose to live without any police protection in Donegal, in a spartan cottage without running water or electricity. It was almost as if this was a form of penance. Several months after moving in, he was shot dead.

The most striking part of Donaldson's story was not his motivation, but the instructions he received from MI5. The history of espionage has many stories of agents provocateurs: government agents who infiltrate a political group and work against it from the inside like a human cancer. They encourage extremists either to become more extreme or to turn against their comrades. In short, they are destructive.

Denis Donaldson could have been told to be an agent provocateur, a gremlin inside the Sinn Féin machine spreading rumours and setting traps to land his colleagues in jail. But he was not. In the 1983 general election, although Donaldson won just a small proportion of the vote in Belfast East, he did significantly better than expected. The local constituency was dominated by Protestants who were never going to vote for a Sinn Féin candidate like him, and this left Donaldson and his SDLP rival to fight over a relatively small number of votes. But in that miniature contest, the MI5 man won. Sinn Féin outperformed the SDLP, mainly as a result of Donaldson's hard work.

Willie Carlin was operating in a similar way. Rather than slow the growth of Sinn Féin, he was doing the opposite, and was acting as an accelerant. Carlin and Donaldson were both trying to move the IRA's political wing towards respectability and electoral success. Rather than being *agents provocateurs* they were more like *agents pacificateurs* helping to steer the party towards peace.

Attitudes inside MI5 were continuing to evolve. During the 1970s, the majority of MI5 officers had watched the Troubles play out with an air of almost fatalistic detachment, as if there was nothing they could usefully do. Now there was a gathering understanding in parts of the service, especially among the younger case officers in Joint Section, that Sinn Féin's success at the polls should be either tolerated or encouraged. This was starting to affect how MI5 ran its agents, and some were being given new instructions and set on very different paths. One of them was Frank Hegarty.

What Are You Smoking?

Frank Hegarty seems to have settled down. It is early 1984, and The General, as he is still sometimes known, lives in Shantallow, north Derry, with his partner, Dorothy. They share a tidy, white-fronted house with their son and daughter, aged four and two, and Dorothy's three children from an earlier relationship.

On most mornings, Frank comes downstairs to school bags, hats, coats, shoes, and a toy or two, knowing that the house will soon be filled with noise, the smell of food and cigarettes, and the bustle of everyone getting ready for the day. In the background, a radio news-reader might be going through the most recent litany of paramilitary attacks. Some families around here have a cousin, a nephew, or a son in jail, and it's rare to get through the day without a reminder of the wider situation.

But Frank is sometimes out of the house before all this begins, as he gets up early to walk the dogs. Each day, he steps out onto a quiet, watchful street. The lemonade man will soon be doing his rounds, and the milkman, the breadman, the postman, the coalman. Frank recognises most of the neighbours around here, and he has friends nearby, who he will see for a pint in a local pub. But Shantallow – 'Shanty' to those who live here – can often feel more like Dorothy's world than his. A part of Frank will always be rooted in Rosemount, several miles away, which is where he grew up and where most of his family still live.

Some mornings, after leaving home early, Frank drives up to his mother's house in Rosemount, where he has a kennel in the garden with space for three dogs. Compared to Shantallow, the front gardens around here are a little neater, the streets quieter, and you're more likely to see lace curtains in the windows.

Frank's mother, Rose, is now in her mid-seventies. She is a proud and matriarchal figure, fast-talking and spirited, and shows no sign of slowing down. Even when Frank's father was alive, Rose was always the magnetic central presence in her household. Like so many women of her generation, she has managed to raise an enormous family while holding down a job in the nearby shirt factory. Rose has nine children, which by anyone's standards is a lot. But in the way they group together, it can feel like three smaller and more manageable families. Her youngest three are all in their twenties, including Noleen, Rose's youngest, who has Down syndrome. Then you have the middle three, who are almost all in their thirties now. Last come the three eldest boys, including her beloved Frankie.

Looking out over the emotional landscape of any family, it is hard to talk about a mother having a favourite child. But most people who know the Hegartys will agree that Rose has, at the very least, a soft spot for Frank. She worries about him and wants to take care of him. She knows that he struggles with his back, and on wintry mornings will help him with his boots before he takes out the dogs. Perhaps she'll have breakfast on the table for him when he gets back. If Rose hears that Frank is going out for a drink with friends, she might tell the others to keep him off the whiskey and make sure he does not drink too much. It's a tease, of course. Frank does not have a problem with drink. But it hints at the way his mother thinks of him, even now. Rose sees him as someone who occasionally needs to be protected, either from the world or from himself. It is hard to imagine how she would react if she found out that for the last few years her son has been secretly working as a British agent.

Frank Hegarty sits down with his army handler about once a fortnight. Although he was taken on by Jack, the pipe-smoking birdwatcher, he is now being run by a different soldier from the FRU, 'Mick', an experienced and imposing man from the north of England, who has already developed a close bond with Frank.

One day in early 1984, Frank goes to see Mick for what he imagines will be a routine conversation. After being picked up in a van, he is taken to the FRU office in Ebrington Barracks and sits down with Mick and another soldier. The room is a jumble of army-issue furniture. There is a map of Derry on the wall, and the scene is lit by a white halogen strip that lets out a faint hum.

Frank knows what to expect from these meetings. He will pass on a few bits of information, Mick will ask some questions of his own, as well as those which have come in from MI5, and Frank will receive his weekly payment of £25. The two men will agree on a date and location for the next pick-up, and he will be on his way.[1]

But this time it is different. Mick tells Frank that they have a new job for him. They want him to join the local IRA brigade, and somehow find a way to get close to Martin McGuinness.

'What the fuck!' Frank says.

'This is what we'd like you to do,' Mick explains, almost as an apology, 'or at least try.'[2]

This is not Mick's idea. It was passed on to him by his boss in the local FRU office, Captain John Tobias, a respected Intelligence Corps officer. When Mick first heard about the plan, he was said to have asked Tobias what he had been smoking.[3] Almost nobody in this FRU office thinks Frank Hegarty has the slightest chance of getting inside the IRA, let alone earning the trust of someone as suspicious and shrewd as Martin McGuinness. Frank is an 'eyes-and-ears' agent. He supplies information he has picked up in the pub and around town. He is not the kind of person you could imagine running around in a balaclava. But Tobias does not back down. That is the job, and now they have to get on with it. Tobias does not say where the order came from, but it is easy to guess.

A local IRA man, Raymond Gilmour, had recently stood up in court and named almost a hundred people with links to the IRA in Derry, and in return become a 'supergrass', meaning he now had immunity from prosecution. The effect on the IRA brigade in Derry was devastating. Most volunteers were either on the run or in jail, and the atmosphere among those left behind was toxic. Martin McGuinness was said to be furious about what had happened, and was telling everyone that he was going to be arrested any day now. But the police never came for him.

Gilmour's testimony had put Martin McGuinness and those around him on edge, and this immediately became a problem for MI5. They needed more intelligence on McGuinness and wanted to recruit agents close to him. But the mood in Derry was so wary that they found it impossible to take anyone on. The targets they approached wanted nothing to do with them. So those in MI5 thought about repurposing some of their existing agents.

The idea of asking Frank Hegarty to join the IRA and get close to McGuinness undoubtedly came from MI5. But when it was first discussed in the FRU office, and ridiculed as something that was never going to happen, it was just that – an idea. Mick had no authority over Frank. He could not order him to have a go at joining the IRA. Frank Hegarty was not part of their military hierarchy and was free to walk away from his undercover work at any time. All that Mick could do, really, was put this idea before him and give him time to think about it.

Frank Hegarty left Ebrington Barracks that day with his head spinning. The thought of trying to infiltrate the IRA so soon after the supergrass Raymond Gilmour had appeared in court was like trying to rob a bank the day after a heist. Security would be tighter than ever. The IRA men were bound to see him coming. Nor was Frank an obvious fit as a paramilitary. Recruits to the IRA tended to be serious, churchgoing, and political. Many of them were in their early twenties and came from republican families. Frank was in his forties, had recently had two children out of wedlock with a married Protestant woman, did not come from a republican family, and often came across as being more interested in looking after his greyhounds than forcing the British Army out of Northern Ireland.

From a distance, Frank did not stand a chance. But he was comfortable with risk. He understood the thrill of placing a bet, the conviction he would sometimes feel that this one was going to come good – even if the odds were long. Frank did not think that he would necessarily be taken on by the IRA, but, as he explained to Mick, once he had had time to think about it, he was willing to give it a try.

Outside the Tent

It is 1984, and the IRA has become a vulcanised version of its former self. Its volunteers are survivors, and are in the habit of second-guessing everyone and everything. So how can you become one of them? How does anyone join the IRA? There is no form to fill out. No recruiting office to visit. Even if Frank Hegarty knows who to approach, the act of asking is the kind of thing that could make him look like a plant. Whatever happens, he cannot appear to be in a hurry or to want it too much.

More than a thousand years ago, Alfred the Great, King of England, disguised himself as a travelling musician before setting off on an undercover mission. He made his way through the night to the camp of his enemy, the Viking leader, Guthrum the Old. When he arrived there, Alfred explained that he had come to play music. The Viking soldiers allowed him to continue on his way and soon he found himself outside Guthrum's tent.

At this point in the story, you might expect Alfred to talk his way in. But he did not. Instead, he sat down outside the tent and began playing the small harp he had with him, as one historian wrote, 'touching the trembling strings in harmonious cadence'. One way to get inside the tent was by letting those inside know that he had something they wanted. After the men in the tent heard his playing, he was 'readily admitted' and 'entertained the king and his companions for some time with his musical performance, carefully examining everything while occupied in singing'.[1] Alfred had come to gather intelligence, and the information he picked up inside the Viking tent was decisive in his subsequent victory over Guthrum – or so the story goes.

If Frank Hegarty is to find a way into the IRA, he needs to show the people inside the tent that he has something they want. He must play his harp and wait to be called in. The challenge lies in making those inside believe they need him more than he needs them.

Which part of the IRA should Frank try to join? Recruits often end up in an 'Active Service Unit', which will mean being asked, at some point, to plant a bomb, hijack a vehicle, take part in a kidnapping, or carry out an armed attack. Even if it's phrased as a question, only one answer is really available. 'In the IRA you're given instructions, and you do what you're told,' a former Special Branch detective explained. 'You don't say, "Well, don't think of me for this job. I don't like loud bangs and explosions. Keep me for next week when you have no shooting to do." Those choices just aren't there.'[2] If Frank joins an Active Service Unit, there is a chance that he will either be killed or become a killer.

Like any handler, Mick feels a profound responsibility towards his agent. He understands the trust that Frank has placed in him and he wants to keep him alive. But he also needs to minimise the risk of Frank being involved in a murder. As much as Mick appreciates the psychological burden Frank will have to carry for the rest of his life if he were to kill someone, he's also worried about the legal side of this.

Frank later recalled one of his handlers telling him that if he committed a serious crime in the course of his work, 'he would be granted immunity from prosecution'.[3] But no handler in the FRU had the power to offer this. Nor had any of them been told precisely what to do if one of their agents was caught up in a killing. The agent-running unit set up years ago by Jimmy Glover prided itself on its 'rigorous training', in everything from weapons handling, photographic interpretation, to how to lose a tail, but the legal side of what they were doing had become a blind spot.[4]

Handlers in the FRU, according to a later military report, were never made 'aware of any guidelines for agent handling'.[5] With no clear set of rules, the soldiers relied on common sense. They told their agents not to carry weapons. They warned them that if the police caught them, then they were on their own (which, in practice, was not always true). A small number of handlers believed that if their agent told them about a crime, this conferred on them some kind of immunity from prosecution.[6] Others let their agents know, without necessarily spelling it out, that if they were involved in a murder, it might be best to keep it to themselves.

From Mick's point of view, the best way to avoid the problem was to have Frank infiltrate a different section of the IRA. Rather than join an Active Service Unit, perhaps he could find a role in one of the organisation's other departments, such as Intelligence, Training, Finance, Publicity, Internal Security, Civil Administration (the IRA's vigilante police force, which administered so-called 'punishment' shootings), or Frank could try to be taken on by the quartermaster's department.

Each IRA Brigade had its own quartermaster. Their job was to source weapons and explosives, store them, and distribute them to local volunteers. If Frank found a way into the local quartermaster's department, he could tell his handlers about where the IRA's weapons were coming from, which were in circulation, and who was about to use them. It would also mean that he could keep his hands relatively clean and he might not be involved in any serious crimes.

Mick talks to Frank about his first move. They agree that he should start by showing his face at the Sinn Féin office on Cable Street, in the Bogside.

'Go round and make yourself available,' Mick tells him. 'Offer to help out, and take round some leaflets.'[7]

On a cold day in 1984, Frank Hegarty walks up to the Sinn Féin office in the Bogside and steps inside. It's an ordinary-looking terraced house, but busier than any other building on the street. Two of the first people he sees in there are Bernie and Briege, the dependable Sinn Féin secretaries who spend most of the day answering the telephone, drinking tea, and typing up minutes on their Olivetti typewriters. The office has been smartened up since the party moved into electoral politics, and the atmosphere that day is lively and full of purpose. There's a sense of momentum and a feeling that things are beginning to change. Upstairs are three small offices, including one on the right that belongs to Martin McGuinness and is reserved for IRA business.[8]

One of the people Frank sees in the Sinn Féin office is Willie Carlin. Neither man knows that the other is a British agent.

'Nice guy,' Carlin would say of Frank. 'A plain guy, but savvy. Sharp as a tack.'

Over the next few weeks, Frank Hegarty continues to show his face at the Sinn Féin office in the Bogside, usually in the mornings after walking the dogs and seeing his mother. He hands out leaflets. He looks for ways to help.

'You had to like him,' one IRA volunteer said of Frank. 'He was a very likeable person. He'd always ask about how you're getting on, stuff like that.'[9]

Frank remains in the background. Interested but not persistent. Helpful but not in a hurry, until he becomes a familiar face in the Sinn Féin office. But he is still outside the tent, which is why he starts to let people know about some of the ways that he can help.

The best greyhound racing in the area is over the border in Lifford, County Donegal, and Frank will occasionally have a dog in a race there, or he will go to see someone else's dog perform and enjoy 'the craic'. Frank is often crossing that border, and his car will sometimes have a dog trailer attached. The IRA has a long history of smuggling. As well as moving weapons and explosives over the border, volunteers will shift goods that can be priced up on the other side of the border, such as alcohol, which can be sold in the Republic for twice what anyone will pay for it in Northern Ireland. One way for the IRA to move contraband is by hiding it in trailers containing dogs. Another is to use horseboxes. 'You couldn't beat horseboxes,' one IRA volunteer explained. 'The Brits' sniffer dogs couldn't get past the smell of the horse. Masses of stuff was moved in those boxes – tons.'[10]

So it is, that in early 1984, Frank Hegarty decides to get back into horses. He and his brother Willie have long had an interest in them, having kept several horses and some goats in a field outside Derry. But Frank now decides to take on a show-jumping horse, and begins to enter it into competitions. This gives him more of a reason to be driving horseboxes across the border, and that makes him more attractive to the local IRA.

Frank is also a 'clean skin', meaning he does not appear on the security forces' lists of known IRA members. Apart from the caution he received as a teenager for driving a car without correctly displaying his learner plates, Frank Hegarty has no criminal record.

The General is now precisely where his handlers want him to be. Frank is sitting outside the tent, waiting to be invited in, when a senior IRA man in Belfast gets wind of what might be about to happen.

17

The Heathen

Ivor Bell has steely blue eyes, a handlebar moustache, and a history of taking things further than anyone else. He grew up as a Protestant, but renounced his faith to become a Marxist, hence his nickname – 'the Heathen'. Bell then joined the IRA, in the 1950s, before walking out in protest after they declared a ceasefire. After joining up again, he was part of the IRA team sent to London in 1972 to negotiate with the British government. He had wanted to turn up in army fatigues to make Willie Whitelaw feel ill at ease, but in the end thought better of it.

When Ivor Bell hears that members of the Derry brigade are thinking about taking on Frank Hegarty, he becomes suspicious. Something about this does not feel right. 'Bell didn't like his background,' Freddie Scappaticci later explained. 'He just didn't fancy him.'

Ivor Bell's main problem with Frank, it turns out, is his association with the *other* IRA. Back in 1972, around the time of Bloody Sunday, Frank Hegarty was said to have joined the 'Official' IRA, also known as the 'Stickies' because their members stuck Easter lilies onto their shirts, whereas the Provos used pins. Others called this original version of the group the 'Red IRA' on account of their Left-wing and more utopian outlook. The Official IRA wanted to

unite the working class in Northern Ireland *before* pushing for unification. Some people dismissed their talk of class solidarity and
bringing together Catholics and Protestants as pie-in-the-sky stuff,
given the reality of everything else that was going on. But Frank saw
enough in this group to join up. Throughout his life, he was drawn
to the promise of a society in which religious divisions were less
pronounced and a future that looked very different to the present.
He believed that people could change.

Ivor Bell is not so sure. He knows about Frank's earlier involvement in the Official IRA. He has also heard that Frank was kicked
out of this group after someone saw him talking to a soldier. The
idea that Frank might have once been an agent makes Bell worry
that he could be doing the same thing now. He doesn't trust him.
But what really concerns Ivor Bell is the department inside the IRA
that Frank might be about to join.

Bell has long felt that the only way to unite Ireland is by force. He
wants to see more armed attacks and a new military campaign, and
over the last two years he has been working hard to smuggle more
arms into Northern Ireland. He has tried to bring in weapons and
explosives from the United States and has made contact with officials
acting for the Libyan dictator Colonel Gaddafi in the hope that he
might also help the IRA. If these supplies ever materialise, they will
be looked after by the IRA quartermaster's department.

Ivor Bell sends a message to Derry saying that Frank Hegarty
must not, under any circumstances, be allowed into the IRA. That
appears to be the end of it. Frank's attempt to join the local IRA
brigade has failed. He has done well to get so close to being taken
on, but there seems to be no way around this. Ivor Bell is on the
IRA Army Council and was recently chief of staff. If someone of
his stature speaks out against you, there is little you or anyone else
can do. Unless, of course, that person is overruled by one of only a
handful of people inside the IRA with even more authority than him.

Martin McGuinness has known Frank Hegarty for years. He has also heard the rumours about him back in the 1970s, and how he was expelled from the Official IRA. But what matters to McGuinness more than any of the stories which have attached themselves to Frank over the years is the intuitive feeling he has for him, and whether he thinks he can be trusted.

'He had an emotional response to people,' Gerry Adams said of McGuinness. 'If he thought you were sound on his first meeting you, then you were sound.'[2] Danny Morrison agreed, saying McGuinness 'was a good reader of people' and could identify 'people's strengths and weaknesses – things I wouldn't have spotted. He was a real psychologist.'[3] Others were not so sure. 'He left school at fifteen,' one former IRA volunteer said, 'he was as thick as two short planks.'[4] But for any of McGuinness's acolytes, and certainly for the man himself, his ability to read people is a defining characteristic, one which has helped him in his rise to the top of the IRA. If he feels good about someone, then that is enough.

The IRA is short of manpower. The General can cross the border without difficulty and has an excuse to be at the Lifford greyhound track in the Republic at least once a week. IRA volunteers can easily meet him there and give him cash to take back to Derry. If the police ask Frank about the money, he can say he was lucky with a bet.

'Sometimes the IRA does what's convenient,' explained former IRA volunteer Anthony McIntyre. 'If someone who you believe to be an agent can get you access to the things you want, and you're getting kudos for that, then you can convince yourself that they're not an agent.'[5] Martin McGuinness knows that standing up for Frank Hegarty is a huge risk, but he can live with that. McGuinness makes his decision. He will vouch for him.

Frank Hegarty has been welcomed into the tent. In being accepted by the local IRA, he has succeeded where pretty much everyone thought he was going to fail. His handlers in the FRU pass on the news to their counterparts in MI5, where it becomes part of a much bigger intelligence picture, one that continues to grow at an extraordinary rate.

Let's go back for a moment to a balmy evening in the summer of 1983, when a crowd of young people gathered outside the Dominion Theatre, in London. The band Duran Duran was on the bill that night. The five-piece from Birmingham had never been so popular and tickets had sold out long ago. They were sexy, stylish, and exotic. Their fans were devoted. The crowd at a recent signing in New York became so frenzied that the police had to close down the surrounding neighbourhood to get the band out of there. The Duran Duran fans in London that day had come in the hope of either getting a ticket on the door or just catching sight of their idols. Most were teenage girls who knew the lyrics to every one of their songs and had spent much of the afternoon singing them together in chorus. A line of police officers in short-sleeved shirts was there to hold them back from the traffic, but most of the cars had slowed down anyway and there seemed to be little risk of anyone being hurt.

Duran Duran filed on stage later that night to play a ten-song set. The concert was in aid of the Prince's Trust, a charity helping young people from disadvantaged backgrounds to find work. Watching from the royal box that night was one of the band's most famous fans, Princess Diana, sitting next to the future King Charles III. The band played well, money was raised, and the night was a success. Very few people realised how close they had all come that night to carnage, tragedy, and a change in the royal line of succession.

Several months earlier, a team of IRA volunteers had arranged to plant a bomb on a long-delay timer behind the royal box in the Dominion Theatre. The plan was to kill Charles and Diana, and others in the theatre, during Duran Duran's performance. The bomb was to be tiled up behind a wall in the public lavatory close to where the royal couple would sit. The IRA bombmaker knew what he was doing, and the plan had been carefully thought through. One of the IRA men involved in this operation was said to have been Ivor Bell.

But there was no explosion that evening. This was because the IRA volunteer tasked with installing the bomb was an agent working for the Irish police who would soon be sharing information with MI5.[6] The heir to the throne and many of the concertgoers that night owed their lives to a vast, unseen enterprise centred on espionage.

The British Army, SIS, MI5, and the local police in Northern Ireland had spun an intelligence web that now covered most of the region and were running the largest 'counter-terrorism' operation anywhere in the world. Information was coming in from international partners as well as SIS officers like Michael Oatley, electronic eavesdropping devices, or specialist soldiers in 14 Intelligence, who would spend days hiding out in people's attics while watching the street below.[7] Most of the information, however, came from their own human sources – a vast array of individuals like Frank Hegarty.

There had never been so many secret agents operating either inside the IRA or close to it. While a small number of them were working for the Irish, the majority were reporting to the British. As well as Frank Hegarty, we know about Willie Carlin in Derry, who provided intelligence on Martin McGuinness and the inner workings of the local Sinn Féin office. In the same city, the MI5 agent 'Infliction' supplied 'an enormous amount of information, many, many hundreds of reports'.[8] Over in Belfast, Denis Donaldson reported on Sinn Féin, and MI5 had access to another agent higher up in the same party who had recently been on the Ard Chomhairle, or Central Committee, and was passing on 'a steady stream of internal policy documents and reports on republican thinking'.[9] The bricklayer and army agent Freddie Scappaticci was producing life-saving intelligence on forthcoming operations, as well as strategic insights into figures like Gerry Adams. He continued to act as both bodyguard and confidant to Adams, and was later described by army sources as the 'jewel in the crown', and 'arguably, the Army's most significant single contribution to the whole campaign'.[10]

Intelligence on Gerry Adams was even coming in from a member of his own family, an individual motivated partly by a desire to get back at Adams's father, Gerry Senior, a committed IRA man who had sexually abused some of his children.[11] This person was followed by another agent close to Adams with a similar reason for supplying information.

But these agents reporting to MI5 or the FRU made up only a tiny fraction of the overall human intelligence effort. Special Branch in Northern Ireland ran many more sources than the army or MI5. This enormous intelligence operation also relied on mass surveillance. Never before had the British state set out to learn so much about so many people. Soldiers at checkpoints were entering into a bespoke computer system the details of more than 27,000 passing vehicles each day – part of 'Operation Vengeful', which had been designed to spot suspicious patterns of movement. The region's most senior MI5 officer had recently introduced 'Movements Analysis', which combined vehicle movements with GCHQ intelligence from tapped telephone lines.[12] Technology was later invented to read vehicle number plates automatically (a system that would be adapted for the London congestion zone). Other soldiers entered information into 'Farmer's Daughter', a digital database with information about people living close to the Irish border,[13] as well as 'Crucible', which gathered intelligence on a wider array of individuals. In the struggle to end the violence in Northern Ireland, computerisation and data management were becoming just as important as the cloak-and-dagger business of running spies.

Frank Hegarty is a single piece on this vast board. Now that he has been taken on by the local IRA, his value to the British has grown significantly and he is starting to be seen as a more important agent.

He has a chance to learn more about Martin McGuinness and he might be able to pass on information from the IRA quartermaster in Derry. But the closer Frank is to the heart of things, the more he might have to do to maintain his cover. As the quality of Frank's intelligence becomes greater, so does the price that might have to be paid to keep him alive.

The Spymaster's Dilemma

Frank Hegarty has just been given his first job for the IRA: the local quartermaster has told him to look after some weapons. Frank's challenge is to find a hiding place for three long-range rifles, two 9mm pistols, and more than a hundred rounds of ammunition. If it has not done so already, the reality of his new life kicks in. This first job is as much a task as it is a test. Get it wrong, and he will be dropped by the IRA. At the same time, if he completes the mission too easily, it might look as if he has had help.

Frank gets to work. He knows he cannot leave the weapons in a place that might be linked back to him, his family, or his friends. So he can't just bury them in his back garden. The location he chooses is both unusual and inspired.

Derry City Cemetery is laid out over a steep plot on the west bank of the River Foyle, and is where Frank's father and most of his relatives are buried. Parts of the cemetery are tidy and neat, while others feel overgrown and unloved. You will often see teenagers chatting in groups and smoking here after school. This cemetery is also where IRA volunteers are laid to rest, in the Republican Plot. The ground here has a sacred meaning for most IRA men and is one of the last places any of them would think of making a 'hide' for a cache of weapons. The security forces know this, which is why they rarely stop to look in here.

Frank goes to the cemetery and finds a place to keep the weapons. He deposits them in their new hiding place – a swift and furtive burial – before heading back to his car and to the rest of his life. The dogs and the horses. Dorothy. His children. His mother, brothers, and sisters, his friends, and his next meet with his army handler, before which he must decide whether he's actually going to tell Mick about what has just happened.

In Elizabethan England, there were laws against government agents providing *false* information, but never anything about when an agent chooses to hold something back. Frank has no legal obligation to tell his handler about the weapons he has just hidden. Beneath the surface of their relationship, a part of it that they rarely see or talk about, lies an understanding that it is up to Frank what to divulge. He knows that if he tells Mick about the weapons, this information could be passed on to the police and that might lead to a raid on the cemetery. Frank would at once come under suspicion as an informer, and there might be a knock at his door from the Nutting Squad.

By this stage in the conflict, the Nutting Squad is mysterious, deadly, and the stuff of nightmares. One of its leaders is said to be obsessed with the occult and devil worship. His henchmen are talked about as if they are psychopaths.[1] There is even a rumour about them having been sent to Libya to study 'bastinado', which involves hanging prisoners upside down and thrashing the soles of their feet to extract a confession.[2]

Frank understands the enormous, life-threatening danger in telling Mick about the weapons. But he decides to put his trust in him. Perhaps he sees this as a way to impress his handler and justify his salary. More likely, Frank wants the weapons taken out of circulation.

Mick writes up his conversation with Frank, and the report is passed on to John Tobias, the young commander of the local FRU office, who shares it with his opposite number in MI5. Now they have a decision to make. The situation might be new, but the dilemma at the heart of it is as old as espionage itself.

One day in May 1941, the senior Allied officer on the Greek island of Crete received an urgent message. He understood that the German Army was gearing up to invade the island. Everyone seemed to know that. But nobody was sure when the assault was going to take place, where, or what form it was likely to take. This officer's job was to deploy the 30,000 troops under his command in a way that would give him the best chance of repelling the attack.

According to the message he had just read, the main German attack was coming from the air. A swarm of parachutists was going to land around the island's airport. An attack like this was not at all what he had expected. But the strangest part of the message came later. The Allied commander was told that he could *not* act on this information unless he was able to find other intelligence reports to back it up. This was not because the British had concerns about the reliability of their intelligence, but the opposite.

The message he had just received was based on 'ULTRA' intelligence from Bletchley Park, where cryptanalysts had begun to decrypt enemy communications sent using Enigma machines. The British were prepared to go to almost any length to make sure that the Germans did not work out that their messages were being read. This new intelligence source was so precious that lives would be lost to ensure that it was not compromised. If ULTRA revealed that a German U-boat was closing in on an unsuspecting Allied convoy, those ships would *not* be rerouted unless a suitable cover story could be put together that would explain their sudden change of course. A reconnaissance plane might be told to fly over the U-boat's location, so that the Germans would think that their submarine had been spotted from the air. But if no reconnaissance plane was available, and nobody could think of another cover story in time, then the British would allow the convoy to carry on towards the U-boat, knowing that lives would almost certainly be lost. Their hope was that more lives would be saved in the long run by keeping ULTRA safe.

The German assault on Crete in 1941 came from the air, as ULTRA had predicted, and after less than a fortnight the island was occupied. More than 3,000 Allied troops were killed, and over 12,000 were captured. The Germans remained unaware that their secret messages were being read.

The dilemma facing John Tobias and his MI5 counterpart in Derry, early in 1984, after being told about Frank's IRA weapons hide, is different, smaller, and in some ways more puzzling than the one before when the British learned of the plans for an airborne attack on Crete. Tobias does not want the stash of IRA weapons to be used. But he also needs to protect his intelligence source. Will he save more lives by acting on Frank's information, or by doing nothing?

One option is to have the weapons 'jarked', which involves taking them out of the cemetery, installing a tiny tracking device inside each one, and returning them to their hiding place. The army can then follow the arms as they move between IRA volunteers and intervene when an attack is imminent. By that stage, the weapons will have passed through so many hands that Frank is unlikely to come under suspicion. In years to come, jarking would involve IRA weapons being flown by helicopter to GCHQ in Cheltenham where highly sophisticated mechanisms could be fitted. But at this stage in the conflict, the process is much more rudimentary. The tracking devices can be spotted by IRA volunteers who know where to look, and the batteries might run out. Plus, the gadgets have a limited range, so soldiers must be nearby to monitor them.

A further problem with jarking is that the FRU would have to work with the Weapons Intelligence Unit, which is partly run by the local police. Although at a very senior level the local police are aware that Frank is an agent, nobody in the FRU or MI5 wants the rank-and-file police in the Weapons Intelligence Unit to know about this, in case his identity leaks out.

Another option is to take the weapons off to a nearby army range and collect their ballistic signatures, so that if any of them is later used in a crime, the police can trace the bullets back to one of the weapons from Frank's hide.

The longer Tobias and his counterparts in MI5 spend with this decision, the easier it becomes. Frank has placed his life in their hands and is vulnerable. If this first job goes wrong, he is unlikely to survive. But if he gets it right, he might become a trusted member of the IRA with access to a stream of hugely valuable intelligence.

The FRU take the arms off to a range before returning them to the cemetery as if nothing has happened.

It's Easter Sunday 1984, and several hundred IRA supporters have begun to march into Derry City Cemetery. This is the same scene that's been played out for decades at around this time of year, and one that Frank Hegarty took part in twelve years earlier, after Bloody Sunday. The atmosphere today is tense and serious. Speeches are made. Allegiances are reaffirmed. Ceremonial shots are fired over the graves of the fallen volunteers.

Only a handful of people in the cemetery that day know about the IRA weapons hidden in the ground near by. Fewer still have any idea that one of these firearms is about to be used.

Several days earlier, Frank Hegarty was approached by someone close to the IRA who asked him to supply a rifle, saying that a volunteer needed it for an upcoming job. Frank did as he was told, before reporting this to his handler. Clearly, an attack was being planned. But neither Frank nor anyone in the security forces know where or when it will take place or what the target might be.

The day after the IRA Easter Parade, two army Land Rovers are driving down Bishop Street, less than a mile from the cemetery, when they are ambushed. Their attackers are teenagers from the Bogside Republican Youth, a group said to be controlled by Martin McGuinness.[3] They are armed with petrol bombs fashioned out of gallon sweet jars. One of these hits a Land Rover and explodes. The vehicle is carpeted in flame and the air supply to the engine cuts out. Burning petrol enters the vehicle. One of the soldiers inside sees that his flak jacket is on fire. He throws open his door and jumps out.

The soldier's name is Neil Clarke. He is twenty years old, barely older than the teenager who has just thrown the petrol bomb. Clarke is a private in the Queen's Regiment, Second Battalion, one part of the enormous military ecosystem which has spread out across the region over the last fifteen years. The world that he inhabits is sweary, loud, and hyper-masculine. His life is turbocharged by testosterone and adrenaline, and he has a strong sense of duty, of what's proper, what's right, and what's out of line. He is also familiar with the anxiety experienced by so many British soldiers in Northern Ireland, which comes from knowing that as soon as you leave your base or step out of your vehicle you might be an instant away from being blown apart by a bomb or killed by a sniper.

One of the people watching Neil Clarke as he leaps out of the burning Land Rover with his flak jacket on fire is an IRA volunteer called Paddy Deery. He is known to his friends as 'Nelson', after losing an eye to a rubber bullet earlier in the Troubles. Deery has his good eye up against the telescopic sight of a long-range rifle. It is the same weapon Frank Hegarty has recently produced from his hide in the cemetery.

Nelson pulls the trigger. The bullet hits Neil Clarke in the head, and he dies almost at once.

On the face of it, Frank's handlers have made a terrible mistake. The weapon used to kill Neil Clarke was recently in their possession, and is one of those that they tested on the nearby army range. Of course, the main responsibility for this attack lay with Paddy Deery, the IRA volunteer who shouldered the weapon, took aim, and pulled the trigger with the intention of killing the British soldier. An operation like this would have been approved at a higher level, so a portion of the blame for this murder belongs to the man who gave the go-ahead – almost certainly Martin McGuinness. But it is hard to escape the fact that if the FRU had taken this weapon out of circulation when they had the chance to do so, then Neil Clarke might still be alive.

And yet, it is too early to know if Frank's handlers have made a mistake. Their decision to keep this weapon in play was rooted in a calculation. They believe that the intelligence Frank might be able to supply in the months or years to come will allow them to save multiple lives. Like every spymaster's dilemma, this one is centred on the notion of an exchange, and a balance that must be struck. As long as the value of the intelligence is greater than the cost, it makes sense to keep going. But sometimes, in the rush of events, these decisions become harder to make, and the scales can start to tip without anyone noticing.

Frank must have known that the weapon he supplied was the one used to kill this soldier. Perhaps he was confused about why his handlers had not acted on his information, and why these weapons were still available to the IRA. At the very least, this murder places a subtle new pressure on him. He is caught up in this now, whatever it is. In theory, he can walk away at any time. He knows that.

It has been made clear to him right from the start. But the reality of his situation has changed now, and it is becoming harder to see a way out.

PART THREE:

BETRAYAL

Operation Kenova

An office block stood on Victoria Street, in central London, a stone's throw from the Houses of Parliament. Most of the buildings in this area gave some indication as to who worked inside or what the building was used for, but this one was different. By the summer of 2017, there was no sign at street level, just a series of numbered buttons. Anyone looking in from one of the blocks across the street might have been able to make out an open-plan office space that was busier than any other. Each day it filled up with some forty men and women who worked at desks with computers – none of them state-of-the-art – and walked around with lanyards around their necks like ordinary office workers. There was very little to indicate that they were detectives, and that this was the Major Incident Room for Operation Kenova, the criminal investigation into the army agent Stakeknife, that was rapidly turning into the largest murder investigation in British history.

Jon Boutcher had been busy over the last twelve months. His first challenge after leaving the press conference in Belfast, in the summer of 2016, was to put together a team. He knew it would be a mistake to take on detectives with any connection to the armed forces, British intelligence, or Northern Ireland itself. He wanted his investigation to be seen as both scrupulous and utterly impartial.

But this created its own problem. The detectives Boutcher had recruited so far were enthusiastic and well qualified, but they knew little about Northern Ireland. Most were recently retired and had spent their adult lives in England at a time when the Troubles received less media coverage than it deserved. So Boutcher arranged for speakers to come into the office and give talks and seminars. He invited military veterans, former intelligence professionals, lawyers, judges, police officers, campaigners, and battle-hardened journalists such as John Ware and Peter Taylor. What was technically a Major Incident Room could sometimes feel like a university campus for mature students.

At the same time, Boutcher set out to meet each of the families who believed their loved one had been killed by 'Stakeknife'. He listened to their stories and gave them his personal phone number, telling them to call whenever they liked. He also assigned to each of these families a liaison officer from his team who would make contact at least once a month. Boutcher even sent personal messages to some of these family members on the dates of significant anniversaries, such as the day they found out their relative had been kidnapped. 'Some families had never been to where these tragic events occurred,' he explained. He arranged for them to visit these places. 'So that they can, even many years later, say goodbye.'

Right from the start, Jon Boutcher had understood that these families would be central to his investigation, and he did everything he could to gain their trust. None of them was used to this. Stakeknife was believed to have been part of the IRA's Nutting Squad, and his alleged victims were men and women who had been accused of being informers. Their families had come to know the stigma that came with this. You rarely saw the families of Nutting Squad victims organising marches or holding vigils. Their grief took on a more private character, and they became used to being overlooked. Most of the families who had lost a loved one to the Nutting Squad did not even receive a visit from the police in the days after the murder, whether to tell them about what had happened or to ask for help with the investigation.[2]

Operation Kenova turned that on its head. The 'Rolls Royce of investigations', as it was later described, was now giving the most attention to those who had, until then, received the least.[3]

'When I meet these families for the first time,' Boutcher explained, 'I always say, "Where are your lever-arch files?" They look at me, but they know what I mean.[4] During his visits, he was shown folders and files containing letters, notes, and newspaper cuttings. 'They've watched every documentary,' he went on, 'they've read every book, they've looked at every article in the media, and they've got their own lever-arch files of what they think happened.'[5]

Among these documents was usually one that stood out, and had an almost sacred meaning for each family. This was the goodbye letter that most Nutting Squad victims were told to write before being killed. It must have been difficult for any family member to read through one of those letters again. The sight of their loved one's handwriting would be enough to bring back the memory of them – how they held their pen, the way they dotted their i's and crossed their t's, their facial expression as they wrote. The message itself conveyed something of the terror they must have felt in their final moments. Boutcher went through these letters with each family, knowing that this was part of the healing process. They were being listened to for the first time. Some of their pain was being witnessed. What Boutcher did not know was that these same documents would later shed light on the murders themselves.

When Jon Boutcher wasn't meeting the families or recruiting more detectives, he spent his time trying to gain access to classified government records. The three organisations with the most material on the army agent Stakeknife were the Ministry of Defence, the Police Service of Northern Ireland, and MI5. Each was cautious about opening up their archives to a criminal investigation, in the way that a restaurant owner might not relish a visit from the food-safety inspector. But the strongest resistance came from MI5.

Boutcher was told that some of the documents he had requested from MI5 were not, in their opinion, relevant to his investigation, and they would not be handing over others because it might endanger national security. The main concern within MI5 was, as always, agent safety. They worried that releasing everything they had on Stakeknife could endanger the lives of other agents and their families. Another worry was that some of their techniques and details of how they had once worked in the field might become widely known. Although much had changed since the Troubles, some elements of their trade-craft remained largely the same.

Boutcher had been here before. He had two options, really. He could push back, or accept that these records were out of reach. The advantage of backing down was that it would keep him on the right side of MI5, which might be helpful later.

In the past, Jon Boutcher had shown that he knew how to collaborate with other agencies. He was known as someone who did not throw his weight around needlessly or pick fights with other departments. In the days after the 7/7 attacks in London, in 2005, in which fifty-two people were killed by Muslim extremists, Boutcher had been a senior figure in the efforts to prevent another attack. On the day after the 21/7 attacks, later the same month, he was second-in-command in the Operations Room during the manhunt for a cell of suspected suicide bombers. His superior was Cressida Dick, soon to be Met Commissioner. Their job was to coordinate the different surveillance teams from a number of different agencies. Tragically, a Brazilian electrician was mistaken for one of their targets, and ran away when he was approached. In the frantic minutes that followed, with Cressida Dick and Jon Boutcher asking questions, giving orders, trying to assess the situation, the man who was being chased, Jean Charles de Menezes, was shot and killed.

Boutcher was questioned at length during the inquest into De Menezes's death. At almost any point in his cross-examination he could have deflected some of the blame onto other people, other agencies, or even his superior, Cressida Dick. This is what a different kind of police officer might have done. But he did not. When asked what had gone wrong that day, Boutcher was unequivocal. 'I am not sure anything did actually go wrong.'⁸ This is what he had come to believe. It was not in his nature to look for colleagues to throw under the bus, and he was loyal and reliable. Perhaps that was part of the reason why he had been chosen to run Operation Kenova.

When faced with MI5's refusal to share certain documents, Jon Boutcher could have easily moved on. Instead, he decided to push back. He pressed for more information about which records existed, the state they were in, and precisely why they could not be shared. He was told that most of the records his team had requested were on paper and some of the catalogues were incomplete. Others were on deteriorating rolls of microfiche or they were digital files that could only be read using obsolete computer systems. Boutcher did not mind. He wanted to see them all.

Operation Kenova was eventually given access to most of the materials requested, and soon they had written agreements in place with the police in Northern Ireland, the Ministry of Defence, and MI5. These allowed Boutcher's detectives to see thousands of sensitive records, which could now become part of the criminal case against Stakeknife.

This was Boutcher's first victory, and it seemed to have come against the odds. Operation Kenova may have been an important investigation, but nobody would tell you that it was a popular one. It had not been the result of sustained pressure over many years from political parties and campaign groups in Northern Ireland. For any detective working on this team, there were moments when it was possible to feel that few people wanted you to succeed. This added to the camaraderie within that open-plan office in Westminster – an us-against-the-world feeling which only sharpened the desire to do everything possible to have their target, Stakeknife, appear in court.

Along the way, however, the detectives' understanding of the man they were investigating was starting to shift. Some of them might have come into this thinking they were on the trail of a cold-blooded psychopath. But the picture beginning to emerge now was more confusing. One of the people they would soon meet was Willie Carlin, the agent in Derry who had once infiltrated the local Sinn Féin office. Carlin knew who Stakeknife was. But he had a very different take on his fellow agent.

'Angel of Death, that's what they call him,' Carlin told the detectives. 'But here's the funny thing about Stakeknife. He saved my life.'[7]

20

The Job

Thirty-two years earlier

It's the summer of 1985, and Frank Hegarty is driving through the Irish countryside with Martin McGuinness sitting next to him. They are in Frank's ordinary-looking Vauxhall Cavalier, which is, in truth, far from ordinary, and contains a hidden network of wires, microphones, and other eavesdropping devices recently installed by a team of British Army technicians.

The two men are travelling through County Sligo, just south of the border in the Republic. The landscape they can see out of the window is different to what they are used to around Derry. It has a softer and more lyrical feel. The horizons are closer, leaving more space for woods and lakes, and the hillsides are spotted with cromlechs and cairns. This is W. B. Yeats country, where the poet spent parts of his childhood. His imagination was shaped by the otherworldliness of this landscape and the stories he heard about mythical spirits hidden among its valleys and fields, as well as pirates and smugglers.

In a way, that is what Martin McGuinness and Frank Hegarty have become. They need to smuggle an arsenal of IRA weaponry into Northern Ireland. Their job today is to find temporary hiding places for these arms, which will be arriving any day now. Frank does not know where these weapons are coming from or how they will be delivered to County Sligo. All he has been told is that a large quantity of arms and explosives is on its way. Once they have been moved across the border, they will be used for a devastating assault against the British.

For months now, senior IRA men have been working on a plan that they refer to as their own 'Tet Offensive' – the name of the onslaught by communist forces in the Vietnam War that was seen at the time as a catalyst to the subsequent American withdrawal. The IRA hardliners wanted something similar to happen in Northern Ireland: an all-out blitz against British military targets that could trigger a full-blown conflict and force the British government to rethink its policy, recall its troops, and agree to a united Ireland.

That's the plan. But the IRA's version of the Tet Offensive requires a massive injection of weapons, ammunition, and explosives. A secret unit has been set up inside the IRA quartermaster's department to oversee this part of the operation. Martin McGuinness's job is to make sure the arms make it safely into Northern Ireland. But he cannot do this himself. He needs someone to look after the weapons while they are held in County Sligo. Given how much is riding on this operation, this person must be a figure he can trust intrinsically.

Frank Hegarty has become a familiar fixture in the local IRA set-up. 'He was trusted,' one IRA source later said, 'and was good at what he was asked to do by us. He was involved in transporting things across the border, and there was no suspicion about him.' Frank has been ferrying money and small quantities of weapons back and forth across the border, usually between IRA contacts in County Donegal and Derry. He is also a popular figure in the local IRA brigade. Most IRA volunteers hiding out over the border would look forward to visits from The General. Frank is usually up for a drink, and is often the first to buy everyone a round. But he is by no means a senior figure in the local IRA set-up, and some people are

Above: Martin McGuinness in the early 1980s, at the start of his political journey.

Left: Greyhound-owner, father and sometime paramilitary Frank Hegarty.

Below: A 1972 IRA parade. Frank Hegarty is at the bottom of the photograph, chatting to the man in the suit.

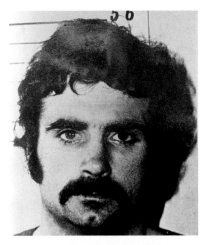

Above: 'Owner of a deep, unwavering, Manson-like stare'. Freddie Scappaticci at the start of the Troubles.

Right: Freddie Scappaticci and Martin McGuinness, colleagues but not friends, around the time of the murder.

Below: Martin McGuinness and Gerry Adams, colleagues and close friends, shortly after the murder.

'Fishers of Men'. Soldiers from the FRU, the British Army's specialist agent-running outfit.

IRA poster, 1974.

Sir General James Glover, Jimmy to his friends, architect of the FRU.

Above: Sinn Fein official and British agent Willie Carlin, who believed that Stakenife had saved his life.

Left: Martin McGuinness and Denis Donaldson, shortly after the IRA found evidence that an informant was living at his address.

Below: Derry City Cemetery.

Left: Brendan Duddy, aka 'The Mountain Climber', who devoted himself to setting up secret talks between the British government and the IRA.

Below: The Grianán of Aileach, where McGuinness and Adams went in the late 1970s to discuss their new strategy.

Above: Funeral procession during the 1981 Hunger Strike.

Right: News report, May 1986, showing the corpse of the British agent.

Below: Margaret Thatcher after signing the 1985 Anglo-Irish Agreement, her greatest regret from her time in office.

Bertie Aherne, George Mitchell and Tony Blair, after helping to deliver the Good Friday Agreement.

'The Chuckle Brothers'. Ian Paisley and Martin McGuinness after being sworn in as First Minister and Deputy First Minister of Northern Ireland.

Above: 'Monaco without the money'. Derry today.

Left: Officer in Overall Command of Operation Kenova, Jon Boutcher.

Below: 'Well, I'm still alive.' Queen Elizabeth's reply to Martin McGuiness, in 2016, after he had asked if she was well.

surprised to hear that McGuinness has chosen him to look after this enormous haul of weapons that will soon arrive in County Sligo.

For the next few hours, Martin McGuinness and Frank Hegarty drive through the lush Irish landscape in search of places to hide the arms. Both men have a lot on their minds that day. McGuinness has been thinking more than usual about betrayal, especially after he was told, only a few months ago, that his friend Willie Carlin was a spy.

'You're talking nonsense,' McGuinness had said. 'Leave him alone.'[2] The evidence was overwhelming, though, and soon the Nutting Squad came for Carlin. But when they arrived at his house, the British agent and his family had gone. Somebody had tipped them off.

The truth about what happened did not emerge for years, but Willie Carlin was right in what he later said to Jon Boutcher's team: Stakeknife had saved his life.

It all began when Carlin's former MI5 case officer, a man called Michael Bettaney, became disillusioned with his life in the West and decided to offer his services to the Soviet Union. Unbeknown to him, however, the KGB man tasked with handling his defection, Oleg Gordievsky, was himself working for the British. Bettaney, the would-be agent, was uncovered by Gordievsky, an actual agent, and was sentenced to twenty-three years in jail. But while Bettaney was on remand, he bragged to an IRA prisoner about having once run an agent in Derry called Willie, someone who worked for Sinn Féin and was close to Martin McGuinness.

It could only have been Willie Carlin. Bettaney also mentioned an army agent in Belfast whose name he had never managed to work out. One of the first IRA volunteers to hear about Bettaney's claims was Freddie Scappaticci – who recognised himself as the army agent in Belfast.

Scappaticci was what locals would call a 'cute hoor'. He was cute in the Irish sense of the word, meaning cunning and quick. He had a genius for self-preservation. Somehow, he explained away the part of the message that referred to him. But there was nothing he could do about the rest of it that pointed so clearly to Willie Carlin. The Nutting Squad was told to find Carlin and extract a confession. But at some point, before they knocked on Carlin's door, the agent later known as Stakeknife called his handler and told them that this man's life was in danger.

Nobody in the local IRA knew the full story – only that they had a mole. Martin McGuinness was the officer commanding the IRA's Northern Command, the most senior IRA man in Derry. This episode reflected badly on him. He had allowed a spy to get close to him, and in the eyes of the IRA hardliners this made him look weak.

At about the same time, McGuinness learned of a different kind of betrayal. He had found out that the man known as the Heathen, Ivor Bell, and a gang of his supporters, were plotting to remove him and Gerry Adams from the IRA and take over themselves. They were angry about the political direction in which the movement was heading and planned to oust McGuinness and Adams at an Extraordinary General Army Convention of the IRA. McGuinness had known Ivor Bell for years, and the two men had gone through a lot together. Both had given a part of themselves to the same struggle. They had campaigned together on the 'Long War' strategy and made huge personal sacrifices in the name of Irish unification. But from the moment McGuinness understood that his old comrade was scheming against him, it was as if a light had been turned out. Ivor Bell was no longer a friend. He was an obstacle.

Martin McGuinness got up before the IRA Army Council and accused Ivor Bell and three others of 'factionalism'.[3] According to the IRA's Green Book, its secret set of rules, this merited a court-martial and was punishable by death. Some of the Army Council men listening to McGuinness that day had recently assured Ivor Bell in private that they would back him if he went for the leadership.

Now they were being asked if the same man should be shot. You might expect them to stand up for their friend. But if there was one thing consistently true of those at the very top of the IRA, and less so of those further down, it was their ability to read the room and be pragmatic about the direction in which the movement was heading.

The IRA Army Council voted to have Ivor Bell and his accomplices tried. Bell did not attend his own court-martial and was found guilty of treachery. That meant death. But Gerry Adams decided to spare his life on the condition that Bell did not break away to form a rival version of the IRA.[4]

Ivor Bell's response was typically, almost comically gruff. Gerry Adams's decision to let him live was proof, he growled, that the IRA had gone soft. 'If it was the other way around,' he said, 'and any of you refused to attend the court-martial, you would be dead by now.' Others came to see this as a masterstroke. Rather than have him shot, Adams made out that Bell had been duped by those around him. According to one former agent, this 'finished off Bell far more effectively than killing him'.[5]

Now Martin McGuinness is being driven around County Sligo by Frank Hegarty. Ivor Bell might no longer be a threat to him, but McGuinness knows that he is still vulnerable after what has happened and must prove to Bell's supporters that he remains, deep down, one of them. He cannot make any more mistakes or do anything to let them think that he is no longer a physical-force man. His reputation within the IRA is precious to him. He needs to make sure these weapons arrive safely in Northern Ireland.

Martin McGuinness and Frank Hegarty call on three local men – one in Coolera, County Sligo, another in Mullaghroe, to the south, and a third in Croghan, County Roscommon. They discuss payment for looking after the weapons. They root around in outhouses, barns, and attics, climbing up ladders and peering into dark holes, before agreeing on three places that they think will work well as hides.[6]

Everything is ready. McGuinness and Hegarty set off for Derry. Both men are quiet by nature, and at times in that journey each would have been caught for a moment in the traffic of his own thoughts. Perhaps McGuinness wonders to himself if Frank is the right man for this job, while, in the same moment, next to him in the car, close enough that they can smell each other, Frank thinks about what he is going to tell his army handler once they get home. If, that is, he tells him anything at all.

Frank Hegarty has heard about Willie Carlin's sudden disappearance, and the news must have been a shock. It is a reminder that as an agent you are never fully in possession of your own fate. There is always the danger that a mistake or decision by some other person will lead to your exposure. Or it might be you that slips up. Every conversation Frank has with a fellow IRA man continues to be a tightrope exercise in restraint and self-control.

The need to bottle up so much of what he is feeling adds to the mounting pressure in Frank Hegarty's life. What makes this harder to bear is knowing that there might be a way out. The journey which began for Frank five years ago, when he met Jack on the Hollyhall Road, does not need to end with death or a new life overseas. A recent piece in the local newspaper told the story of a man who claimed to have been an army agent, like Frank, before handing himself in to the local IRA. 'I thought there was nothing I could do,' he was quoted as saying. 'Now I realise it's never too late. You're better off coming forward.'⁷

The IRA will put out a version of this story every few months. Come to us with a confession, and you will be spared. Wait until you are caught, and you will not. Frank's head tells him never to trust the IRA, and he knows more than enough about the Nutting Squad and what happens to informers. But after a long or difficult day, his heart might start to lead him off in a different direction. As the burden of his secret life weighs down on him, the idea of coming clean only becomes more attractive. Frank knows that with one conversation, just a few words to the man sitting next to him, he can bring down the curtain on his performance as an agent. Salvation, forgiveness, and redemption could be just a few sentences away.

Martin McGuinness and Frank Hegarty arrive in Derry, and each man goes home to his young family.

The Gear

Adrian Hopkins manoeuvred his ship alongside the other one and cut the engine. In the background, he could see the dry, jagged cliffs of Gozo, an island off Malta. Men from the other vessel called out in greeting. Ropes were tossed over the silky Mediterranean water, perfect for swimming at this time of year, and the two ships were soon bound together.

Hopkins was the captain of the 65-foot-long *Casamara*, a seiner fishing vessel from Arklow, County Wicklow. For years it had worked the waters around Ireland, its crew using weighted nets to encircle schools of herring, pilchard, and mackerel before pulling on the purse lines to haul in their catch. Now, in August 1985, this ship was being put to an altogether different use.

The vessel next to it was the *Samra Africa*, which had set out the day before from the Libyan capital of Tripoli. It was carrying 300 heavy wooden crates. These were transferred onto the deck of the *Casamara*, and later moved down into the hold. This was a dank, windowless space where you would have once seen glittering mountains of fish. Now it was slowly being filled with the mysterious wooden boxes. They were dry, lacked a distinctive odour, and had recently been painted white. Although there were no markings on any of the boxes, it was possible on some of them to see underneath the paint the words: 'LIBYAN ARMED FORCES'.[1]

Hopkins left the waters off Gozo with 10 tons of weaponry in the hold of his ship, including eighty AK-47s, spare magazines, bayonets, cleaning kits, eighteen Taurus semi-automatic 9mm Parabellum PT92 pistols, more than eighteen thousand rounds of ammunition, and seven Soviet-made RPGs, or rocket-propelled grenades. It was, according to one former soldier, 'enough weaponry to provide a medium-sized military force with the capability to mount full-scale terrorist attacks'.[2]

The arms had been sent on the orders of the Libyan president, Colonel Muammar Gaddafi, a dictator who could be brutal, paranoid, and erratic, and whose response to criticism was savage. Gaddafi loathed Britain. He saw the country as an avatar of imperial arrogance, greed, and foreign interference. Much of this went back to the moment earlier in his reign when he learned that the British had backed an attempted coup against him.

By the summer of 1985, Gaddafi's animus towards Britain had acquired a new edge. Diplomatic relations between Britain and Libya had recently been broken off after a gunman inside the Libyan Embassy in London opened fire on a crowd of protesters and killed Yvonne Fletcher, an unarmed police officer. Gaddafi now wanted 'to create a problem for Britain', as he said, 'and to drive a thorn in her side'.[3]

In the hours after Yvonne Fletcher was shot, there had been a stand-off between the police and those inside the Libyan Embassy. This was settled by a team of negotiators which included a Libyan intelligence officer called Nasser Ashour. Some months later, Ashour travelled to Dublin for a meeting with several IRA officials, including Ivor Bell. Ashour told the IRA men that his boss, Colonel Gaddafi, wanted to supply them with 300 tons of weaponry and $10 million in cash. There was one condition. All of it must be used against the British. The British Army, the British state, the British people – it did not matter, as long as it registered as a series of attacks against Britain.

The IRA rarely showed any scruples about where its funding came from, and in the past had asked for support from the Soviet Union as well as Nazi Germany. Gaddafi's offer was, one historian later wrote, 'the paramilitary equivalent of a lottery win'.[4] The IRA hardliners said yes. The following year, Nasser Ashour was on board the *Samra Africa* as the first batch of Libyan weapons was transferred to the Irish ship.

Several days later, Adrian Hopkins weighed anchor off Clogga Strand, a curving, sandy beach south of Dublin. His men used three high-speed Zodiac dinghies to move the cargo ashore, a job which would have taken most of the night. Each of the 300 crates had to be heaved out of the *Casamara*, ferried to the shore, and hauled up the beach. You can imagine the burn in the men's forearms as they dragged the wooden boxes up from the shoreline, and the strange striations left in the sand.

Gaddafi's weapons were loaded into a series of lorries beyond the beach, which then thundered off into the night. The crates were moved across Ireland in stages, until most had arrived on the other side of the island, in County Sligo, where they were transferred into three transitional dumps which had been prepared several days earlier by Martin McGuinness and Frank Hegarty.

Frank's handler could hardly believe what he was being told. The size of the shipment of arms that had just arrived in County Sligo was unheard of, and this was the first anyone on the British side knew about it. They needed to see the weapons before working out what to do. But the three hides that Frank had been told to look after were in a different country. They were in Ireland, and the British security forces had clear instructions never to cross the border. But, at the same time, if these weapons went into circulation, hundreds of lives could be lost.

Frank and his handler went on an illegal road trip into Ireland. They drove past the locations where the weapons were stashed without getting too close, as Frank did not want to be recognised. Once they were back in Derry, Frank's handler tried to pinpoint the locations of the dumps on a map. The trouble was, he couldn't remember exactly where they had gone. Fortunately, the recording equipment had been turned on in Frank's car, and one FRU soldier spent the next two days transcribing the conversation in the car and cross-referencing what had been said with driving times, distances, and speeds. Eventually, he worked out the locations of the three IRA hides. A specialist unit was then given the job of photographing Gaddafi's weapons in their hiding places.

Now Frank's handlers had to work out their next move. It was the spymaster's dilemma all over again, but with a twist. First, the weapons were outside the United Kingdom, so they could not have an SAS team lie in wait nearby. For the same reason, it would be difficult to 'jark' the weapons and have soldiers remain close as they moved across the border.

One option was to pass on the locations of the weapons to their Irish counterparts, but this would finish Frank's career as an agent. It would also reflect poorly on Martin McGuinness, given that he had overall responsibility for the safety of these weapons. Allowing this enormous cache of Libyan weapons to be smuggled into Northern Ireland was a tremendous risk. But it was one they would probably have to take.

Their decision might have been different, however, if they had known about the secret discussions that had recently finished in London. A political storm was on its way to Northern Ireland, one that would change Frank's life forever.

The Project

Margaret Thatcher had an unusual relationship with Ireland. Everyone knew that she was a Unionist to her core and believed passionately in the union between Northern Ireland and Great Britain. When one of her aides suggested that in a hundred years' time there might be a united Ireland, her response was: 'Never! Never!'[1] But she was sometimes puzzled by Unionists themselves. She admired them, but rarely seemed to show them any affection, as if she felt that they were tainted by their connection to Ireland, a country she had still not forgiven for remaining neutral during the Second World War. When Thatcher heard a civil servant suggest that the people of Britain and Ireland had been intermarrying and mixing for centuries, she recoiled, saying, 'I am completely English.' (Her great-grandmother was Irish.)

Thatcher's ideas on how to bring peace to Northern Ireland often sounded rushed, like she was answering the final question in an exam and had run out of time. One of her suggestions was to surround Northern Ireland with an enormous fence.[2] She was told that a border like this would be difficult to patrol on account of its length. She thought for a moment and proposed redrawing it as a straight line. Another time, she asked if there was a way to remove Catholics from Northern Ireland altogether and have them relocated south of the border. 'After all,' she said, 'there was a big movement of population in Ireland, wasn't there?'[3]

Her aides looked at each other. One asked if she was referring to the ethnic cleansing that took place under Oliver Cromwell, a man known to most Irish schoolchildren as the 'Butcher of Ireland'.

'That's right,' she said, 'Cromwell.'

As one of the civil servants later explained, 'The idea of a population transfer was not pursued'.[4]

Margaret Thatcher was consistently more impressive on other subjects, such as Britain's relations with the United States, the Cold War, the threat posed by the Soviet Union, anything, really, other than Irish affairs. And her attitude contributed to the lack of policy across Whitehall. During most of Thatcher's time in office, there was a strange ambivalence towards the situation in Northern Ireland, a collective shrug, or what Jimmy Glover, the army officer who set up the FRU, called a 'sloppy failure to think about what we are doing'.[5] Most civil servants and politicians agreed with each other that there was no point working on a political solution until peace had been restored. But they had it the wrong way around. The military conflict could only end once a political agreement was under way, and this would involve compromise.

Although Margaret Thatcher did not have a good grasp of Irish politics, she had a deep and, at times, intuitive understanding of the people who voted for her and their attitude towards the IRA. When the Conservative pressure group the Monday Club sent her a list of ideas on how to tackle the IRA, it included 'mining the border', 'a "quick-kill" policy', and 'executing terrorists'.[6] The *Sun* later ran a front page describing 'Gerry Adams' as 'the two most disgusting words in the English language'.[7] Most of Thatcher's supporters wanted her to have no engagement with the IRA or its political wing, Sinn Féin – a feeling that hardened as Left-wing politicians

such as Ken Livingstone and Jeremy Corbyn expressed support for
Martin McGuinness and Gerry Adams.

Even without this, Thatcher had personal reasons to keep her
distance. Irish paramilitaries had murdered her close friend and
advisor Airey Neave. She knew that the IRA wanted to kill her too.
Although she rarely projected vulnerability during her premiership,
after leaving office she described the effect of these IRA threats, and
how she found the experience of walking into any crowd 'absolutely
terrifying' and would always scan the faces in the gathering for
anyone who looked as if they were about to attack her.[8]

Margaret Thatcher was surrounded by people who wanted to see
Sinn Féin and the IRA either defeated or destroyed, and their leaders
locked up for the rest of their lives. But in one part of Whitehall a
very different attitude had taken root – one that contradicted almost
everything she had ever said on the subject of Northern Ireland.

At around this time, an MI5 officer in Northern Ireland sat down
with a man he hoped to take on as an agent. He did not realise that
he was being secretly recorded.

'Steve', as the MI5 man introduced himself, began by talking about
what he and his colleagues were trying to do in Northern Ireland.
They were recruiting men and women with the 'potential' – his
word – to be 'worked into key positions within Sinn Féin'. Rather
than take on agents purely to gather intelligence, Steve wanted people
who could move into the upper echelons of Sinn Féin. 'I'm not interested in collecting evidence so that I can put someone in court,' he
went on. His office wanted to shape Sinn Féin's direction and policy.
If one of his agents found their path to the top blocked, then MI5
would look for ways to get the competition 'off the scene'.[9]

The MI5 strategy that Steve described was for a series of agents,
or 'plants', as he called them, to 'implement and push policies' from
the British that would continue Sinn Féin's move towards peace.

They wanted the party to become a force that Protestant politicians would be willing to negotiate with and work alongside. This was 'a long-term operation', the MI5 man went on, 'spanning ten to fifteen years', and he wanted the person sitting next to him – the one who was secretly recording him – to become a part of it.[10]

The recruitment came to nothing, but the recording survived. It was later played to the journalist Peter Taylor, who wrote about it in a book. This tape remains one of the most interesting insights into MI5 strategy at the time. It seems to confirm the idea that some MI5 officers were looking for ways to accelerate the IRA's shift into politics, and that this meant exerting a subtle influence on Sinn Féin. What had once been a thought experiment was, by the mid-1980s, becoming more of a reality. Even as Conservative politicians railed against the growing popularity of Sinn Féin, MI5 was running agents inside the party who were working hard to improve its performance at the polls.

How did MI5 persuade Margaret Thatcher to sign off on this? The strategy was entirely at odds with her position on Sinn Féin and the IRA. The idea of her agreeing to this is one that strains at the edge of credulity. But in all likelihood, she never did.

'Very little' MI5 activity at this time, according to security expert Mark Urban, was 'specifically authorised by the government'. MI5 officers might be required to outline in broad terms what they were up to, but they could often leave it at that. There was no day-to-day scrutiny of MI5 operations and the service enjoyed 'a constitutional freedom of the kind senior managers at SIS and GCHQ could only gaze upon with envy'.[11] Unlike every other government department, MI5 was self-tasking. It could set its own agenda and had a long history of keeping its strategies and goals to itself. MI5 was required to ask the home secretary for legal authorisation to carry out particular tasks, but it was not subordinate to the Home Office, and the relationship between the two was more distant than many people imagined.

David Mellor, who was minister of state at the Home Office at the time, recalled that during almost five years in office, he 'never had any direct dealings' with anyone from MI5.[12] Although some civil servants in the Cabinet Office (specifically, the Joint Intelligence Secretariat and the Intelligence Assessments Staff, which included officials seconded from MI5) had a fairly good idea of what MI5 was doing in Northern Ireland, none of them could see the entire picture.

From a distance, it might sound as if MI5 was trying to keep Thatcher in the dark about some of its work in Northern Ireland. But the evidence suggests that she was happy to maintain a certain distance from MI5, and to let them do what they judged to be right. The prime minister had a romantic and at times deferential attitude towards the country's intelligence agencies. She trusted them in a way that her two predecessors in No. 10 Downing Street had not. This left some MI5 officers with an incipient sense that they had more leeway than before, and a licence to be bolder and more crea-tive. One of them admitted to Willie Carlin that their desire to turn Sinn Féin into a respectable political force was not one shared by 'the main body of government'. Another told him that most government officials 'don't know about this project'.[13]

This project.

MI5's 'project' was counterintuitive and bold, as well as risky. One danger was that it might leak out. A whistleblower could go to the press, or an agent be forced to make a confession. Then again, their whole approach could be wrong. Perhaps the solution to the Troubles lay in flooding the region with soldiers and trying to defeat the IRA on the battlefield. Another concern was that they might have backed the wrong men.

Were Gerry Adams and Martin McGuinness capable of bringing the rest of the IRA with them? The attitude among many IRA hard-liners until then had been: 'If it's good enough for Martin, it's good enough for me.' But what if that were to change? And if either Adams or McGuinness was to find himself facing jail, how far should MI5 go in an effort to keep him out?

One of the questions they did not consider, but probably should have done, with hindsight, was whether another government department could be about to launch its own initiative to end the Troubles, one that was in many ways the opposite of theirs.

Anglo–Irish

'I think I would like to do something about Ireland,' Margaret Thatcher had said one night in December 1982, while sitting by the fire at No. 10 Downing Street. She was holding a glass of whiskey and soda, and it was late.[1]

Most of the people with her that night gave little thought to this remark, apart from one. His name was David Goodall. He was a diplomat with a keen memory, and he hung on to Thatcher's words that night and saw in them a mandate to act. The following year, when an Irish diplomat mentioned the vague possibility of a new agreement between Ireland and the United Kingdom at some point in the future, Goodall leaped at it. He contacted his friend Robert Armstrong, the cabinet secretary, and together they came up with a plan that they hoped would change the relationship between Britain and Ireland and bring the Troubles to an end. At the heart of it was their desire to head off the rise of Sinn Féin. They were also driven, Goodall explained, 'by a desire to make amends for Britain's ill treatment of Ireland down the centuries'.[2] Goodall recognised that they were not playing entirely by the book, and that some might argue they were going beyond their remit as unelected officials. But they went ahead with it anyway.

Over the next two years, a small group of Irish and British civil servants met thirty-six times in secret to discuss this new agreement between the two countries. Their meetings were unusual for several reasons. One was the extraordinary level of secrecy. Everyone involved knew that the idea of these conversations taking place was enough to spark a political explosion in Northern Ireland. That was because they were discussing closer cooperation between the north and south of the island, which for most Protestants was a step towards unification. The other thing that set these talks apart was that right from the start both sides were basically in agreement.

Garret FitzGerald, the Irish Taoiseach, was bemused. 'Ultimately, it was not a negotiation,' he said. 'Ultimately, everybody was convinced that something should be done. "How do you persuade the prime minister?" was the question.'[3]

Thatcher became the obstacle they needed to overcome. Robert Armstrong and David Goodall 'never definitely overstepped the mark', according to one of Thatcher's private secretaries, but 'they were all going behind her back. Their meetings were principally to discuss how to handle her.[4] Goodall agreed that 'it is very fair to say that we were all trying to persuade her' and that 'we did a bit conspire'.[5]

It was hard to overstate Robert Armstrong's subtle influence over Margaret Thatcher, or how completely different their views were on the subject of Northern Ireland. She was a proud Unionist. He was not. Armstrong saw himself as a European. He believed in consensus and internationalism and was convinced that the only way to end the Troubles was by making concessions to the Irish government. Armstrong also wanted to strengthen political parties in the centre, such as the SDLP, the left-of-centre Irish nationalist party, and he hoped to weaken Sinn Féin, which he saw as an impediment to peace. Either he thought the MI5 'project' to encourage the growth of Sinn Féin and keep McGuinness and Adams in position was a mistake, or, much more likely, he was unaware of it.

Armstrong and Goodall chipped away at Thatcher's resolve for months, telling her that this new agreement could be the first step towards a lasting peace. They also reminded her that the American president, Ronald Reagan, appeared to be keen for this agreement between Britain and Ireland to go ahead and had hinted that it could lead to more economic assistance from the United States.

But before Margaret Thatcher could reach a decision, she was nearly killed by the IRA. In October 1984, she went to Brighton for the annual Conservative Party conference. Northern Ireland was far from her mind, and the IRA did not feature in the speech she planned to give. In the early hours of the morning, an IRA bomb eviscerated the hotel in which she was staying. The device had been tiled up behind a bathroom wall, just as it would have been in the plot to kill Prince Charles and Princess Diana the year before. But this time, the job of installing the bomb had not been given to an agent known to MI5.

Five people were killed that night and thirty-one injured, but the principal target, Margaret Thatcher, survived. Her thinking on Northern Ireland might have changed in the days after this near-death experience, and she could have shut down the attempt by her civil servants to build closer relations with Dublin. Instead, she gave in to their arguments, and less than a year later a draft of the Anglo–Irish Agreement went before the British Cabinet. Even if nobody around the table was hugely enthusiastic about the text, there was no spirited opposition either.

It was not long before Garret FitzGerald and Margaret Thatcher sat down together in the drawing room of Hillsborough Castle, outside Belfast, and signed the agreement. Thatcher had a detached, almost spectral air as she scribbled her signature. It was as if she already knew that she was making a mistake. Later, she would describe signing this treaty as the greatest regret she had from her time in office. One private secretary compared her feelings on this 'to Queen Mary I of England's terrible sadness at the loss of Calais'.[6]

Several hours before signing the document in front of the cameras, Thatcher had heard that her close friend Ian Gow, a committed Unionist and Conservative politician, had resigned in protest. (Gow would later be murdered by the IRA.) That was just the start of it. More than 100,000 Protestants then gathered outside Belfast City Hall to vent their fury. Ian Paisley, the energetic, roaring leader of the Democratic Unionist Party, was at the head of the crowd. 'Never!' he bellowed into the microphone, eyes bulging. 'Never! Never!'[7] All fifteen of the region's Unionist MPs resigned. The Northern Ireland secretary was spat at in the street. There was talk of a strike. Thatcher was told that some senior Protestant politicians were even thinking about ways to turn Northern Ireland into a breakaway state with its own provisional government.[8]

'The reaction was', Thatcher conceded, 'much stronger than we thought it would be.'[9]

Many of the Protestants who took to the streets were upset about more than the agreement. In a deeper and more personal sense, they felt betrayed by Thatcher herself. Until then, she had been a saviour figure and seemed to be one of them. Now she had crossed a line and become an enemy.

'Oh God,' Ian Paisley growled into a microphone, 'take vengeance against this wicked, treacherous and lying woman.'[10]

Thatcher desperately wanted to give the likes of Paisley proof that this agreement might still work and that she had done the right thing. One of the reasons for signing the treaty had been to improve intelligence sharing with Ireland. 'We received far better intelligence cooperation', Thatcher recalled, 'from virtually all other European countries.'[11] But in the days after the agreement came into being, nothing had changed, and little intelligence was being exchanged between the two countries. In one meeting, Thatcher was asked to 'press the Irish for results on this front'.[12] It was vital, according to her foreign secretary, Geoffrey Howe, 'to find positive ways of demonstrating to the Unionist community that the agreement is ultimately in their best interests'.[13]

But how? The British government needed something – anything would do – to show that this agreement had been worth the trouble. Senior civil servants thought about ways to kickstart the intelligence-sharing relationship. Some wondered if the best way to do this was to hand their Irish counterparts a precious piece of intelligence – one so valuable that the Irish would have no choice but to give something back in return.

24

Kidnapped

'What's happening? What's wrong?' Dorothy asks Frank. But he won't say.

She presses him again.

'You wouldn't understand.'

It is January 1986. Dorothy Robb and Frank Hegarty have been having versions of this conversation for weeks. She knows that something is up. She can sense that his mind has been taken over by doubt or fear, it's hard to say which, but he won't let her in, and their relationship has begun to feel strained.

Frank's life is now a carousel of meetings, conversations, and places to be, and there are times when he struggles to keep up. The dogs will always need to be walked and looked after, and often there's a friend who wants him to see to their greyhound, or there are his horses to think about. He goes to visit his mother, as well as his brothers and sisters. His youngest children, now aged five and three, might need taking somewhere or looking after. Then there are IRA men who appear without warning to ask about a weapon, or money that they need him to take across the border. And, of course, he must remember to see his army handler.

Frank knows how fragile this edifice has become. With one slip, the whole thing might come crashing down. A word out of place. A pick-up that goes wrong. Something he knows and is not supposed to know. He also understands that the less he tells Dorothy and the more elliptical he is with her, the safer she will be. His silence comes from a place of love.

The constant in Frank's life – the one thing that will always be there and whose presence is a kind of solace – is Derry, his home. He has never felt so rooted in this place. It may not be a city that everyone falls in love with. 'I had never imagined Europe could look so threadbare,' the travel writer Paul Theroux wrote after a recent visit. 'Little brick terraces, and drink shops, and empty stores, and barricades, and boarded windows, and starved dogs, and dirty-faced children – it looked like the past in an old picture.'[1] But behind this Dickensian façade is a torrent of life. The city that Frank cannot imagine leaving is close and intricately connected, and he can place most of the people he meets with the question: 'Who's your father?'[2] Even if the violence has pushed many people away from each other, others are now closer than ever, bound together by the memory of what they have been through. Nor has life stopped for the Troubles. Open a local newspaper, and you'll see adverts for local pantomimes and roller discos, fundraisers, dinner-dances, pub quizzes, concerts, and bingo, alongside the news that Seamus Heaney will be reading his poetry next week in the city's Guildhall, or the actor Stephen Rea has begun to rehearse *Double Cross*, a play about William Joyce, better known as 'Lord Haw-Haw', who was also a British agent in Ireland.

Some of the MI5 agents operating in Derry will be taken by their case officers for short trips to the countryside or overseas to give them a break from what they are doing and, for a moment, remind them of the world beyond the goldfish bowl that is Derry. But not Frank. Either this is not offered to him, or he is not interested in it.

Frank Hegarty has faith in his handlers and knows that they will protect him. When they decided, finally, to seize the cache of weapons that he had long ago hidden in the city cemetery, they did so in a way that meant he would not come under suspicion. The police appeared to have stumbled across them by accident. It was reported the next day that this weapons' hide contained 'two 9mm pistols, over 100 rounds of ammunition, a quantity of command wire and detonators, boiler suits, gloves, woollen face masks and false faces', as well as the rifles used in three murders, including that of the British soldier Neil Clarke.[3]

One of the people questioned by the police in relation to this discovery was Martin McGuinness. Not long after Christmas Day 1985, at dawn, a queue of police officers bundled into McGuinness's home to carry out a search. They knew that they were unlikely to find anything, because McGuinness always kept his hands clean, but they rummaged around in his house all the same before arresting him and driving him to Belfast.

'Isn't it wonderful, Mr McGuinness,' he remembered being told by one Special Branch man, 'we can take you out of your bed in Derry at 6am and bring you to Belfast and keep you for a week. And we can do it again and again and again.[4] During the seven days that he was held, Martin McGuinness reportedly said nothing.

A month later, Martin McGuinness could be seen sitting on a stage by Free Derry Corner, the iconic end-of-terrace building emblazoned with the words 'YOU ARE NOW ENTERING FREE DERRY'. This was where the Battle of the Bogside took place at the start of the Troubles, when British soldiers were deployed for the first time. McGuinness was there to mark the fourteenth anniversary of Bloody Sunday. In front of him was a small crowd of people, and next to him on stage was the Labour MP Ken Livingstone, who gave a speech in which he promised that a Labour government would never repress the people of Derry. He went on to attack the recent Anglo–Irish Agreement, which he dismissed as just 'another gimmick in a long line of gimmicks fostered on the Irish people'.[5]

Martin McGuinness had a distant look on his face as Livingstone spoke. Just before he took to the stage, someone had told him the news. The three IRA weapons dumps in Ireland, the ones set up by him and Frank Hegarty, had been raided that morning by the Irish police. Five people were now under arrest. Ten tons of IRA weaponry had been found, in what was already being described as the Irish police's 'biggest ever arms haul'.[6] The first person he had to find was Frank. Someone had tipped off the authorities.

Rose Hegarty has no idea where her son is. She has been saying this all morning to the men calling up to ask after him. She has not seen Frankie, and does not know what has happened to him. One of the most persistent callers is Danny, a close friend of Frank's, and a well-known member of the local IRA. Rose wants to find out where Frank is as much as anyone else and is soon on the phone to Dorothy, who is also under siege. She does not know where Frank has gone either, as she keeps telling everyone. But she can see that his car has disappeared, and so has he.

The night before, Dorothy tells Rose, she went out with Frank. Nothing unusual about that. It's what they did every Saturday night. 'We were having a drink. And he said to me, "You know, I'm going away tomorrow". He said, "If I don't make it tomorrow, you won't see me for a long time". I had asked him what was he doing. He said, "I can't tell you".[7] But he did mention something about going to Sligo. If everything was alright, he would see her again after that on Sunday night.

Dorothy is used to this kind of uncertainty. She could have needled him for more, but usually there is no point. She knows that Frank has it in him to be gregarious and lively, just as he has a reflexive ability to clam up if anyone prods at him too many times.

Rose calls up Danny, Frank's friend, to pass on what she has heard. She also remembers Frank talking about a football match down in

Sligo. A little later, Danny appears at Rose's door, accompanied by someone she knows a lot about – he's known in Derry as 'one of the big boys' – but has never seen in the flesh.[8]

Martin McGuinness is bigger than he looks on television, and fills the doorframe to Rose's house as he walks in. The two IRA men carry on through the hall, past the picture on the wall of a long-haired Jesus cradling a Sacred Heart, before settling down in the living room of the house where Frank once lived. McGuinness is close to his own elderly mother and knows how to behave around a respectable matriarch like Rose Hegarty. He is polite and deferential, and Rose has no reason to be hostile towards him. She offers them tea, and they sit down to talk. McGuinness peppers her with questions about Frank, and they speak for a while. Once he is satisfied, he says it is time to go. Pulling himself to his feet, he thanks Rose for the tea and says goodbye.

Outside, darkness has fallen. The streets are lit by spoonfuls of yellowish lamplight as Martin McGuinness makes his way into the night. One of his next stops is Dorothy's house in Shantallow. Again, he makes himself at home and listens to her story. He tells her that he will be in touch.

Up in Rosemount, Rose hears the phone ring.

She picks up.

It's Frank. He is upset and frantic. He tells his mother that he is only allowed one phone call and will probably never see her again.

Rose asks him what has happened.

Frank tells her that two men abducted him earlier that day as he left Dorothy's home, and he has no idea where he is being held or why.

That's it. The call ends. Rose passes on what she has heard to Frank's sisters, who go to the police and report that their brother is missing. The police note down what they have said and assure them that Frank is not being held by either them or the army.

Word spreads that Frank Hegarty is saying he was kidnapped.

Later that night, Dorothy hears a knock at the door. She opens it to see several local IRA men, including one she knows. They say that she and her youngest children need to come with them.

Outside, it has started to pour down. Or as they say in Derry, the rain is lifting lumps out of the street. Dorothy goes upstairs to her children, rouses them, gathers some clothes, and helps them downstairs to where the IRA men are waiting. Dorothy and her children are then driven over the border to the Republic to a house of a man who knows McGuinness. Elsewhere in Derry that night, every IRA volunteer who has known Frank is told to disappear. Most of them pack a bag and head for the border.

Rose Hegarty wakes up the next day to a strange, distended reality. Time seems to telescope ahead of her to the moment when this will all be over. Her son has been taken. Two of her grandchildren are no longer at home. She does not know where they all are and she has begun to live with the terrible fear that she might never see any of them again.

25

Exile

Frank Hegarty left Derry in a rush, but he was not kidnapped. The night before his departure, he received a call at home from his handler. This was unusual, and would only happen in an emergency. His handler explained that they needed to meet at dawn the following day, and that this was urgent. Frank would not have been told over the phone about what was going to happen, or that his life might be in danger. But he knew it was serious, and he went out with Dorothy that night aware that something big was about to happen.

The following morning, Frank Hegarty woke up before anyone else in the house. Perhaps he went to see his sleeping children and kissed them goodbye. On the other side of the border, the Garda were preparing to raid the hides. Frank did not have long. He left his home in Shantallow and went to the Foyle Bridge, where his handler was waiting for him. The situation was explained to him, and he was soon on a plane to England. That evening, he called his mother to tell her he was safe.

The next few days must have passed in a blur. Frank was debriefed, moved from one place to another, and finally taken to an army safe house in Sittingbourne, Kent, where he tried to adjust to life as an exile.

Frank's new home was a semi-detached house opposite a hospital.

He had two soldiers with him at all times and was well protected. But everything around him felt off and a little out of kilter. Each night he went to bed alone and woke up in a place that smelled like someone else's house. Frank missed Dorothy, his mother, his brothers and sisters, his friends, Derry, and the touch of his children. And he thought often about his dogs. With none of these around, time itself seemed to slow down. The intensity of Frank's desire to return to Derry and see his family was matched only by his understanding that this was the one thing he could never do. It must have felt as if he had lost a part of himself.

The two soldiers in the safe house encouraged Frank to think about 'next steps'. They took him on trips to the local bookies, so that he could place a few bets to take his mind off things. They tried to lift his spirits by talking about a new life overseas or somewhere in Great Britain. But this didn't appeal to Frank in the way that it might have done to someone else. He had never been one of those Derrymen who dreamed of maybe moving away and starting again 'across the water'. Some of his friends thought about emigrating to faraway places like Australia or the United States, making a success of themselves, and returning in a blaze of triumph. Northern Ireland at the time had one of the highest rates of emigration in the world. But Frank was different, and every day he spent in that safe house was less like the start of a new life than another twenty-four hours in purgatory.

The soldiers wanted Frank to paint over these feelings each day with a fresh coat of optimism, but this was difficult. He was still angry about what had happened, and probably traumatised by how suddenly he had been removed from the world he had known all his life. He felt let down by his handlers in Derry. He wouldn't be in this situation if it wasn't for them. He also felt sorry for the men in the Republic who had allowed the IRA to use their outbuildings as weapons hides and had since been arrested.

What Frank did not know – and could not know at that stage – was that the decision to pass on his intelligence to the Garda had not originated with his handlers. It came from elsewhere, and the soldiers who had been looking after him were livid when they heard about how Frank's information was going to be used. They knew what this would mean for him. But there was nothing they could do. Their job was primarily to gather intelligence and pass it up the line; other people had the final say on how it was acted upon.

Once Frank had settled into his life in the safe house, he was allowed to make regular calls to his mother, and soon he was on the phone to her every day. He heard from her about Dorothy and their children going over the border with the IRA men, and spending ten days in a house outside Ballyshannon, County Donegal, before being put on a bus back to Derry. It must have been difficult for Frank to hear about this on the phone, knowing there was nothing he could do.

But then it seemed as if there might be. Perhaps he could go home, after all.

In the weeks after Frank's disappearance, Martin McGuinness began to pay regular visits to Rose Hegarty. He went round to see her, she remembered, 'practically every other day'.[1]

US President Bill Clinton later hailed Martin McGuinness as someone who was 'good about sticking with something he decided to do'.[2] Or as Sinn Féin president Mary Lou McDonald put it: 'Once Martin McGuinness committed himself to a course of action, that was it'.[3] British civil servant Jonathan Powell said that when McGuinness promised 'to deliver on a particular deal, he actually then did deliver on it – he didn't sort of wimp out halfway through'. But Powell also mentioned another quality. 'When I say he was a man of his word, I don't mean a man who's necessarily always telling you the truth about what happened.'[4]

Martin McGuinness had made a decision and was going to stick with it: he would do everything in his power to lure Frank Hegarty back to Derry. Each time he went to see Rose, he assured her that her son was safe to return, and he would personally vouch for him. This went on for weeks. Some of Frank's siblings were suspicious of McGuinness and did not like having him in the house, but Rose was at least willing to listen to what he had to say.

'Martin portrayed himself as a friend,' according to a source familiar with these events; "'I'm someone who can deliver. Yes, you can trust the IRA. No harm will come to your son. He just has to come back.'"⁵

Rose passed on the message to Frank. Then, one day, her son called up from England while Rose had McGuinness in the house with her. The IRA man indicated that he would like a word with Frank. Rose passed over the phone.

'Come back,' McGuinness said to Frank over the phone. 'You will be safe.'⁶

Now Frank had a decision to make. Perhaps he really could go home. Perhaps he would be safe. Everything turned on whether he could trust Martin McGuinness. The choice bore a startling similarity to the one faced long ago by his namesake, Father Hegarty, as he swam away from the Redcoats.

'Come back,' they had said. 'You will be safe.'

High-priority Target

It's been several weeks since Frank Hegarty arrived in the safe house in Kent, and he's still struggling to work out where his future lies. He has heard Martin McGuinness tell him that he is safe to come back to Derry, but he is not yet sure what to do next.

The soldiers looking after Frank are worried about him, and decide to try something different. They arrange for a colleague to contact Dorothy, Frank's partner and the mother of two of his children, and ask if she would like to visit Frank in England. Dorothy agrees, and is soon on the train to Antrim station, outside Belfast, where she is met by a British government official. The pair of them fly to Gatwick Airport, where a different official takes her by car to the nearby Copthorne Hotel. On the way, this other man makes a point of admiring the houses they pass. Once they reach the hotel, Dorothy is led to a room where Frank is waiting for her. The door closes behind them, and they are alone.

This reunion is not an easy one. Since they have last seen each other, their lives have been torn apart. Frank has been uprooted and knows that there are people who want him dead. Dorothy and her children have had to leave their home for a time, and, back in Derry, have begun to experience the stigma of knowing someone believed to have been an informer. As they sit together in the hotel room, Frank tells Dorothy that the British have made them an offer: if she is willing to leave Northern Ireland and start a new life with him and the children, they will be set up with a new house similar to the ones she passed on the way in from the airport. They will also get a car, a trust fund for their children, and £100,000 in cash. But there is a catch. This offer only extends to Dorothy's youngest three children, and not to the older two or her elderly mother.

Frank is not expecting Dorothy to decide right away, but he can see that she does not leap at this idea. Dorothy is soon on a plane home, and that night she is with her family again. At some point before midnight, there is a knock at her door. It is Martin McGuinness, who has already heard about her trip to England.

Dorothy tells him about what happened. She also hands over a tape that Frank has recorded in the safe house in which he gives an account of how he ended up in England. In the recording, which was made for McGuinness to hear, Frank claims that he never told anyone about the location of the IRA weapons, and was taken away from Derry against his will. His voice throughout is preternaturally calm, but at the same time he doesn't really sound like himself. Yes, it is him. But his choice of words is stilted, as if he is reading from a script that has been prepared for him.

Dorothy also tells McGuinness about how the British have offered them £100,000 to start a new life overseas.

'I'll double that,' Martin McGuinness says. 'I'll offer you £200,000 to stay.'

He is serious, and at the same time he is not. Dorothy does not imagine that the IRA chief is about to hand over a briefcase containing £200,000 in cash, nor would she ever take money from him. But his reaction confirms what she has already begun to suspect. McGuinness will do whatever it takes to bring Frank back to Derry.

Dorothy thinks more about the offer from the British but, in the end, realises that she cannot abandon her older children and mother. She decides to stay where she is.

At around the same time, Margaret Thatcher receives a message about 'a very well-placed agent who has been supplying us with valuable information for some time'. It's Frank. He is 'an extremely high-priority target' for the IRA, she reads, as a result of 'certain intelligence successes against them'. He is being looked after by the army, and every effort is being made to find him a 'permanent settlement abroad', but – and this is the problem – the agent himself is not sure what he wants to do.[1]

This is probably the first time that Margaret Thatcher has heard about Frank Hegarty. She knows that at some point this man has passed on important information to the British, and that his life is now in danger, and he is trying to work out where to live. What she does not know about Frank is how he ended up in this predicament, and the way his fate is bound up in her recent decision to sign the Anglo-Irish Agreement.

Why did Frank's career as an agent come to an end? The details are hard to pin down, but the overall shape of the narrative is clear. In the weeks after Thatcher signed the paperwork on the treaty, and as Protestants across Northern Ireland reacted with fury to what had happened, someone, somewhere in Whitehall – either from the prime minister's office or the Northern Ireland Office – asked what could be done to kickstart the new intelligence-sharing relationship with the Republic of Ireland. So far, nothing had changed. Was there some valuable piece of information that the British could pass on to the Irish, in the hope that they would then return the favour?

One of the suggestions that came from the DCI in Northern Ireland involved the three IRA weapons dumps over the border, that were being looked after by Frank. Sharing their location with Irish intelligence might allow the British government to salvage something from the Anglo-Irish Agreement. It would also, of course, remove the possibility of these weapons ever being used against soldiers or civilians. The only problem was that doing this would mean resettling the agent who had provided the information.

Several weeks after the first message about Frank Hegarty, Margaret Thatcher receives another one.

'Unfortunately this man has disappeared from the protected accommodation,' she reads. 'We suspect he may be intending to be reunited with his common law wife and family.'

Nobody knows where he is, but they are trying to locate Frank, the message goes on, because if Frank returns to Derry he will 'probably be killed'.[2]

Thatcher underlines this last phrase in thick blue ink. No doubt she is alarmed by what she has just read. It is essential that the British find this man before the IRA does.

Cricket

Gerry Doherty was known around Derry as 'Mad Dog'. He had been jailed earlier in the Troubles for the attempted murder of a British soldier and two bombing offences. As a seventeen-year-old, he had set off a 120-pound explosive device outside Derry's Guildhall, one of the region's most iconic buildings, shattering its stained-glass windows. Thirteen years later, in 1985, Mad Dog returned to the Guildhall in a different capacity. He had come to hear the results of the local council elections in which he was standing as a candidate for Sinn Féin.

Doherty made his way up the stairs to the main hall. On his way, he passed a marble statue of Queen Victoria that had lost both of its arms in his explosion. He lined up with the other candidates and waited for the results. At last, his name was read out. Mad Dog had won. The former IRA volunteer was now a Derry city councillor.

The celebrations in the room were frenzied and loud, with the sound amplified by the soaring vaulted ceiling. The newly elected Sinn Féin representative was then carried down the steps of the Guildhall on the shoulders of his supporters. In the background came the joyful chant, sharp and clear – 'I, I, IRA, I, I, IRA, I, I, IRA!'[1]

One of the men carrying Mad Dog down the stairs that day was Martin McGuinness. With each electoral victory like this, he and Gerry Adams were turning paramilitaries into politicians. Reluctant politicians, sometimes. But politicians all the same. They were starting to get there. The journey that McGuinness and Adams had begun eight years earlier on their long walks out of Derry to the Grianán of Aileach was picking up speed.

Sinn Féin won an impressive fifty-nine seats in these 1985 local elections, the first they had ever contested, and the party attracted more than 11 per cent of the popular vote. McGuinness and Adams seemed to be edging towards a situation in which a political settlement might be within reach. But there was more to what they were doing than their activities on behalf of Sinn Féin.

Gerry Adams would soon secretly be in touch with John Hume, the leader of the SDLP, and was also about to start a clandestine correspondence with the British government. A trusted local priest, Father Alec Reid, would pass on messages to the new Northern Ireland secretary.[2] This was a huge gamble for Adams, especially given that he had not cleared it with the IRA Army Council. He was risking his life by writing these letters to the British. But he felt the danger to himself was justified by the scale of what was at stake. He was part of a conflict which had the potential to keep going for the rest of his life unless he decided to act.

The replies that Gerry Adams received to his letters appeared to come from the then Northern Ireland secretary, Tom King. His signature was always at the bottom of the page. But the text of these messages had been written by officers working for MI5. Anything to do with Gerry Adams or Martin McGuinness, and the 'project' to bring the IRA closer to a political solution, was MI5 business.

The replies from MI5 to Gerry Adams were both encouraging and firm. The British government was open to finding a political settlement, they said, 'as long as it was not imposed by force'.[3]

A dialogue was under way. MI5's faith in McGuinness and Adams was beginning, slowly, to pay off. But they recognised the other side to this. Neither man had turned his back on violence. Several months after Martin McGuinness helped to carry Gerry 'Mad Dog' Doherty down the steps of the Guildhall, he set out with Frank Hegarty to find suitable hiding places for 300 crates of Libyan arms. McGuinness presented himself as a respectable Sinn Féin politician, while also giving the go-ahead for IRA attacks on British military targets, authorising murders, and telling Rose Hegarty repeatedly that her son was safe to come back to Derry.

For all this, Martin McGuinness and Gerry Adams still represented the most realistic path to peace. That was the uncomfortable truth. It was probably in Britain's interest for these two to stay out of jail and in control of the IRA. They also needed to keep them alive.

The year after Gerry Adams began his secret correspondence with British government officials, the British Army learned about a plot by Protestant paramilitaries to kill him. A landmine was going to be attached to his car. The response from MI5 was emphatic: 'the attempt on Adams must not succeed'.[4] The landmine was located and disabled, and this attempt on his life failed. But that may not have been the first time the British intervened to keep him alive.

Three years earlier, Adams was attacked by two gunmen from the Ulster Freedom Fighters (UFF), who fired twenty rounds into his vehicle, hitting him four times. The gunmen had been standing no more than 15 yards away. But the surgeon who later treated Adams said: 'I don't think he was particularly close to death from the actual injury he sustained'.[5] According to one former soldier, the reason for this was simple. The FRU had been tipped off about this attack and had jarked the ammunition. They were able to reduce the charge in each round so that the bullets were extremely unlikely to kill anyone.

Some years later, in the 1990s, a group of IRA hardliners put together their own plan to kill Gerry Adams. According to former Northern Ireland secretary Michael Mates, on this occasion Adams was warned directly by MI5, who then ensured that the IRA man behind this plot was arrested in relation to a separate matter. Another attempt on Adams's life had come to nothing.[6]

Sometimes a strategy will succeed not because it is the best idea there is, but because it has been in place longer than any other. There were a number of different British approaches to ending the Troubles, but the one that was starting to outlive the others was built around the idea that to end the violence, those on the margins needed to be brought into the centre and given a share of the political power, even if this involved difficult compromises. There was also an under-standing that this process was going to take time.

'One thing about the Brits,' a local priest used to say, 'remember, they play cricket. Nice and long and slow.'[7] Cricket was seen by some Irish people as an unfathomably English type of game. As a Catholic in Northern Ireland, showing an interest in cricket was a bit like talking about your love of *EastEnders* or the BBC. It was the kind of thing that might make some people call you a 'West Brit' or 'Brit lover'.

One Northern Irishman with a fascination for cricket was Martin McGuinness, something he kept to himself during the Troubles. 'I thought it was really interesting,' he later said. 'It was a game where discipline was required. An intriguing battle between bowler and batsman. I became very interested in the different techniques and strategies that were deployed around it.'[8]

Martin McGuinness had spent most of his life in bat against the British, and understood that it would only take one wild or rash stroke to bring his innings to an end. What he did not know was that some of the bowlers on the other team did not actually want to get him out. All he knew was that he had to keep going. He recog-nised the need for restraint, and, at the same time, the importance of keeping the scoreboard ticking over. If Frank Hegarty were to reappear in Derry, McGuinness felt that he had to do something to restore his reputation among the IRA hardliners, just as he had to be careful not to do anything that was reckless or might later come to haunt him.

The Revenant

Late April 1986. The harbour at Cairnryan, southern Scotland, where a ferry is about to leave for Northern Ireland. The air is spiced with diesel. It's late afternoon, and the light has started to thin. Passengers are driving their cars into the hold of the ship at a sluggish, best-behaviour speed, with men and women in bright jackets waving them on. Behind them, the hills pour into the waters of Loch Ryan, which gives onto the Irish Sea.

Somewhere in this scene is Frank Hegarty. Not exactly hidden, but not wanting to draw attention to himself either. He has come to meet a person he knows well and has not seen since leaving Derry three months ago. Their relief on seeing each other is overwhelming. Frank left the safe house several days ago. He is tired and does not look his best. But seeing this person is transformational for him. It is the first real sign that he might make it home, after all, and that perhaps everything will be alright.

How has he got this far? One version of the story is that he escaped from the army safe house in Kent after going to the local bookies with one of the soldiers and then slipping out the back of the shop. In another, Frank had help from someone in the IRA. In some ways, it does not matter. The soldiers looking after him had no authority to detain him, and Frank was not their prisoner. He was there for his own protection, and if he decided to leave, there was a limit to what they could do to stop him.

Frank and his companion drive into the hold of the ferry. The crossing takes just a few hours, and they soon arrive at Larne, north of Belfast. The ferry doors grumble open. Cars stream out in single file. If Frank is going to be stopped by the port authorities, this is when it will happen.

Their car is waved through. They drive away from the port and set out for Derry. Out of the window, Frank can see familiar landmarks. They come at him like the lyrics to a favourite song. The signs by the side of the road saying how many miles to Derry act as a countdown to the scene he has imagined so many times over the last few months.

At last, they reach the outskirts of Derry. Frank knows the curves of the road before they come, which traffic lights are around the corner, and where the army bases are. He can see the oak trees coming into leaf. Then he catches sight of the River Foyle, wide and moody as it sweeps out in silence to the sea. Next comes the soaring arc of the new bridge, where he met his handler on the morning of the Libyan arms raids. The Foyle Bridge is steep, and as the car climbs to the highest point there is a moment, only a second or two, when it is as if they are flying, high above everything and everyone and free from suspicion or blame, before they roll down the other side, back to reality, and weave through the city until they reach Rose's house.

The handbrake crunches up. Engine off. Seatbelts released. Frank steps out of the car and walks up to the house he knows so well. The place he has run to is the place from which he has come. Moments later, he is in his mother's arms.

Rose Hegarty is overjoyed. She is also shocked by the state of her son, who has not had a bath in days. She sees that his feet are covered in blisters from all the walking he has done since leaving the safe house. That night, she fills a bowl with hot water and soap, and tells him to soak his feet. She does everything she can to look after her son, for, as she later says, 'He had walked for a lot of miles to try to get away from his capture'.[1]

His capture. This is the story that Frank has decided to tell. He was captured, he says. He was taken by the Brits and held somewhere outside London before making his escape. No, he doesn't know why they took him, but he's relieved to be home and to have the whole business behind him.

Later that night, Rose calls up Dorothy to say that Frank has made it home. Dorothy drives up from Shantallow and is relieved to see him. But at the same time, she notices some of the ways in which he appears to have changed. Frank is on edge, which is understandable, and, perhaps she's imagining it, his accent sounds different and more English than before.

Frank tells Dorothy that he won't be coming home with her tonight and will stay here with his mother.[2] This must be hard for Dorothy to hear; they have two children together, and have lived for years under the same roof. But things have changed between them and Frank is not yet ready to come back to her. Even if he can understand why she chose not to start again with him overseas, as it would have meant leaving her mother and eldest children, this has changed the complexion of their relationship. He also knows that he cannot go back to her and how things were until he has sorted everything out. There are people he needs to see before his life can go back to normal.

The next day, Rose Hegarty hears the phone ring. It is Dorothy. Martin McGuinness has just been round, she says, and is now on his way up to see her. Minutes later, there's a knock at the door. McGuinness is standing in the doorway. He is wearing a heavy fisherman's jumper that day and a tweed jacket. He asks to see Frank, but it's a rhetorical question, really. McGuinness gets his way in

Derry, and he is expecting to hear Rose call up the stairs for Frank. But she does not.

Rose tells him that nobody is seeing her son today.

McGuinness pushes back.

'He gave me an absolute guarantee that nothing would ever happen to Frankie,' Rose remembered. 'Everything could be worked out. He did not have to go and liaise with anyone. "You know what I'm saying," he said.'

But Rose Hegarty has made her decision and that's final. Frank is shattered. He has travelled for three days straight, and he will not be seeing anyone until he has had some rest.

Eventually, Martin McGuinness accepts this, but says that several people need to speak to Frank. Rose tells him that he can come back on Friday, four days from now. As a parting shot, McGuinness tells Rose that in the meantime her son would be best advised to stay inside. The implication is clear. Several days earlier, it was reported that IRA men had dragged a naked man through the city centre 'screaming like an animal caught in a trap' in a so-called 'punishment' attack.[3] There are some IRA men who can't be controlled, McGuinness seems to be saying, and who might, on seeing Frank, decide to mete out their own form of justice.

Martin McGuinness is entitled to feel a kick of frustration as he leaves Rose Hegarty's house. He has worked hard to bring Frank back to Derry and he wants, at the very least, to see him for himself. But he is not worried about Frank running away, and there is probably no harm in waiting until the end of the week. Besides, he has other things to worry about.

Earlier that day, McGuinness attended the funeral of Séamus McElwaine, an IRA volunteer responsible for a string of brutal attacks, including the attempted murder of the policeman John Kelly, father of Arlene Foster, the Unionist politician alongside whom McGuinness would later work. He spoke at McElwaine's funeral, just hours before going to see Rose Hegarty, denouncing the 'British terrorists' who had killed McElwaine, and other 'terrorists such as Thatcher and Reagan'. He went further than usual in his speech that day. To anyone reading a newspaper report of what he said, it sounded as if he was trying to get a reaction from London or Washington, DC. But all he was trying to do was get through to the IRA hardliners.

Martin McGuinness has still not recovered from the loss of the Libyan arms. A powerful clique of physical-force IRA men are seething about what happened, and some blame him for the raids. One or two would later say that they asked themselves if McGuinness had secretly intervened to make sure the weapons were seized, because he did not want the IRA to launch a new military campaign. Others may have begun to wonder to themselves if there was an entirely different side to McGuinness and if he might be protected by the British or working for them as an agent. But none of them make the mistake of saying any of this out loud – because that could get them killed.

Martin McGuinness has been here before. He knows that the cloud of suspicion will not blow over by itself. He needs to act. But he also understands that he must not go too far. His challenge is to be two different things at the same time. He needs to be feared as a paramilitary and respected as a politician, even if there are times when this seems to be almost impossible.

May Day, 1986. The film *Top Gun* is playing in cinemas across Derry, and 'Rock Me Amadeus' is the song you're most likely to hear on the radio. The mood out on the streets is buzzy and bright. The local football team, Derry City, has just won the League of Ireland's inaugural First Division Shield, after more than a decade in the football wilderness, a fairy-tale victory that has given local people a lift. In other parts of the city, there is growing excitement about Northern

Ireland taking part in the football World Cup, which begins in Mexico later that month.

But unknown to anyone in Derry, the clouds forming over the city that day are not as they seem. Last week, a catastrophic nuclear explosion at Chernobyl, in the Soviet Union, launched millions of radioactive particles into the atmosphere. Carried away by the wind, a heavy concentration of them has now formed above this part of Northern Ireland. Any day now, it will be washed onto the streets of Derry.

Beneath this radioactive sky, Martin McGuinness walks up to Rose Hegarty's front door and knocks. Four days have passed since he was last here. He is accompanied by two local solicitors. Rose opens the door, and the three men are shown into the living room where Frank is waiting for them. The door closes, and they are left to speak in private.

McGuinness has brought the solicitors with him because he wants Frank to give a sworn affidavit setting out exactly what happened. McGuinness might be angry, but he is not in a rush. This is a man who likes to fish in his spare time and has the patience to tie his own fishing flies. For the next three hours, McGuinness probes Frank about his time in England, moving slowly and carefully. The solicitors take notes. Occasionally, they ask Frank to repeat a detail or spell out a name. The atmosphere is tense and watchful.

Once they have finished, McGuinness asks Frank to sign the affidavit that has been put together. As well as setting out his account of what happened, it states that any information Frank might have supplied to the British was given 'under duress'.[4] It also says that he will never testify in court. McGuinness's overriding fear is that Frank Hegarty could become another supergrass, like Raymond Gilmour.

Frank signs the document, and McGuinness tells Rose that

everything is fine. He has nothing more to ask. Frank has answered all his questions.

Martin McGuinness has come a long way in his reinvention as a peace-loving Sinn Féin politician. He recently took part in a BBC documentary, *At the Edge of the Union*, in which he portrayed himself as a teetotal churchgoer, loving parent, and man of peace. The programme made almost no reference to his paramilitary past and the days when he was known around the world as the IRA's 'boy general'. McGuinness has worked hard to change how he is seen, and Frank's return to Derry is a chance for him to go further. He could call a press conference to present Frank – loveable greyhound owner, proud Derryman – as a former British agent who has come home to seek forgiveness and who trusts Martin McGuinness, the respectable Sinn Féin politician. Yes, some IRA hardliners might think to themselves that he has gone soft, but others will see this as another milestone on the journey away from violence.

As for Frank, he has survived. But it does not yet feel like that. He continues to spend his days holed up in his mother's house, and it is still not safe for him to go anywhere he likes in Derry. He knows that he won't be able to until he has been exonerated in public by the IRA. And there is really only one person in Derry who can do this. 'His precise title is irrelevant,' one Derryman later said. 'There wasn't a single person on either side of the sectarian divide in Derry, or among the security forces on either side of the Border, or among the media, who thought McGuinness was anything other than the leading figure in Sinn Féin and the IRA in Derry.'[5] Martin McGuinness is Frank's greatest hope and his greatest fear, and until he makes up his mind about what to do, Frank will remain in limbo.

Frank sleeps, he sees his dogs, he eats his mother's food, and he smokes. He goes out for the occasional walk, but only to places where he is unlikely to be recognised. He spends one night talking to a local priest. Slowly, he starts to feel more like himself.

One day, Frank goes on a trip with Dorothy and their children to the Grianán of Aileach, the fort above Derry. They walk around the structure, like an ordinary family on an ordinary day out. Ryan, his five-year-old, tells him that one day he would love to have a motorbike. Frank tells his son that he will see what he can do. All around them, the view arrows off into the distance as far as they can see, and at times it is possible for each of them to think about the future and feel some underlying sense of hope. Towards the end of the outing, Ryan sees his father pull a ring from his finger and hand it to Dorothy. He then says something to her about giving it to Ryan when he is older. After that, they make their way back to Derry.

Martin McGuinness has come to see Rose Hegarty again. Once they have settled down, he tells her that three 'prominent men' over the border need to speak to Frank. 'And he said to me,' Rose recalled, 'he got down, and he said to me, on his knees: "There's nothing going to happen to Frank. I'll bring him back."'

Rose passes the message on to Frank.

The IRA does not exactly control this part of Derry, and if Frank wants to escape, then his chances of making it out are good. If he is having second thoughts, he can leave town again. But he does not. He has heard from his mother that McGuinness has promised nothing will happen to him. Frank also knows that he cannot spend the rest of his life in hiding. If he is going to start again in Derry, which is why he has come home in the first place, he needs to straighten things out with the IRA.

'I know what I have to face,' Frank tells Dorothy, 'but not who.' Going to see the three men over the border is the last bridge he must cross on his path to freedom.

On Wednesday, 21 May 1986, at around sunset, Frank Hegarty says goodbye to a group of family members. He is wearing jeans, a flat cap, and a sandy-coloured leather jacket. His sideburns reach down to a point just below his cheekbones. He has a warm face and a kindness in his eyes. His family watches him as he walks out through the back garden, so that nobody on the street will see him leave. Frank is forty-five years old. He is sturdy without being overweight, and moves with his familiar and friendly gait, almost a swagger. He and a close family member then step into a car and drive away.

Frank arrives later that day at a hotel in Buncrana, a seaside village across the border in Ireland where he and his brothers used to go when they were little. The smell of the place brings back summery memories of messing about in the sea, ice creams, the pink Buncrana rock, and the bright lights of the arcades. Perhaps it reminds him as well of visits as a child to Father Hegarty's Rock, just a few miles away beyond the town.

Frank gets out of the car and sees a man waiting for him in the shadows. They walk off together into the night.

The next day, Rose asks Martin McGuinness when her son will be coming home. He tells her that she has nothing to worry about, and that her son is probably wolfing down a curry as they speak. He says that Frank will be home tomorrow.

But Frank does not return the next day, and Rose becomes worried. It is a full moon that night, and Rose has a dream that she will never forget. She imagines seeing her son laid out on a sloping patch of ground with one eye open and the other closed. She can also make out several men standing nearby, figures she does not recognise. They are looking down at her son in a menacing way. She bends down to pick him up. At this point she notices that the ground is wet and his clothes are soaked through. She cradles his body in both arms, like the Madonna in a *pieta* carrying the body of Jesus, and realises, to her horror, that she cannot tell whether he is dead or alive.

When Rose wakes up, she is distraught. She cannot shake the

memory of her dream. Her daughters are so worried about the state she is in that they call the family doctor.

Later that day, a woman comes by the house to drop off a tape. It is a recording of Frank reading out a statement. At one point, he addresses his family directly, and says, 'I don't know if I'll ever see you again'.[6]

Judas Goat

'You may find these pictures disturbing,' the newsreader, Eamonn Holmes, began. Television screens across Northern Ireland were filled suddenly with footage of what looked like a man asleep by the side of an unmetalled lane. His head was cushioned by a pillow of turf, his hair was tousled and slick from the night's rain, and the supple shape of his limbs made him look relaxed and peaceful, like a farmhand resting up after a long day in the fields.

It was Frank Hegarty. He had been killed in the night on a country lane outside Castlederg, County Tyrone. His corpse would soon be taken for a post-mortem at the mortuary in Altnagelvin Hospital, where they found no trace of alcohol in his blood and judged that he had been healthy at the time of his death.

The news report cut to a wider shot that included policemen and bystanders who moved around with the self-consciousness brought on by a proximity to death. Next came a close-up of Frank's hands. The fingers on his right hand had closed around a tangle of brown cord, and you could see the leather strap of his watch and the cuff of his white shirt, part of the outfit he had chosen before going to meet the three senior IRA men.

The police investigating this murder found four bullets at the crime scene, a detail that did not appear in any of the news reports.

One of these bullets was buried in the ground beneath Frank's head. It had travelled through his skull before tunnelling 4 inches into the earth below. Clearly, it had been fired at close range, and after Frank had fallen to the ground. The killer would have leaned over him or bent down for this final shot.

Everything about the murder scene suggested an execution, and that the killer – or killers – knew what they were doing. The location of the corpse was also revealing. Frank's body had been discovered only 100 yards from the border crossing near Castlederg. There was no military presence here, and although a set of concrete bollards prevented cars from passing through, it was possible to cross on foot.

A member of the IRA's Nutting Squad later described their *modus operandi*. They conducted their interrogations in the Republic, then 'the body is dumped in the North. The forensics are in the South and then the people who have to investigate that murder are the RUC. It fucks up their investigation.' Finding Frank's corpse this close to the border pointed clearly to the Nutting Squad. It was their signature move.

In all likelihood, Frank was held somewhere in Donegal before being driven to the border, with masking tape over his eyes, and then walked into Northern Ireland before being shot. But some parts of this story did not add up. It was unusual to find a Nutting Squad victim over on this side of Northern Ireland. Most were discovered closer to Belfast or South Armagh, near the home of the senior Nutting Squad man at the time, John Joe Magee. Another detail that jarred was that the rope around Frank's wrists had been cut, presumably while he was still alive. It hinted at some element of trust between him and his captors, or at least an understanding. Perhaps Frank knew the people who killed him, which backed up the idea that those responsible for his death could have been from Derry and were not part of the Nutting Squad, which was dominated by men from Belfast.

The most puzzling detail was the masking tape over Frank's eyes. There was something almost macabre about the care with which this had been applied. It seemed to imply, in Truman Capote's words, 'a certain twisted tenderness'.[2] Why do this? What was the masking tape meant to achieve?

Frank Hegarty's body was later taken to his mother's house for the wake. Rose sat in her living room with Dorothy by her side as the place filled up with family members and Frank's friends. His wife was also there, as well as others from the neighbourhood, and the greyhound world to which he had belonged. Some people stayed away because of what they had heard about Frank being an agent, but most did not, and soon the queue to get into the house meandered down the street.

A wake, in the Irish tradition, is lively and unpredictable. You throw open your doors without knowing who is going to turn up. 'Sorry for your trouble,' people will say, which to an English ear sounds like a bloodless euphemism, but this is 'trouble' from the Irish 'troibloíd' with connotations of grief, loss, and compassion. In saying it, you want the relative to know that in some way you share in their sorrow. What made the atmosphere at Frank Hegarty's wake different was how the family's sadness was infused with a sense of terrible injustice. Whatever it was Frank may have done, he did not deserve this.

The next morning, at half-past-nine, Frank's coffin was taken from Rose's house to St Eugene's Cathedral, where 500 people attended a Requiem Mass. The chief concelebrant was a cousin of Frank's. 'The circumstances of Frank Hegarty's death', the priest said, 'were cruel, unjust and brutal. Such taking of life is murder and cannot be called by any other name.' He asked the congregation to pray that whoever killed Frank might find 'the grace to repent'.[3]

Later that day, to many people's surprise, Sinn Féin councillors proposed that the local council take steps 'to alleviate the suffering caused by the continued use of paid perjurers'.⁴ They argued that the responsibility for Frank's murder did not lie with the IRA, who had just released a statement taking responsibility for his death, but with the British armed forces for being in Northern Ireland in the first place. Some of the SDLP councillors could hardly believe what they were hearing.

'Grotesque and callous', said SDLP leader John Hume of Frank Hegarty's killing. 'When those who carried out these acts can kill human beings, including fellow Irishmen, in such ready and grotesque manner, people have to ask whom or what exactly can they claim to be defending?'⁵ Hume would say a similar thing after other IRA atrocities. In these acts he saw a terrifying kind of arrogance, a feeling among those inside this paramilitary organisation that they were more Irish than anyone else, they had the right to dispense death and destruction, and that the British were always to blame for what they had done. The likes of Martin McGuinness saw themselves as 'the keepers of the holy grail of the nation,' Hume would later say. 'That deep-seated attitude, married to their method, has all the other hallmarks of the fascist'.⁶

John Hume did not call out Martin McGuinness by name on the day of Frank's funeral, but it was as if he had. 'Condemnation from Mr Hume and clergymen are pathetic in the circumstances that we find ourselves in,' McGuinness said later that day. He was then asked to condemn Frank's murder. 'I don't condemn it,' he said, 'although I feel for his family. I am obviously concerned that they have suffered in this whole affair. From a republican point of view, I don't condemn the IRA action. I understand it and I understand that the IRA have a responsibility to protect themselves and equipment'.⁷

It must have been hard for Rose Hegarty to hear Martin McGuinness say he *felt* for her. McGuinness, the same man who had practically begged her son to come home, and who might, for all she knew, have pulled the trigger himself. She could have kept quiet in the days that followed about who she believed to have been behind her son's death. But she did not. Rose was not afraid of this man, and began to tell her neighbours and friends, and anyone else who asked, that Martin McGuinness was personally responsible for Frank's death.

The response from McGuinness was cruel. He told reporters that Rose Hegarty was an old woman who had got herself in a muddle. He said that he had only ever told her that her son would be safe *in Derry*, and that once Frank had left the city there was nothing he could do.

The Hegartys began to refer to Martin McGuinness as the 'Judas goat', after the animal in an abattoir that leads unsuspecting sheep to slaughter. Frank's family wanted justice. They wanted McGuinness to be arrested and tried for his role in Frank's murder. As a Catholic living in Derry, you were not supposed to speak out against Martin McGuinness, but the nature of Frank's death and the brazen injustice of what had happened had an emboldening effect.

Soon after Frank's funeral, the journalist Peter Murtagh visited Frank's partner, Dorothy, after hearing that the Hegartys were 'unhappy, very unhappy, with McGuinness, and blamed him for the killing'. Murtagh had not met Dorothy before but was welcomed into her house and told that 'Martin McGuinness had things to answer; that he promised Frank would be safe'.

Just seconds after the conversation began, there was a knock at the door. 'Two men came in. One stood directly in front of me,' Murtagh recalled, 'cutting me off from the women. The other engaged the woman who had been talking to me. I was ushered out, out to a waiting car. Inside the car sat Martin McGuinness.'

'The family is very upset,' McGuinness told him, adding that it wasn't a good time for anyone to speak to them. 'In fact, they really couldn't talk right now.' Murtagh understood this was not a negotiation and that the interview was over.[8]

Already, McGuinness could see that something about this IRA killing was different, and that it was not about to be forgotten.

Many of Frank Hegarty's friends found it hard to come to terms with his death. The most difficult part was not knowing exactly what he had done. Was he really working for the British, as the IRA claimed? It seemed so unlikely. Perhaps this was a sly rumour which had been put about for some unknown reason. The British security forces would neither confirm nor deny. That was their way. Frank's friends were left to play detective in their heads, picking over their memories of being with him. That time when he asked to be dropped off in the middle of nowhere, was he off to see his handler? Those days when he had more money than usual, was that from a bet which had come good or payment from the Brits?

Willie Carlin, the other agent from Derry, began to be haunted by the story of Frank Hegarty's death, in part because he had so very nearly suffered the same fate. Carlin knew that after he had fled Derry, the year before Frank was killed, Martin McGuinness went to see his mother-in-law and said to her: 'Tell him to come back and I'll do everything in my power to see to it that he's safe.' It was almost word for word what he later said to Rose. Carlin and Hegarty's paths had run in parallel before diverging at the last moment. When the Nutting Squad came for Carlin, he was saved as a result of intelligence from Stakeknife. But if the Nutting Squad also came for Frank, as presumably they did, why hadn't Stakeknife pulled the same trick and warned his handler?

Mick, Jack, and the other handlers who had known Frank experienced a different kind of sadness. Each had had his own relationship with Franko, or The General, and had shared secrets with him and earned his trust. But the pain they felt was heavier than grief. They were left with a sense that in some way their side had let him down. Frank had put his life in their hands and done everything they had asked of him, but now he was dead. Earlier in the Troubles, one army handler in north Belfast, on learning that four of his agents had been killed by the IRA, chose to take his own life.[10] It is hard to overstate how hard this feeling can weigh down on anyone in this situation, and the strength of the bond that can form between handler and agent.

Ian Hurst was a corporal in the Intelligence Corps and had met Frank Hegarty after being posted to Derry. He was a shortish, round-shouldered man with a high-pitched, Mancunian lilt. Hurst had been part of the support staff in the local FRU office, and would sometimes pick up Frank and drive him to a meet. Several years later, he joined the Special Intelligence Wing, a small unit which took care of army agents after they had been moved into the military equivalent of witness protection, and in this capacity, he was posted to the army safe house where Frank was staying.

Hurst became close to Frank. They bonded over a shared love of greyhounds. 'We talked about Derry and how much he missed it. I asked him if he would return, and he said he would at some stage,' he recalled. 'He seemed convinced he could talk his way out of it.' Hurst remembered Frank as 'a wonderful man, a typical working-class Derry man', who reminded him of 'Stanley Ogden of *Coronation Street*; that's exactly how I'd describe him. A working-class gentleman who enjoyed gambling. I was gutted when he died.'[11]

But there were also times when Ian Hurst wondered if he could have done more to talk Frank out of going back to Derry. He struggled as well with some of the other questions surrounding his death. After Frank had fled the safe house, why wasn't he picked up when he arrived in Northern Ireland? Had a decision been made at a higher level to let him return to Derry, on the assumption that he would be killed? Or perhaps it was nothing more than a mistake by the port authorities, who who failed to spot him on his return to the region.

The most puzzling reaction to the news of Frank Hegarty's death, however, came from Freddie Scappaticci. At the time, he was thought to be the army's most valuable agent in the region. He had infiltrated the IRA, just like Frank. But he did not belong to the same unit, so it was hard, on the face of it, to think why he should feel anything out of the ordinary about Frank's death. And yet he did. He seemed to mind about what had happened to him.

PART FOUR:

JUSTICE

30

Try Not to Get Caught

One day, in the early 1980s, the course of Freddie Scappaticci's life took a sudden turn. He was approached by a senior IRA man who told him that he had been chosen to join the Nutting Squad. At first, Scappaticci did not know what to do. He sensed this could be a trap. The IRA was paranoid about spies, and one way to find out if a volunteer was secretly working for the other side was by asking them to do a job that was 'dirty', meaning it could involve taking someone's life. Anyone who refused might be an agent. The assumption within the IRA was that the British would never let one of their agents participate in a murder.

Freddie Scappaticci went to his handlers for advice. They knew that there were huge intelligence benefits to having an agent inside the Nutting Squad. This unit had already become like a junction box for the IRA. Its members had access to almost everyone inside the organisation. They also had an aura of being feared and untouchable, like a Praetorian Guard. An agent inside the Nutting Squad could transform Britain's understanding of the IRA. But at what cost? What was the legal, moral, and human price that might have to be paid for intelligence from inside this unit? Scappaticci's handlers understood that if their agent agreed to join, then at some point he could be told to abduct an IRA volunteer, which in itself was a serious crime. But worse could follow, and the order might come from the IRA Army Council to have this person killed.

Scappaticci's handlers knew that there were steps they could take to mitigate the risk. They could supply their agent with sick pills disguised as over-the-counter medication, so that if he heard a job was on, he could pop one, and would soon be vomiting uncontrollably. Another pill had a similar effect, but it only worked in the presence of certain chemicals, such as those found in aftershave. So Scappaticci could take one at the start of the day and activate it later, if needed, by giving himself a quick spritz of aftershave as he left the house. Or the army could fit his home with a panic button made to look like a switch on a household radio, and install listening devices to monitor what was being said inside the Scappaticci home. This might reveal where an interrogation was going to take place, which would allow the security forces to intervene. They could also encourage Scappaticci never to carry a weapon, making him less likely to be chosen by the IRA as the 'trigger man'.

These interventions might reduce the chances of Scappaticci taking someone else's life, but they did not rule it out. Ultimately, his handlers were up against another version of the spymaster's dilemma, and they had the added pressure of time. Scappaticci had to go back to the IRA with an answer. Could the value of his intelligence ever outweigh the devastating cost? Would more lives be saved if he said yes, or if he said no?

Thousands of miles away, at around the same time, an American philosopher published a paper that cast this dilemma in a slightly different light. Judith Jarvis Thomson, a professor of philosophy at the Massachusetts Institute of Technology, had recently finished an experiment in which she built on the work of Philippa Foot, a philosophy lecturer at Oxford University.

Almost two decades earlier, Foot had set up an experiment that explored how we respond to complex moral challenges. She asked her respondents to imagine a scenario in which a runaway train was hurtling towards five railway workers stranded on the line. The participants in Foot's thought experiment had a choice: either they could allow the train to plough into the five men, killing them all, or they could pull a lever that diverted the train onto a separate track, but – and here was the catch – this would mean killing a different railway worker. By intervening, the participant saved five lives at the cost of one. By standing back and doing nothing, they would save one person's life, while letting five people die. Most participants chose to divert the train.

At about the time that Scappaticci's handlers were presented with their dilemma, Judith Jarvis Thomson decided to give Foot's experiment a twist. She imagined the same runaway train and the same five railway workers stuck on the line. But in her new scenario, the participants could not pull a lever to divert the train. The only way to prevent it from killing the five workers was by pushing an over-weight man off a bridge and onto the railway line below. The overall effect is the same. One person dies, five people are saved. But in this new version of the experiment, the participant must use their own physical force to commit murder.

In a legal sense, the two scenarios are surprisingly similar. Had you chosen to intervene, your defence in each case would be founded on the doctrine of double effect. Your aim was to save the five workers, and the other man's death was an oblique effect you had foreseen but not directly intended. But in a moral sense, as the two experiments showed, the two scenarios are wildly different.

In the years after Foot and Jarvis Thomson published their findings, other researchers presented the same scenarios to people around the world. They tested for variations between young and old, conservative and liberal, wealthy and poor, male and female, and yet, to their surprise, the results remained essentially the same.

In the first experiment, roughly nine out of ten people will choose to divert the train. But when asked to push a man off a bridge, most people had the opposite reaction. Nine out of ten people prefer to stand back and do nothing, even if they know that the five railway workers will die.

Why? The simplest answer is that the thought of using our own physical force to end someone's life has the effect of scrambling our minds. It closes down our ability to assess a situation in cold and pragmatic terms. We would rather have more people die than live with the memory of having pushed an innocent man off a bridge. But when asked to end a life at one remove, simply by pulling a lever, our approach is completely different.

We are used to thinking of human morality as fluid. Look at our changing attitudes to same-sex marriage or capital punishment, and how these have evolved over time. But the results of these experiments hinted at a deeper set of human ethics, a core morality that belied geography, history, class, creed, and gender. They suggested an inherited sense of right and wrong that had developed over millions of years.

Freddie Scappaticci's handlers were, in this sense, the same as you and me. We share with them an innate human morality. The dilemma they faced after their agent came to them and said that he had been asked to join the IRA's Nutting Squad was, in an abstract sense, the same as the earlier of the two philosophical experiments described above. The handlers were not being asked, in moral terms, to push anyone off a bridge, but to pull a lever. The intelligence their agent could supply from inside the Nutting Squad would almost certainly save more lives than it might cost. And the safeguards they could put in place (such as the sick pills) would reduce the chances of his being involved in a murder. Telling him to turn down this promotion, however, would not save anyone's life, as the IRA could find someone else to do the job. It might also put Scappaticci at risk, because by refusing to join the Nutting Squad he could mark himself down as a potential spy.

In the end, though, Scappaticci's handlers knew this dilemma was not entirely theirs. They could only offer their agent advice. They knew he would listen, but they did not have authority over him, and the decision was ultimately his.

Freddie Scappaticci agreed to join the IRA's Nutting Squad. At the time, it was run by two men known as 'the Bodysnatchers' – one from County Derry, the other from County Tyrone. These two were said to have murdered more IRA volunteers in the early 1980s than were killed by the British Army during the same period. Only some of their victims were supplying information to the security forces. Once it was clear that they were out of control, Gerry Adams – who has always denied being part of the IRA – is alleged to have been behind the decision to remove the Bodysnatchers from the Nutting Squad and replace them with two Belfast men.[1] One was a former Royal Marine called John Joe Magee, who would run the unit. His deputy was a man who Gerry Adams had come to know during his time inside Long Kesh: Freddie Scappaticci.

Perhaps this was the moment for Scappaticci's handlers to pull the plug on this experiment. They could have urged him to move to a different part of the IRA, or they might have cut their ties with him altogether. But they did not. The reason was simple. The information now coming in from Scappaticci was so valuable, and so extensive, that it was starting to change the shape of the conflict in Northern Ireland. As second-in-command of the Nutting Squad, Freddie Scappaticci knew who had joined the IRA or was suspected of being a spy, the locations of weapons, the outlines of some forthcoming IRA attacks, and even the identity of IRA agents inside the Irish police and the Irish Army.[2] He was also supplying important strategic intelligence on senior IRA figures such as Gerry Adams, who would open up to him while sitting in the passenger seat of his car, unaware that his words were being recorded, or that edited transcripts of what he had said would later be picked over in Whitehall. Senior politicians such as Margaret Thatcher were sometimes played excerpts of these recordings from Scappaticci's car when they came to visit Northern Ireland.[3]

Scappaticci was producing so much material of such high value that the British could not act on all of it, because doing so would expose their source. He had become a one-man Bletchley Park. After years of having too little information, the British were almost in danger of having too much.

But at what cost? How far was Freddie Scappaticci being asked to go to maintain his cover inside the Nutting Squad?

By the time of Frank Hegarty's murder, in 1986, Scappaticci and his boss, John Joe Magee, were known throughout the IRA as merciless and inscrutable interrogators. But they did not always rely on violence. Magee's most effective weapon in an interrogation was his patience. Being cross-examined by this balding, heavy-set man was like sitting a never-ending exam. 'John Joe was an ignorant big shite,' one former Nutting Squad man recalled, 'but he was very methodical. He was a details man. I'd never seen anything like it.[4]

Nutting Squad victims were usually taken to a safe house close to Magee's home on the Cooley Peninsula, where they were stripped, given a boiler suit to wear, and led into a darkened room with cloth over the windows. A solitary chair was turned to face the wall. The suspect was told to sit with their back to Magee, who would ask questions in a polite and clear voice. He might spend up to a week going over the victim's story, listening as much to what was being said as to the way it came out. 'A good, consistent flow,' Magee explained, 'without hesitations, contradictions, or gaps, tended to indicate that the subject was telling the truth.[5] Rather than rely on his own judgement, Magee sent tapes of his interviews to an IRA commander in South Armagh who had a machine that he claimed could detect stress in audio recordings.

Freddie Scappaticci had a different style. If Magee wanted to hear the whole story, no matter how long it took, Scappaticci was only interested in the ending. He would tell the suspect that he already knew what they had done. He just wanted to see how much they were going to volunteer to him. Scappaticci was hard to predict. One moment he could be shouting at you from the opposite end of the room. The next, he was whispering in your ear. He might threaten to beat you up or ask which road you wanted to close – meaning where would you like your corpse to be left. Then he held out the prospect of salvation, just as you were losing hope, telling you that the IRA Army Council might be lenient if you made a full confession. As Scappaticci himself later said, 'Everybody has a breaking point'.[6]

'He was a bastard,' one man said of Freddie Scappaticci.[7] 'There were very few people in the Provisional IRA for whom I felt genuine loathing and fear,' another volunteer added. 'He was one of them.'[8]

Scap presented himself as a model IRA volunteer – someone who enjoyed his work in the Nutting Squad and was unencumbered by doubt. Behind this façade was an entirely different person, an alter ego. The same energy and terrifying intensity that Scappaticci put into his interrogations, he was also giving to his work as a spy. He was working *for* the IRA almost as much as he was working *against* it. As 'Scap', he was being told by the IRA to take lives. As a British agent, he was often trying to save them. The mental strain must have been overwhelming. Sometimes he shared this with his handlers, asking them for assurances that he was doing the right thing. In all likelihood, they told him not to worry, and that they would do their best to protect him.

But none of these soldiers fully understood the legal side of what was going on, and how it might look in court. The laws on agent-running were not exactly confusing or difficult to interpret. They simply did not exist. The document which army officers had been told to use in Northern Ireland as a legal guide to agent-running was a set of non-statutory Home Office guidelines issued *before* the start of the Troubles. It bore almost no relation to the situation in which they found themselves and was later described by the government as 'an embarrassment'.[9] Very soon after the murder of Frank Hegarty, the FRU issued a new set of 'Directives and Instructions' on agent-running in an attempt to clear things up. The timing of this is suggestive. But these directives were inadequate and would later be dismissed by a judge as 'manifestly unsatisfactory'.[10]

The legal adviser at MI5 urged the attorney general to draw up new legislation on whether agents could be authorised to break the law, but nothing happened. The defence secretary described the situation as 'unacceptable'.[11] He, too, pressed the attorney general for action. Again, nothing.

On at least one occasion, the problem was raised with Margaret Thatcher. Raymond White, the senior Special Branch officer in Northern Ireland with responsibility for handling informants, said to the prime minister: 'I'm asking these agents to do things that technically could be construed as criminal acts.' White had a law degree, and understood the need for clear legal guidelines. 'The message that came back from the prime minister's office was, "It's too hot to handle. We appreciate what you're doing. Please continue to do what you're doing. But for goodness' sake, try not to get caught."'[12]

At about the same time, several thousand miles away, the American journalist Janet Malcolm argued in a long article that most societies around the world are built around 'an unspoken agreement whereby we are given leave to bend the rules of the strictest morality, provided we do so quietly and discreetly. Hypocrisy is the grease that keeps society functioning in an agreeable way,' she went on. 'You never come right out and admit you have stretched the rules for your own benefit. You do it and shut up about it, and hope you don't get caught.'[13]

Malcolm meant this in the broadest sense. But it would be hard to find a better example of this 'unspoken agreement', the stance of *try not to get caught*, than the relationship at that time between the people of Britain and their spies. The British are fluent in the language of secrecy, and have been for centuries. 'Secrecy', wrote historian Peter Hennessy, 'is as much a part of the English landscape as the Cotswolds'.[14] It is in our character, how we tilt at the world, and the way we speak. We grow up knowing what it means to keep our lips sealed, keep mum, keep schtum, or keep something under our hat, behind closed doors and under wraps, as well as the importance of being able to hold our tongue, cover our tracks, take it to the grave, keep everyone else in the dark, and never spill the beans, dish the dirt, give the game away, sing like a canary, or let the cat out of the bag – because if we did, that would make us a nark, a snitch, a sneak, a leak, a blab, a grass, a tout, a weasel, a squealer, a tittle-tattle, or indeed a rat. Combined with a historic deference towards a handful of powerful institutions, this deep familiarity with secrecy has meant that for much of the twentieth century most British people have been willing to accept the government's notion that there was no secret service, while knowing all along that there was.

'Try not to get caught' seemed to reflect a broader outlook on espionage and official secrecy – one that was emphatically British, and at the same time familiar around the world. It was an inherited attitude, rather than a new one. But in the years after Thatcher heard about what was happening in Northern Ireland, and responded by turning a blind eye, this stance would begin to be seen in a different and less forgiving light.

Thirty years after Frank Hegarty's death, Freddie Scappaticci, his accomplices, and those who had been running him were under criminal investigation. That's because Scappaticci was the army agent referred to in the media as 'Stakeknife'. His actual codename was

'Steak Knife', but the misspelled version was the one that stuck. Jon Boutcher's team of more than seventy detectives had, by the start of 2018, spoken to over 129 men and women about Stakeknife, taken more than 1,000 statements and seen at least 12,000 classified documents from the archives of MI5, the Ministry of Defence, and the police in Northern Ireland. They had also made a series of breakthroughs on the forensic side of their investigation.[15]

One of Boutcher's forensics experts had looked at the letters written by Stakeknife's victims to their loved ones shortly before they were killed. They found traces of DNA that did not belong to either the victim or the victim's family. After these letters were written, they were handed to a member of the Nutting Squad who would have read them to check that they contained nothing incriminating. Some of the letters were then sent by post, at a time when stamps needed to be licked. The backs of these stamps were a treasure trove of genetic material. The IRA prided itself at the time on its forensic awareness, but nobody in the Nutting Squad in the 1980s had imagined that this kind of technology might ever exist.

The case against Freddie Scappaticci, some of his handlers, and other members of the Nutting Squad, was becoming stronger. One of the murders to which Scappaticci had been linked was that of Frank Hegarty. Boutcher's team had seen the 'murder box' put together at the time of the original investigation in 1986. It contained police reports, photographs of Frank's corpse, and other materials relating to the case. The detectives also heard an audio recording made in the early 1990s, which seemed to unlock the secret of what happened to Frank and who was responsible.

The story of how this tape came into being and why it was then covered up begins in 1990. It is as much about the murder of Frank Hegarty as it is a way into the hidden history of how the Troubles ended, and it starts on a cold night in Derry, when a middle-aged SIS officer went to have dinner with an old friend.

31

Operation Chiffon

It was dark by the time Michael Oatley reached the house, a plain-looking building on the Glen Road, one of the more sought-after streets in this part of Derry. During his long career in intelligence, he had been stationed all over the world, rarely staying in any place for more than a few years. But this particular building was more familiar to him than most and kept drawing him back, even now, in October 1990, on the eve of his retirement.

Oatley stepped into the front garden and carried on past the carefully pruned rose bushes and the pocket-sized lawn up to the front door. He was soon being welcomed in like a prodigal son. The house was warm, the air filled with the smell of food. Before long, Oatley was locked in conversation with the man he had come to see: Brendan Duddy – local businessman, Catholic, pacifist, former cross-country runner, and all-round dynamo.

It had been almost six months since Michael Oatley and Brendan Duddy last saw each other. Perhaps each one quietly scanned the other for signs of change, as men over a certain age will do. Both were in their fifties now, and Brendan was less active these days. His hair had lightened and his face was softer around the jowls. But he had lost none of his vigour. Michael Oatley had a similar though less expressive energy and had aged in a different way. His hairline had retreated and his eyebrows were thicker. Yet he remained much the same man he had been when he first met Brendan Duddy seventeen years earlier: courteous, open, driven, and blessed with a voice like honey.

Usually, they would meet in Duddy's house, just up the road, but tonight they were in the home of Brendan's friend Bernadette, or Bernie, who was in the kitchen making supper. 'Friend' was the preferred euphemism. Brendan was married to Margo but spent a lot of time with Bernie, who used to be a long-distance runner like him and shared his stamina. Margo accepted this situation and had become close to Bernie over the years. Sometimes the two women would even go away on holiday together, leaving Brendan to look after the kids. There were two women in Brendan's life, and one stayed with him in the big house, while the other lived here, in a smaller house less than a hundred yards down the road.

Brendan Duddy was comfortable in the kinds of relationships most people find uncomfortable. He got on well with the SIS man, Michael Oatley, and with the IRA man, Martin McGuinness. He could play different parts, and had an instinctive understanding of creative ambiguity, always seeming to know when to speak and when to hold back.

For Brendan and Bernie, a visit from Michael Oatley was a special occasion, and usually this meant a roast dinner of meat and vegetables steeped in gravy. The three of them began to catch up. But no matter how warm or light the mood in the conversation became, it retained an edge. Oatley was their friend, but he was also a serving British intelligence officer. It might have been hard to explain who he was and what he was doing if an unexpected visitor walked in.

The relationship between Michael Oatley and Brendan Duddy had grown over the years to include much more than their various attempts to create dialogue between the IRA and the British government. Each knew about the other's family, his children, his private life, his hopes and aspirations, his health, and his worries about money. Later, they would both serve on the board of the same Derry hotel. They had a real affection for one another and understood the risks the other was taking by continuing this relationship. Duddy also knew that Oatley's career in SIS was now drawing to a close, and it was not exactly the ending his friend had wanted.

Michael Oatley was about to turn fifty-five, the age at which most SIS officers retire. He had been SIS Controller for the Middle East and run SIS operations in Europe, and had been in contention for the top job at SIS as 'C', which would have meant staying on for longer. But he had recently found out that the position was going to someone else.

With his career in SIS soon to be over, Oatley had begun to look back over what he had achieved. He kept returning to memories of his time in Northern Ireland. He and Brendan Duddy had come so close to ending the violence years ago in 1975. During the second hunger strike, in 1981, there were moments when again, they seemed to have brought the two sides closer than ever. Perhaps now, in 1990, there was time for a final roll of the dice. 'I'd developed a feeling that in my last year in government, that I would like to make use of my connections one more time', Oatley said, 'to see if I could have any influence on the situation before I retired. Seemed to be a pity just to walk away and leave it all as something one simply remembered.'

Brendan Duddy knew that Oatley wanted to speak to a senior IRA figure, and, at the same time, that his friend could never actually ask him to arrange this. The British government did not engage with the IRA. Full stop. But Duddy understood Michael Oatley better than most people, and recognised in him the same maverick streak he saw in himself.

They had just finished eating when they heard a knock at the back door.

'Who the fuck is that?' Bernie said.

Oatley must have felt a pinch of anticipation. He knew how close some of his colleagues had come to being killed in Northern Ireland. The SIS officer who replaced him in 1975, after recruiting KGB officer Oleg Gordievsky in Copenhagen, had to be rushed out of the region after a source revealed that the IRA was about to murder him. The order to kill this man had reportedly come from Martin McGuinness.

'I forgot to tell you,' Brendan said. 'That's Martin.'

If the adrenaline had not yet kicked in, it did now. Oatley could see that Bernie was also on edge, but for a different reason.

'I don't have enough dinner left!' she said. 'We've eaten it all.'

Brendan gave her a look. 'He's not here for dinner.'[2]

Martin McGuinness walked in. He was taller than Duddy and shorter than Oatley. In the seconds that followed, Michael Oatley could have left the room. Technically, that's what he should have done, as a Crown servant who found himself unexpectedly in the presence of a senior IRA official. But he did not, and was soon locked in conversation with Martin McGuinness.

Brendan Duddy was riveted. 'It was like a couple wanting to get together,' he remembered, 'to enter a courtship.' On both sides, he could see a degree of respect, the oxygen of any negotiation, but he also noticed the change which had come over his IRA friend. It was, he said, 'a McGuinness that I'd never actually saw before'.

Oatley described McGuinness as 'very serious and responsible about the situation that he occupied', and was interested by the fact that he did not come across as 'somebody who actually enjoyed getting people killed. So, I found him a good interlocutor. Rather, in some ways, like talking to the ranking British Army officer of one of the tougher regiments, like the Paras or the SAS.'[3]

Michael Oatley and Martin McGuinness moved through to the living room without Brendan. Once they were alone, Oatley spoke more openly about the British government's policy towards the IRA, Anglo–Irish relations, and the future. He also explained that although he was about to retire, he wanted this secret line of communication through Brendan Duddy to continue. Then he gave McGuinness his own assessment of the situation in Northern Ireland. Violence had not worked, he said. By his reckoning, McGuinness had only a few years left in which to act before the next generation came through. Now was the time to push for peace.

Martin McGuinness listened to Michael Oatley talk, and promised to discuss this with his colleagues, by which he basically meant Gerry Adams. Then came the most surprising part of the conversation. They had been speaking for several hours when Martin McGuinness began to talk about fishing.

We all reveal ourselves at one remove, often communicating in the words we don't say as much as the hidden meaning of those that we do. It was close to midnight as Martin McGuinness, paramilitary and politician, opened up to the British spy about his love of fishing and how much he was looking forward to being able to visit the British mainland. He could not currently do this because he was subject to an exclusion order that prevented him from entering Great Britain. This had been in place for most of his adult life. The first thing McGuinness planned to do once this was lifted, he went on, was pack up his rod, his waders, and a box of flies and take a holiday in Scotland. He had it all worked out. He had taken the time to research the best bed-and-breakfasts, had a list of places with the finest salmon and trout fishing, and knew the order in which he planned to visit them.

Michael Oatley recognised this for what it was. The most powerful man in the IRA had decided, within himself, that the violence would end, peace was coming, and soon he would be free to travel where he liked. Even if there were younger members of the IRA agitating for a new military campaign, for whom any kind of ceasefire was a defeat, Martin McGuinness had a different vision of the future.

Michael Oatley eventually said goodbye and left Bernie's house.

The next day, he arranged to see Sir John Chilcot, permanent secretary at the Northern Ireland Office, and John Deverell, senior MI5 officer in the region, to tell them about what had happened.

They were astonished. Officially, yes, Oatley had exceeded his remit. But they accepted that he would never have been given the green light to proceed with a conversation like this if he had come to them first. As the Northern Irish saying went – better to ask for forgiveness than permission. Direct contact had been made between the British government and the IRA. Michael Oatley and Brendan Duddy appeared to have made a breakthrough.

Less than a month later, Margaret Thatcher stepped down as prime minister. Almost at once, the British political landscape was transformed. This was a reflection of the mood inside the country as well as the extraordinary changes taking place elsewhere in the world. The Berlin Wall had just come down. The Soviet Union was falling apart and the Cold War appeared to be over. In Bulgaria, Romania, Hungary, Poland, Albania, Czechoslovakia, and East Germany, brutal communist regimes had been replaced by democratically elected governments. Apartheid was being dismantled in South Africa. The Israelis and Palestinians were closer to peace than they had been for decades. Even Colonel Gaddafi, the Libyan dictator, was trying to improve his country's relations with Britain and was about to share with SIS details of all the arms he had ever supplied to the IRA.

Reconciliation was in the air. Maps were being redrawn. Enemies were sitting down to talk. For many people, there was a sense of history carrying within itself the possibility of an ending. But the reaction in MI5 to the news that Michael Oatley had sat down with Martin McGuinness appeared to come from a different place.

Stella Rimington, soon to be MI5 director general, was one of those who did not think the government should trust Martin McGuinness.

Some senior MI5 officers were deeply wary of entering into talks with the IRA. This was partly because they felt that if they waited a little longer, there might not be much of an IRA left to deal with.[4] By that point in the Troubles, as many as eight out of ten IRA operations were either being called off or broken up by the security forces.[5] Sometimes this was down to a mistake on the part of the IRA, or because someone had fallen ill, but most of the time they were being abandoned as a result of British intelligence work.

The IRA in Belfast had become, as one volunteer put it, 'a hall of mirrors'.[6] Nobody knew who to trust and who might be a spy. The paranoia was infectious. The smallest coincidence was enough to have an operation cancelled. The IRA had reached a point where it could move 'very, very little', renowned IRA man Brendan Hughes later said. 'I think that's what the technology did and what the intelligence services were able to do. I think they were able to effectively stop the IRA and contain it.'[7]

Although everyone in MI5 recognised that Oatley's conversation with McGuinness represented a significant development, some were suspicious of the fact that it had involved an SIS officer, and not one of their own. It was impossible for those in MI5 to know precisely what Oatley had said to McGuinness, and how to interpret this meeting. They also wondered if Martin McGuinness was trying to negotiate from a position of weakness. Perhaps he realised that the game was up, and this was his way of salvaging something from a military campaign that had ultimately failed.

Others disagreed, arguing that parts of the IRA were in extremely good health, and the organisation was able to keep going for many years. Shortly after Michael Oatley had sat down with Martin McGuinness, IRA volunteers successfully launched a mortar at No. 10 Downing Street; it was the second time in fewer than ten years that this organisation had come extremely close to killing a British prime minister. Although IRA units in places like Belfast and Derry had been heavily infiltrated by British agents, some of the rural units were much harder to penetrate, and appeared to have the resources and motivation to keep going indefinitely.

MI5's senior officer in Northern Ireland, John Deverell, acknowledged that there were arguments against speaking to the IRA. But he also felt they had a moral duty to explore this opportunity now that it had been presented to them. Their task in Northern Ireland was to end the violence. Oatley's conversation with McGuinness gave them a chance to do that, and they had an obligation to act on it.

In public, the new prime minister, John Major, described the thought of negotiating with the IRA as one 'that would turn my stomach', adding, simply, 'we will not do it'.[8] His government's position remained the same as it always had been. There would be no talks with this illegal paramilitary organisation. Nor would anyone be allowed to hear its leaders speak. It continued to be illegal within the United Kingdom to broadcast Martin McGuinness's voice on television or the radio. The same was true for all IRA or Sinn Féin representatives (and a similar broadcasting ban was in place in the Republic of Ireland). Apparently, the British government would neither talk to the IRA nor listen to them.

In private, however, MI5 was authorised to launch 'Operation Chiffon', a secret initiative designed to bring about talks between the British government and the IRA and a ceasefire in Northern Ireland. The smallest exposure to the outside world would be enough to kill this operation. It depended on a small group of people on different sides being able to pass secret messages to each other, and keep doing this for an extended period of time. But if any of these individuals, such as Martin McGuinness, was either killed or unexpectedly sent to jail, the whole process would collapse.

The further Martin McGuinness went as a politician, the more he seemed to be pursued by his past. Just as Gerry Adams was starting to be linked in public with the 'disappearance' of Jean McConville, a widowed mother of ten from Belfast, McGuinness continued to be asked about his role in one particular incident: the murder of Frank Hegarty.

In 1988, an hour-long BBC *Panorama* programme, presented by Peter Taylor, focused on Frank's death and the role McGuinness had in it. Dorothy had been interviewed, as well as McGuinness himself. Even if the programme did not lead to a police investigation, it reinforced the link in many people's minds between Martin McGuinness and this particular murder.

Rose Hegarty had decided not to appear in this television programme, but still desperately wanted to see Martin McGuinness face justice. She longed for him to have his comeuppance – to be tried in court for his part in her son's killing and sentenced to time in jail. Then, one day, she was contacted out of the blue by someone who seemed to be offering her the chance to make this happen.

'Evil is Too Good a Word'

Roger Cook was the kind of journalist who sometimes received death threats in the post. He was famous for presenting *The Cook Report*, an investigative television programme in which he confronted conmen, thieves, and other criminals. The man accused – and usually it was a man – might run away, slam the door in Cook's face, or attack him. Each episode delivered a pure hit of moral justice. Viewers loved it.

By March 1993, *The Cook Report* was the most popular current-affairs programme on British television. When two young boys were killed that month by an IRA bomb in Warrington, Cheshire, the team behind *The Cook Report* decided to make a programme about this paramilitary organisation. They wanted to name the IRA man who had authorised the Warrington attack.

Over the next few months, the producers carried out their research. Although they never found out who had given the go-ahead for this particular operation, they were told repeatedly about one man who had authorised many other IRA attacks and was responsible for countless deaths, including the 1986 murder of a suspected informer from Derry called Frank Hegarty.

In August 1993, the programme went out.

'Tonight, we name Britain's Number-one terrorist,' Roger Cook began in his voiceover, sounding both indignant and languid. 'The man who controls the IRA. Martin McGuinness.'

'He's killed people himself,' a silhouetted former paramilitary said of McGuinness.

'Now,' Cook continued, 'he passes himself off as a benevolent politician.'

The footage cut to an image of Frank Hegarty's corpse by the side of the road.

'Some politician.'

Cook paused to let this sink in.

'McGuinness, as we'll show tonight' – the screen went to a close-up of Frank's body – 'personally lured this unfortunate man to his death.'

The next shot was of Rose Hegarty. Neat grey perm, glasses like goggles, generous blazer dress with a sharp white lapel, rosary in her hands.

'Do you hold McGuinness responsible for your son's death?' the interviewer asked.

Rose paused. 'Well, nobody else can be held responsible.'

Revenge comes in different forms. Often the best way to get back at the person who has hurt you is not to attack them physically but to shame them in public. You can only do this, though, if you understand where their weakness lies and how it can be exposed. Martin McGuinness's vulnerability lay in the glaring contradiction between his life as a paramilitary and a politician. His ability to be these two different things at the same time depended on people being afraid of speaking out. He knew that the best way to protect himself was by making himself terrifying.

'He was like God in Derry,' one *Cook Report* producer later said of Martin McGuinness.[2] The only people who had ever been brave enough to break this omertà and 'talk out of school' were disgruntled former paramilitaries, who would sometimes appear in television documentaries like this one. But they were always filmed in silhou-ette, often with their voices disguised, and their accusations rarely left a mark on McGuinness. Rose Hegarty's testimony was immedi-ately different. The families of three other IRA victims had at first agreed to appear in the programme, but they pulled out just before filming began. Rose was the only one willing to go through with it.

After Roger Cook had explained what happened to Frank, the programme cut again to Rose.

'I feel very bitter now and full of regret that I ever let him in the door,' she said. 'That's how I feel.'

'What do you think of Martin McGuinness?' the interviewer asked.

'He's an evil man,' Rose replied, pausing to reflect on what she had just said, adding, 'evil is too good a word for him.'

It was not just what Rose said that stayed with viewers but how it was framed. Rose was not in hiding. She was sitting in front of the cameras in St Eugene's Cathedral, where Frank's funeral had taken place and where Rose herself had been married more than sixty years before. The priest had agreed to let the cameras in only because he had known Rose for so long, and she was a valued member of the congregation. This religious and serious setting gave her testimony more weight. The fact that she was not a former paramilitary and did not come from McGuinness's world also added to its impact. She came across as a respectable, God-fearing Derrywoman: exactly the type of person McGuinness had always claimed to be looking out for.

Towards the end of the broadcast, Roger Cook said Martin McGuinness was a 'man who by any normal standards should be locked away in jail', before pausing again. 'But he isn't. Why?'

In terms of ratings and reviews, this episode of *The Cook Report* was a hit. More than 10 million people tuned in to watch it. But the programme also had a political impact. Unionist MPs responded to what they had seen, and to Rose's testimony, by calling in Parliament for McGuinness to be arrested. It also seemed to change the popular perception of this man, making him less powerful. One of Frank's sisters even went up to him in the street shortly after the broadcast and whacked him with her umbrella, something nobody had dared to do before. McGuinness also had journalists coming to his door in the days after this programme went out, which, again, he was not used to.

'I'm not a member of the IRA,' he told one of them angrily. 'I'm not chief of staff of the IRA,' he went on, 'and I'm not Britain's number-one terrorist.'[3]

The local police seemed to disagree. In the days after the broadcast, inspired by what they had seen, a team of detectives in Northern Ireland launched a new investigation into Martin McGuinness's alleged crimes. It was codenamed 'Operation Taurus' and was run out of a large Nissen hut in police headquarters in Belfast. Detectives from Operation Taurus began by questioning everyone who had appeared in this episode of *The Cook Report*. They soon had the skeleton of a criminal case against Martin McGuinness centred on three witnesses who were willing to testify against him in court.

This was it. After years of trying to prosecute this notorious IRA chief, the police had what they needed. Unless something very unusual happened, Martin McGuinness was going to jail.[4]

For Rose Hegarty, the experience of being interviewed and then watching the programme go out was both enervating and exhausting. Speaking to the television producers had brought back the memories of those tight, airless days after Frank's death, the wake, the funeral, and the emptiness of the weeks that followed. Rose had worried that some people might think she was wrong to speak out on camera, which was why so few people in Derry had in the past agreed to do something like this. It took courage for her to go through with it. But the response she received was over-whelmingly supportive, and her home was soon filled with flowers from well-wishers.

Few people who saw this episode of *The Cook Report* would forget the way Rose Hegarty spoke about her son. She had become the face of this story. Frank's murder began to be associated less with espionage than with his mother's grief, and how Martin McGuinness had abused her trust.

Rose had had her revenge. But that might be just the start of it. Her interview had already triggered a new police investigation into McGuinness's activities, and this could lead to him spending years in jail. It also seemed to have had a profound effect on a man who knew a lot about Frank's murder.

Two days after Rose's interview was broadcast, the producers of *The Cook Report* received a call from a man with a thick Belfast accent. He said his name was Jack, and he had information to pass on.

'The stuff you put out there,' he said over the phone. 'It was, well, it was nothing.'

Jack wanted to talk to them specifically about what Martin McGuinness had done.

'Is it worse than what we said?' the producer asked.

'Yes.'

'And can we prove it?'

'Well,' he said, chuckling, 'I don't know now, that's the problem.' He did not want to say more on the phone, so they arranged to meet in the car park of the Culloden Hotel, just outside Belfast.

Jack arrived on time. Even if he gave the impression of having just got there, he had in fact carried out several passes of the car park to make sure that this was not a trap. The producer watched this man as he walked over to the car. He looked smart. Crisp white shirt.

Ironed blue trousers. Meaty shoulders. Low centre of gravity, and a way of moving that projected pure certainty. But this man was not everything he seemed to be, and his name was not Jack.

It was Freddie Scappaticci.

'More Things in Life Than Killing'

Freddie Scappaticci opens the door to the car and clambers in. The man already inside the vehicle is Frank Thorne, a producer for *The Cook Report* and previously a reporter with the *Daily Mirror*. A few moments ago, Thorne pressed record on a device hidden in one of the car's air vents. When Freddie Scappaticci interrogates suspects for the Nutting Squad, he usually begins by scanning the room with an electronic bug detector. But this is different, and he has left his scanner at home. The two men are soon joined by another producer from *The Cook Report*, Clive Entwistle, who sits in the back seat. A third producer, Sylvia Jones, is watching from the hotel, and has taken down the number plate of the vehicle in which this man, 'Jack', has arrived. She asks a friend in the police to run a trace. *The Cook Report* team still has no idea who he is.

Freddie Scappaticci begins by giving the producers a crash course on the inner workings of the IRA. He tells them about who controls the IRA bombing campaign in England, how the IRA Army Council works, and the names of those tasked with interrogating suspected informers. Right from the start, what's unusual about this is the fluency with which he speaks, and how open he appears to be. The producers are used to IRA men being tight-lipped and tense. This man is completely different. He is talkative and calm, and appears to hold nothing back.

The programme they put out a few days before only really scratched the surface, Scappaticci says, but he's glad it was broadcast.

'Exposed him for what he is,' he says of Martin McGuinness. 'And, see, that woman that came on, she was right in what she was saying, like, he is an evil person.'

'Mrs Hegarty?'

'Yes,' Scappaticci says, in a warm, almost musical voice, 'because he gave the go-ahead for Frank Hegarty, right, Frank Hegarty . . .'

'Can I ask you how you know that?' a producer interrupts.

Scappaticci sucks in his breath and makes an involuntary 'ach' sound.

'I know what we're talking about is really tough,' the producer goes on.

'I know,' Scappaticci says. 'It's . . .' At this point in the recording there is a small slap, like someone throwing their hands onto their thighs, a moment of indecision, an *I'd-like-to-tell-you-but-I-can't.*

'You know,' the producer says. Not 'you know' as a conversational prefix, but as a way of saying Scappaticci *knows* what happened; he *knows* how Frank Hegarty died.

'Aye,' Scappaticci replies.

For the first time since stepping into the car, Freddie Scappaticci sounds unsure of himself. The silence runs on, until it is broken by one of the producers. 'We've talked to a lot of people who have been very trusting with us, as you can see from the nature of the programme.'

'Aye,' Scappaticci says again. He seems to be seconds away from unburdening himself.

'The only reason I ask you', the producer adds, 'is because we only put out part of what he did there with Mrs Hegarty.'

'Well, I'll tell you what I know about it, right,' Scappaticci begins. 'McGuinness was on the phone to Frank Hegarty when he was in England,' he says. '"Come back, you'll be okay, blah, blah, blah."'

Convinced him he'd be okay, and convinced the mother, right. He then come home, and McGuinness was the instrument of him being taken away and shot.'

The way Scappaticci talks about McGuinness as 'the instrument' of Frank's death is striking. It's as if he wants to play down the importance of who pulled the trigger and focus everyone's attention instead on the man that gave the order.

'Do you know that story because—' the producer begins.

'No, no, no,' Scappaticci interrupts.

'*We* know it because the family have told it. I mean, do you know it because McGuinness told you?'

'Well, I know it because . . .'

He trails off, and again the car is silent.

Scappaticci could have just agreed and said that he knew this because McGuinness had told him. But he does not. He knows about the details of Frank Hegarty's murder for some other reason. Perhaps he is weighing up whether to name the person who killed Frank, and in the silence that stretches out comes the possibility that he is on the brink of a confession.

'If we want to be straight here,' Scappaticci starts, 'I was at the heart of things for a long time, right. I'm no longer at the heart of things, right. Haven't been for two or three years, right. But I know what I'm talking about.'

The change in Freddie Scappaticci's life came about four years after Frank's death, in 1990, when a Nutting Squad operation went wrong. He had been part of the IRA team which had been told to abduct a police agent called Sandy Lynch. They took their victim to an IRA safe house in West Belfast, where Scappaticci told him he would soon be hanging upside down in a cowshed. He said he would skin him alive, and was going to kill him, just as he had recently killed Joe Fenton, another suspected informer.

Then some of the IRA men on this team decided they were not

safe where they were. But Scappaticci insisted they stay put. This was because he had just told his handler that this was where they were holding Sandy Lynch, and that the Army Council had decided he should be killed. Scappaticci needed them to stay where they were because this was the address that had been given to the police.

Scappaticci slipped out of the back door moments before the police burst in through the front. Almost everyone in the house was arrested, including Danny Morrison, former Sinn Féin director of publicity, but Scappaticci got away.

The IRA became suspicious. They knew that the police had swept the building for fingerprints, and that Scappaticci had left behind his anti-bugging device, which would have been covered in his prints. Why had he not been arrested?

Scappaticci's solution was to act as if he were 'on the run'. He moved south of the border to Dublin, and stayed there for the next twenty-two months, meeting his lawyer occasionally in the local McDonald's (Scappaticci's order was a quarter-pounder with cheese). His army handlers worked on an alibi and, eventually, Freddie Scappaticci was able to return to Belfast. He was arrested, but told the detectives that his fingerprints were on the battery of the anti-bugging device because he had been doing some electrical repair work in the same building earlier that week. His story was corroborated by the homeowner – who had been told what to say. The police did not press charges.

Freddie Scappaticci was back in the Nutting Squad, but after nearly two years away, he found that his standing had slipped. He had broken an IRA rule by speaking to the police, and he wasn't being listened to in the same way as before. To win back some of his power, Scappaticci came up with the idea of investigating a rumour that a British spy might be on the IRA Army Council. This would involve interrogating everyone on the council – the seven most powerful men in the IRA. Chief of staff, Kevin McKenna, was apoplectic when he heard about the plan and had the entire Nutting Squad stood down, including Scappaticci.[2]

Throughout his life, Freddie Scappaticci responded badly to any loss of status. His decision to become an army agent in the late 1970s was partly a reaction to being kicked out of the IRA. Now a similar thing had happened. He wanted revenge on those who had moved him out of the way, and at the top of his list, it seemed, in block capitals and underlined, was Martin McGuinness.

Freddie Scappaticci tells the two producers from *The Cook Report* that Martin McGuinness is every bit as bad as Rose Hegarty made out in her interview. He is the one with the final say on whether an informer is killed.

At this point, the tape used for the secret recording runs out. The device is hidden inside an air vent so they cannot change it. Instead, one of the producers uses shorthand to take down the rest of the conversation.

'Hegarty was an affront, he took it very personally,' Scappaticci says of McGuinness. 'Before Hegarty was shot I knew about it. A friend of mine was to interrogate Hegarty. But McGuinness' – and at this point Scappaticci says the name of a senior IRA figure who cannot be named here for legal reasons – 'and Kevin McKenna interrogated him.'[3]

These were the three 'prominent men' that McGuinness had alluded to when speaking to Rose Hegarty. But who was Scappaticci's 'friend', the one that was supposed to interrogate Frank? Until then, Scappaticci has named everyone he's talking about. So why talk about a 'friend' here? Why disguise this person's identity? The answer might be that there is one individual he likes more than any other and wants to protect. Or the 'friend' who thought he was going to interrogate Frank Hegarty was Freddie Scappaticci himself.

'McGuinness ordered his shooting,' Scappaticci adds, a point he has already made.[4]

Scappaticci then says that he is no longer part of the IRA. One of the producers asks why.

'There are more things in life than killing.'

The Cook Report producer follows up by asking if he has killed anyone.

Scappaticci does not reply, and the interview soon comes to a close.

That might have been the end of it, but before Scappaticci leaves the producers persuade him to meet up a second time. He does so. Again, the conversation loops back repeatedly to the murder of Frank Hegarty. Something about this episode has a grip on Scappaticci. He says that Frank was 'a dead man' from the moment the Libyan arms were seized by the police.[5]

'It's not important who pulled the trigger,' Scappaticci goes on, unprompted. 'McGuinness wouldn't dirty his hands with that.'

Which again suggests that he knows who *did* pull the trigger.

Then something happens which is both unusual and significant. Freddie Scappaticci begins to talk about Frank's murder in a way that indicates he is not just passing on a story that he has heard.

Frank Hegarty 'threw himself on the mercy of the Army Council', Scappaticci says. 'They went into another room, said, "No – take him out and give him it." A real kangaroo court. They would have blindfolded him and assured him they were taking him home, then would have taken him from the car and told him to keep walking. A bullet in the back of the head. Four bullets is normal, usually by two people so that they are both implicated in the murder.'

It may not sound like much, but one detail stands out. None of the media reports of Frank's murder mentioned *four* shots in the night. Most referred to there being just one. And yet, Scappaticci is right. The police found four bullets at the crime scene, a detail that only became public many years later.

Freddie Scappaticci might have made a guess. As he said himself, four bullets was 'normal'. Or he mentioned four bullets because the sound of those shots breaking the night, as we know they did in the early hours of 26 May 1986, deep in the Irish borderlands, continued to echo in the halls of his memory. Maybe Freddie Scappaticci arrived in County Donegal that day thinking he was going to interrogate Frank Hegarty. Maybe he planned to pass on the location to his handlers or find some other way to save Frank's life. Maybe he found that Martin McGuinness and the others had already carried out the interrogation and now wanted him to take Frank away and kill him, and he felt that there was no way to get out of it.

This would explain some of the intense resentment Freddie Scappaticci feels towards McGuinness, and why he keeps dragging the conversation back to the person who ordered Frank's murder, rather than the one who carried it out. When he came close to killing a fellow agent the year before, after Willie Carlin came under suspicion, Scappaticci intervened to save his life. It follows that he would have wanted to do the same for Frank.

Either that, or it really was a friend of his who was due to interrogate Frank Hegarty, and Scappaticci has simply heard about what happened from someone who was involved.

The conversation ends. Freddie Scappaticci makes his excuses and leaves. He gives the producers no way of contacting him. It is the last time they will ever see him.

MI5 has a problem. The same is true of the police in Northern Ireland and the British Army, and their problems are connected and can be traced back to Rose Hegarty's appearance on *The Cook Report*. Without that, Freddie Scappaticci would not have spoken to the producers, who now have enough material for a sensational follow-up programme. This new episode would do well in terms of ratings, but it might also result in Scappaticci being court-martialled by the IRA and killed. There is a good chance that in the fallout from this programme it will emerge as well that the British have for years been running a spy inside the IRA's Nutting Squad.

Another problem for MI5 is Operation Taurus, the new police investigation into Martin McGuinness, also triggered by Rose Hegarty's appearance on television. The detectives working on this investigation are confident that they now have enough evidence to prosecute Martin McGuinness for a number of serious crimes, and that he will soon be behind bars. The problem for MI5, and for the British government, is that jailing McGuinness will finish off Operation Chiffon and the prospect of peace talks. Either they grant Martin McGuinness some kind of informal immunity from prosecution, which would be troubling from a legal perspective as well as a political and moral one. Or they accept that criminal justice must be allowed to run its course.

What makes the decision facing MI5 so much harder is the timing of it. Operation Chiffon appears to have stalled. The IRA leadership and the British government have exchanged a number of messages over the last two years, with Brendan Duddy, codenamed 'Roadrunner', handing on communications to Martin McGuinness, codenamed 'Penguin', and representatives from both sides have repeatedly expressed a broad desire for peace. At times, they seem to be within touching distance. MI5 have even purchased a bungalow in Northern Ireland where they imagine the actual peace talks will take place. Stephen Lander, the MI5 officer running Joint Section, is at the stage of having worked out who will provide the catering during these talks, and has lined up a team of SAS soldiers to protect the building during the formal discussions.

But there is still no agreement, and it is hard to see how this will change. The IRA hardliners, meanwhile, have escalated their military campaign. In recent months, bombs have gone off in the City of London, Belfast, Portadown, and Magherafelt, as well as those in Warrington. The physical-force men seem to be moving away from peace, not towards it. The worry for those in MI5 is the same as it ever was: that Martin McGuinness and Gerry Adams might be unable to bring all of the IRA with them. Perhaps Operation Chiffon was a mistake.

MI5 make their decision. They have come this far, and will keep going. They push to have the police investigation into Martin McGuinness shut down.[6] Although there is a strong desire within the local police to finish the job and charge McGuinness, the prospect of peace is judged to be more important. The detectives working on Operation Taurus are told that this IRA commander and Sinn Féin politician will not be prosecuted. The Nissen hut that was the nerve centre of this investigation begins to empty out and will soon fall quiet.

Clive Entwistle, senior producer on *The Cook Report*, who has begun to think about how to use the audio recording of Freddie Scappaticci, is taken aside and told that Scappaticci is 'somebody that British intelligence relied on a great deal', and that the broadcast of this secret recording could lead to his death.[7] Entwistle agrees to spike the programme, before storing the recording in a safe place.

Operation Chiffon is still alive, Martin McGuinness has avoided jail, and Freddie Scappaticci has survived.

So, too, has the possibility of peace.

One cold December day in 1993, the British prime minister, John Major, and the Irish Taoiseach, Albert Reynolds, appear in front of No. 10 Downing Street for a press conference. Major announces that the two of them have reached an agreement known as the Downing Street Declaration.

'It is a declaration for democracy and dialogue,' Major says, 'and it is based on consent.' There is now 'an opportunity to end violence in Northern Ireland for good,' he goes on. It is, he adds, 'the first stage in the peace process.'[8]

Over the coming months, paramilitary groups and political parties in Northern Ireland gravitate slowly towards each other, and the violence becomes less intense.

Then, on a bright day in August 1994, the IRA announces an unconditional ceasefire. The headline in the *Belfast Telegraph* that day is simple: 'IT'S OVER'.

Gerry Adams and Martin McGuinness appear that afternoon at the Sinn Féin office in Belfast, where they are handed flowers by someone in the crowd. Both men look giddy and tired. It later emerged that McGuinness spent most of the day before making the case for peace to recalcitrant members of the IRA Army Council. While some of them refused to come over to his point of view, enough of them eventually did.

The Troubles are drawing to a close, and Operation Chiffon has come to a successful end. The extent of Britain's infiltration of the IRA and Sinn Féin remains a tightly guarded secret, and the idea that MI5 might have quietly intervened to keep Gerry Adams or Martin McGuinness either alive or out of jail is, for now, the stuff of spy fiction.

Late into the night, people can be seen celebrating on the streets of Belfast and Derry. Some are hanging out of the backs of cars, grinning and holding Irish tricolours. The darkness that settled long ago over the landscape is starting to lift.

Good Friday

Tony Blair was only half joking when he said he had a 'Messiah complex'. The former British prime minister knew that people made fun of him about this, but he didn't mind too much because he felt there were times as a leader when you needed a Messiah complex, especially if you wanted to bring about historic change. Proof of this, he felt, looking back on his career, was the part he played in ending the Troubles.[1]

When Blair came into office, after Labour's landslide victory in the 1997 general election, peace talks were already under way in Northern Ireland. They were overseen by an owlish US senator called George Mitchell. His challenge – and at times it seemed impossible – was to engineer an agreement between the Irish government, the British government, Sinn Féin, the SDLP, the Ulster Unionist Party, Progressive Unionist Party, Ulster Democratic Party, Alliance Party, Labour Coalition, and the Northern Ireland Women's Coalition on how the region should be run. After nearly two years of this, Mitchell was losing faith. He told Tony Blair they had reached an impasse, and it was probably best to call off the talks.

'I took the decision then and there', Blair remembered, 'to take complete charge of the negotiation.'[2]

Four days later, at 5.26pm on Good Friday, 10 April 1998, they had a deal. The parties had agreed on a 11,687 word-long text, formally called the Belfast Agreement, which would be known around the world as the Good Friday Agreement. It was radical, far-sighted, and brave. The signatories had committed to peace and to laying down their arms. Convicted paramilitaries would be released from jail. People in Northern Ireland would be able to choose between British and Irish nationality, or they could take both. The constitution of the Republic of Ireland would no longer assert sovereignty over Northern Ireland, and the status of the region would only be allowed to change with the consent of people living on the island of Ireland. This agreement also sketched out plans for a new legislative assembly in which power could be shared between the different parties, with the ten departmental ministries divvied up between Protestant and Catholic representatives according to a precise mathematical formula.

'There are decades when nothing happens,' Vladimir Lenin once said, 'and there are weeks where decades happen.' This seemed to be one of them. After almost thirty years of bloodshed and uncertainty, the Troubles had come to an end.

In the silence that follows the end of any conflict, it is in our nature to look for a victor. But the situation in Northern Ireland was unusually hard to read, and many people struggled to work out who had won. As the news of the Good Friday Agreement spread around the world, the only ones who looked in any way triumphant in the press photographs accompanying the story were those who had helped to broker the deal. This agreement was hailed as a victory for Tony Blair and New Labour. The story put out by the communications team at No. 10 Downing Street, led by Alastair Campbell, was, essentially, that four enlightened outsiders had flown into Belfast, knocked some heads together, and ended the Troubles.

There was some truth to this. Bill Clinton, the US president, had been on the phone to the key participants in the frantic final few hours of negotiations, and was, Blair remembered, 'a total brick throughout'.[3] Bertie Ahern, the Irish Taoiseach, played a vital role and so did George Mitchell, while Tony Blair himself had been crucial in those final few days. The prime minister was later compared to a man having seven affairs at the same time, in that he often found it hard to say no – a quality perfectly suited to closing the Good Friday Agreement. (That same need to keep a variety of people happy would later characterise his relationship with US President George Bush and play a part in Britain's involvement in the Iraq War.)

The Troubles ended when they did partly because of the involvement of Blair, Clinton, Mitchell, and Ahern. But really these four were finishing off a job which had begun years ago. By the time these peace negotiations began, most of the heavy lifting had been done and the two major impediments to peace were no longer there: Sinn Féin had become a genuine political force, and the IRA leadership realised that military victory was out of reach. What's interesting is why these obstacles had disappeared.

When the Good Friday Agreement was signed, very little was known about Britain's intelligence operations in Northern Ireland. The various agencies involved had taken on a Cinderella role – overlooked and underestimated. But in the decades that followed, a huge amount of new information came to light. Slowly, it became clear that by the mid-1990s, the IRA and Sinn Féin had been infiltrated by the British at almost every level.

The size of this intelligence operation is sometimes hard to grasp. One very senior British intelligence officer said that as many as one in three of the IRA's most senior figures at this time was either close to a British agent or was themselves being run by a handler or case officer.[4] This is a staggering figure. According to another reliable source, by this stage 'a majority of the seven-person IRA Army Council were effectively compromised because of their proximity to high-level agents'.[5] A local priest who was later shown classified government papers in his capacity as a member of the Consultative

Group on the Past said that the British had been running as many as 800 agents in Northern Ireland. One intelligence source scoffed when he heard that figure. The real number, he said, was much higher.[6]

This army of secret agents helped to end the Troubles in a variety of ways, but they represented just one part of an even larger enterprise. The main strand in this vast operation was 'tactical' intelligence: scraps of information from agents like Frank Hegarty and Freddie Scappaticci, or details that came in from an array of increasingly sophisticated electronic listening devices, all of which could be used to break up IRA attacks. This was essential in reducing the IRA's military capability, bringing parts of the organisation to a standstill, and moving it, often against its will, towards peace.

'Strategic' intelligence was also vital. Sources close to decision-makers such as Martin McGuinness and Gerry Adams gave the British a detailed and up-to-date understanding of what was going on inside the IRA and Sinn Féin. Without this, there would never have been a project to preserve McGuinness's and Adams's leadership, and on several occasions these two might have been either ousted by the IRA hardliners or killed. Strategic intelligence also played a part in the Good Friday Agreement itself. Several years later, it was reported that Martin McGuinness's telephone had been tapped during the negotiations and one of his drivers was an MI5 agent. McGuinness had been Sinn Féin's chief negotiator in the talks. Tony Blair's skill as a communicator played a part in getting the deal over the line, but the team around him also benefitted from knowing a lot about what everyone else was thinking, and some of these insights came from secret sources.

Agents like Denis Donaldson and Willie Carlin also played a vital part in ending this conflict. Many of them worked for Sinn Féin while reporting to the British, and although they were not simply 'agents of influence', they were often encouraged to keep steering the party towards peace and do what they could to improve its performance at the polls.

Stephen Lander, a future MI5 director general, described the fourth way that intelligence work helped to end the Troubles. Without the back channel to the IRA set up by Michael Oatley, he said, 'there would have been no peace process'.[7] Covert diplomacy provided the breakthrough which led, ultimately, to the Good Friday Agreement. The British saw Brendan Duddy's contribution to ending the Troubles as so important that he was later given a pension by MI5.[8]

The final way that intelligence helped to end the Troubles in Northern Ireland was mass surveillance. Much of this was slow and unremarkable work, involving thousands of soldiers and policemen entering information every day into a network of connected computers, while others analysed and interpreted enormous data-sets. But the intelligence produced by this was often the foundation on which some of the more eye-catching operations were built.

Without the secret work of the local police, MI5, the British Army, SIS, and GCHQ, it would have taken longer for Sinn Féin to become a genuine political force, and for the IRA leadership to recognise that military victory was not possible. The Troubles might have continued for many more years.

What makes this intelligence effort so unusual is not just the size of it, but the impact it had. The world of spies and secret information is fascinating to outsiders as well as heroic and romantic. But conflicts tend to be won by soldiers, not spies. They turn on questions of manpower, weaponry, motivation, supplies, and tactics. Not who has the best agents. Scroll through the annals of global warfare, and you will not find any other conflict in which intelligence is thought to have played the decisive part.

The story of the Troubles was different. Even the military men agreed. 'The insurgency could not have been broken and the terrorist structure could not have been engaged and finally driven into politics,' the British Army's official report on the Troubles began, 'without the intelligence organisations and processes that were developed.'[9] Jimmy Glover's experiment in agent-running, the FRU, was later described by one officer as 'by far and away the most successful thing we managed to achieve inside Northern Ireland'.[10] Former SIS chief Maurice Oldfield had been right with the prediction he made after being sent out to Northern Ireland in the late 1970s: intelligence was the match-winner.

But for all the agents in play at any one time, the British never *controlled* the IRA or Sinn Féin, and nor was the IRA defeated. Agents and electronic surveillance provided a level of coverage that was often unnervingly good, but it was never complete. In places like South Armagh, the IRA remained almost impossible to infiltrate. The same was true of most IRA cells in England. There were also problems on the British side. Although the different intelligence agencies coordinated well, their desire to outdo each other sometimes led to gaps in their coverage. Within MI5, there was also an understanding that they could never cross the line between influence and control. The service had come dangerously close to this in the past with its infiltration of the Communist Party of Great Britain, and senior officers working on Northern Ireland recognised the risk of something similar happening again. There was a limit to how many agents they wanted to have inside the IRA or Sinn Féin.

In the years after the Good Friday Agreement, Britain's reputation within the wider world of espionage began to change. What had happened in Northern Ireland seemed to reflect a new and more modern approach, one that provided a sharp contrast to the earlier, clubbier image of British intelligence. Senior officers from MI5 became go-to experts in counter-insurgency. Lessons learned during the Troubles by the local police, MI5, SIS, and the FRU would later be applied in Afghanistan and Iraq. As one MI5 director general put it, the service's experience in Northern Ireland meant that 'we were better prepared to deal with Al Qaeda; we had protocols in place to deal with terrorist threats'.[11] When the Taliban tried to establish a back channel for peace negotiations, the American response was informed partly by the story of Michael Oatley and Brendan Duddy. Britain's record in Northern Ireland also helped to establish a powerful new axiom: that the response to any terrorist threat must be centred on intelligence.

But there was another side to all this; a shadow tale that took longer to emerge. The corollary to relying so much on intelligence in Northern Ireland was that agent handlers had been making countless life-or-death decisions about how to use the information in front of them. They were living, sometimes daily, with the spymaster's dilemma. They had to ask themselves repeatedly the same question: will I save more lives if I act on this intelligence, or if I don't?

The story of Freddie Scappaticci epitomised this. He was the portrait in the attic. The man who had once been Britain's most valuable intelligence asset in Northern Ireland was now its darkest secret. Perhaps this was the price for peace. Scappaticci's career as Stakeknife remained an obsessively guarded secret, and the Ministry of Defence was primed to block any newspaper report that so much as hinted at what he might have done. And this was not just to avoid a scandal. It was to protect the fragile peace in Northern Ireland.

Oblivion

'There was this great gasp went around the Assembly chamber,' one man remembered. 'You might as well have been nominating the devil himself to be in charge of our children.' It had been more than a year since the Good Friday Agreement, and Gerry Adams had just stood up in Stormont, the seat of the New Northern Ireland Assembly, to nominate Martin McGuinness as the region's Minister of Education.

Some commentators thought McGuinness should have been facing charges for war crimes, not overseeing their children's education. Others worried that he might not be up to the job. But if there were two constants in this man's life, they were his determination to succeed and his quicksilver capacity for reinvention. The boy from the Bogside who had failed his 11-plus exam and left school at fifteen would make a go of it, and he refused to be held back by his past. Nor did he like to be reminded of it.

In his new guise as a respectable politician and peacemaker, Martin McGuinness gave the impression of being someone who wanted nothing to do with the story of the Troubles. Some people found this infuriating and hard to accept, including the Reverend Ian Paisley, the fiery leader of the Democratic Unionist Party, who had recently stood up in Parliament to launch a detailed attack on McGuinness.

'Who are these IRA people?' Paisley asked the house testily. 'One is a man called Martin McGuinness,' he answered, before reading out an article which took the form of a letter to McGuinness. 'Mrs Rose Hegarty must long to know,' he began. 'You promised, on bended knee, that her son was safe to return from exile.' He went on. 'You promised and cajoled and charmed her into telling him to come home. "A few boys would question him and he'd be free to go," you told her. His sister drove him to the appointed place,' he said. 'He was shot and his body unceremoniously dumped. Those women long for the truth behind that atrocity. They won't hold their breath waiting for you to speak it.'[2]

The murder of Frank Hegarty had become a political shorthand. It stood for Martin McGuinness's refusal to talk about his IRA past, one that Ian Paisley found unforgivable. Several years later, he was on his feet again in Parliament to make the same point, only this time he described Frank's murder in more detail.

Paisley did not go after other IRA men like he pursued McGuinness because they were less prominent and had not been involved in as many serious crimes. But they also seemed more willing to acknowledge parts of their past. McGuinness, according to Paisley, had 'never once breathed a regret that those things should have happened'. Many people shared Paisley's desire to hear McGuinness talk with contrition and honesty about what he had done. But at the same time, some felt an almost unconscious need for the opposite to happen, and preferred to see if it was possible, for now, to look the other way.

After the Athenian civil war in the fifth century BC, citizens were told to take an oath 'not to remember the recent misfortunes'. Bitter religious hostility in sixteenth-century Britain was followed by the 1560 Treaty of Edinburgh that included an 'Act of Oblivion'. At the close of the Thirty Years' War, the following century, the Treaty of Westphalia introduced 'a perpetual Oblivion' to cover the crimes 'committed since the beginning of these Troubles', effectively a legal amnesty. The 1660 Act of Oblivion in England went further, handing out fines to anyone found guilty of trying 'to revive the memory of the late differences'. The message from one Italian newspaper in 1945 on the day that Hitler died was simply, impossibly, 'Forget as soon as possible!' After the 1975 death of General Franco, the Spanish dictator, the government introduced El Pacto del Olvido, designed to encourage people to move on from the past without interrogating it.

In the history of civil wars and bitter internal conflicts a clear pattern emerges. If one side appears to have won, there is usually some public show of justice and retribution. A small number of people might be imprisoned, killed, exiled, or put on trial. In South Africa, a Truth and Reconciliation Commission was set up after the end of apartheid, in which those who agreed to speak out about what they had done were offered immunity from prosecution. This satisfied some of the collective need for a reckoning. But it was only possible because most people agreed on who had won the struggle that had just ended.

When a bitter, inward-facing conflict finishes with both sides feeling that they have won, a desire for justice is almost always subsumed by the need for peace. Some kind of amnesty will often be accompanied by a call to forget – at least for now.

This is roughly what happened in Northern Ireland. There was no clear moral victor. Paramilitaries were released from jail early, while the focus in public was on the future. The Good Friday Agreement was detailed and courageous, but it contained very little on how to deal with the legacy of the Troubles.

More than 50,000 men and women had been either injured or killed, and few Northern Irish families had not been affected in some way by the conflict. A book released the year after the Good Friday Agreement called *Lost Lives*, by the journalists David McKittrick, Seamus Kelters, Brian Feeney, and Chris Thornton, which described every killing that took place during the Troubles, became a bestseller.

The queues to buy the book stretched out of bookshops into the streets. Each copy was more than a record of who had died. It was also a silent memorial to what had happened. In their own way, often in the privacy of their homes, the people of Northern Ireland were starting to make sense of the past for themselves.

One of them was Ryan Hegarty, Frank's son. He was seventeen when the Good Friday Agreement was signed. 'Every day I think of him,' he said of his father. Indeed, Ryan struggled to remember a time when he did not feel that he was living in the shadow of Frank's murder. 'Your dad's a tout, and so are you,' they chanted at school. He was bullied and taunted, and asked if his house was bugged. Soon he found that certain pubs in Derry refused to serve him because of who his father had been. Even now, in the new age of peace and reconciliation.

This had a hardening effect on Ryan, and he found it difficult to put his trust in other people. Nor could he find a way past the sheer injustice of it all. Why should he go through life answering for what his father had done? And had Frank really done anything wrong? 'In the eyes of the IRA,' Ryan later said, 'he committed the ultimate crime. But in my eyes, he saved people's lives.'[3]

Ryan Hegarty also had to live with the knowledge that those responsible for his father's death had never been charged for their crimes. Martin McGuinness, the man widely believed to have lured his father to his death, was now Minister for Education, and being feted by world leaders as a man of peace. Perhaps they were correct, perhaps he had changed. But that did not diminish Ryan's right to justice. The police had a duty to investigate his father's murder, and the people responsible should be tried. Ryan Hegarty needed to know who had taken his father's life, and he failed to understand why nothing was being done.

36

Scap

A former British soldier was out shopping one day in 1999, soon after the Good Friday Agreement, when he wandered into a bookshop and picked up a book that had caught his eye. It was called *Killing Rage* and was a memoir by former IRA volunteer Eamon Collins, who had once been part of the Nutting Squad. The man now leafing through this book was Ian Hurst, formerly of the FRU, who had helped look after Frank Hegarty while he was in an army safe house in Kent. As he went through the book, he skimmed through some of the passages. Then he read something that made him feel physically sick – a section in which the author recalled a conversation with the men who ran the Nutting Squad, and how they had joked about a murder they claimed to have carried out. But this was not the detail that made Hurst's stomach turn. The moment when he thought he might vomit came when he saw one of the men's names. This was the second-in-command of the Nutting Squad, who was described in the book as 'Scap'.

Hurst knew immediately who this was. Scap was Freddie Scappaticci. He had known for years that Scappaticci was a prized army agent. But he'd had no idea what his role inside the IRA was. The idea that this British agent had been part of the Nutting Squad left Hurst reeling. He quickly joined the dots. If Scappaticci had been a senior figure in the Nutting Squad in the late 1980s, then he was probably part of the team that killed Frank Hegarty. Perhaps he was the one that actually pulled the trigger. One British agent inside the IRA might have murdered another. Or was the truth even darker than that? Hurst wondered if the British, rather than the IRA, had ordered Scappaticci to kill Frank Hegarty. Perhaps they were trying to protect another source they had higher up in the organisation, someone like Martin McGuinness.

Ian Hurst could not reconcile himself to the idea that his friend, Frank, the man he had helped to look after, might have been killed by another British spy. His relationship with Frank made this feel inescapably personal. Hurst felt an overwhelming urge to do something about what he had found out, and decided to become a whistleblower. He contacted the *Sunday Times* reporter Liam Clarke. After a number of conversations, they agreed to collaborate on a series of pieces.

The first article came out on 8 August 1999 under the headline 'The British Spy at the Heart of the IRA'. It described a mysterious army agent who went by the codename 'Steak Knife', and was 'earning up to £60,000 a year for vital information'. 'Steak Knife was and is the crown jewel of British intelligence in Ulster, a man at the heart of the IRA's war effort who had to be kept happy at all costs.'[1] But the article did not reveal who Steak Knife was, which made the story even more compelling.

The machinery of official secrecy came to life immediately. The Ministry of Defence applied for, and was granted, injunctions against both Ian Hurst and the *Sunday Times*. Hurst reported that his house was broken into and that documents mentioning Scappaticci were stolen. One of these items, he said, was later produced in court by lawyers acting for the Ministry of Defence.

But it was too late. The Stakeknife story could not be squeezed back into its tube. Hurst fought back against the injunction, and so did Liam Clarke, the *Sunday Times*, and the other journalists who had begun to report on this. One of them was Greg Harkin, who, after several years of legal wrangling (in which the spelling of Steak Knife changed to Stakeknife), put together a piece for the *Sunday Tribune* in which he named this agent as the former IRA volunteer Freddie Scappaticci.

The evening before the story ran, Greg Harkin decided to visit what he believed to be Scappaticci's house, in Andersonstown, West Belfast. He wanted to let him know about the piece that was about to be published, and to ask him for his reaction.

The door was opened by Scappaticci's grandson.

'Granda', there's someone at the door.'[2]

Freddie Scappaticci had hurt his back earlier that day on a building site and was laid up inside on his settee. Eventually, he staggered out to the door. He was wearing an Italian football shirt and shorts and was friendly in a way that Harkin found disarming.

'Have you seen this article?' Harkin asked, waving a copy of the piece due to be published the next day.

'What article?' Scappaticci said.

'Well, the *Sunday Tribune* is running an article that says you're a British agent.'

'You're joking.'

Harkin handed him the article. Freddie Scappaticci got as far as the headline, which said he had been paid £80,000 a year.

'Eighty thousand pounds a year? Are you serious? I'm out breaking my back building concrete blocks and I'm getting eighty thousand pounds a year? You must be joking.'[3]

The piece was published the next day. At first, the reaction was as you might expect. Man is accused of being a mass murderer and spy. Man disappears.

Freddie Scappaticci had vanished. According to one rumour, he was flown by helicopter to a British Army base where a party was held in his honour. Another story was that his handlers spirited him away to Cassino, in central Italy, where he thought about whether to start a new life. Then the narrative took a mad turn. Rather than stay wherever he had been taken to, Scappaticci reappeared in Belfast and went to see two members of the IRA Army Council.

This sounded like suicide by proxy. By thinking that he could talk his way out of this, Freddie Scappaticci appeared to have made the same mistake as Frank Hegarty. But his circumstances were different. Scappaticci was too big to fail. He had been so senior within the IRA, and had seen so much, that the people he was speaking to had almost as much to lose from his exposure as he did. The IRA and Freddie Scappaticci came to an understanding. He would admit to nothing, and in return he would not be killed.[4]

'My statement basically is that I am Freddie Scappaticci,' he began, several days later, at a press conference to which just two reporters had been invited. The IRA's head of intelligence was said to be watching from a building across the street. Members of the British security forces were also said to have the property under surveillance. Scappaticci was being carefully monitored by those he had worked against and those he had worked for.

'I am telling you I am not guilty of any of these allegations,' Scappaticci went on.

'Were you at any stage involved in the IRA or the republican movement?' one journalist asked.

Scappaticci paused, looked away, and licked his lips. 'I was involved in the republican movement, thirteen years ago, but I have had no involvement these past thirteen years.'[5]

That was it. The whole thing lasted fifty-five seconds.

Freddie Scappaticci had completed his task, which was to deny the allegation that he had been Stakeknife. But if he imagined that this was going to be the end of it, he was wrong. There were more articles, and more journalists came to his house.

Then Scappaticci surprised everyone again by turning up at the offices of his local newspaper, the *Andersonstown News*, looking anxious and on edge. He said that he wanted to give an interview. He felt he hadn't been given a chance to put across his side of the story.

For the next hour, Freddie Scappaticci spoke about what had happened to him since the story broke, as if he was the survivor of a terrible assault.

'I said to myself, "Jesus!" I was physically sick, just sick,' he said of seeing the first newspaper reports identifying him as Stakeknife. 'And to tell you the truth, the first thing that came into my head was, Jesus, what are my family going to think when they see this?'⁶

Freddie Scappaticci was the victim, he insisted, of a witch-hunt. 'My family has been tortured by the British media and gutter press, coming to my house, banging on the door, windows, putting letters through the door, wanting to know where I was, wanting to write something derogatory about me and my family.'⁷ He then described the effect of all this on his youngest daughter, then sitting her A levels, who was now so worried about her father's safety that she had been taken out of school.

Priests and nuns had called to the house, Scappaticci added, each of them offering their support, and promising to say Masses for his wife. Neighbours had come by to ask if there was anything they could do, and had refused to speak to the media in a show of solidarity. Scappaticci also made a point of thanking 'the republican movement' who had been, he said, 'fantastic'. 'Without the help of the republican movement I don't think I could have got through this. That's the thing that has been keeping me going.'⁸

The journalist asked if he had ever been a spy.

'Never,' was Scappaticci's emphatic reply. 'According to the press I am guilty of forty murders,' he went on. 'But I am telling you this now: after this has settled, I want to meet the families of the people that they said I murdered. And when I do, I will stand in front of them and say, "I didn't do it. I had no part in it." And I will look them straight in the eye when I do it.'⁹

Scappaticci had a way of speaking that made him sound both natural and incredibly authentic. He came across as someone you wanted to believe, in spite of yourself. This interview was either a bravura performance, or the heartfelt testimony of a man who had been terribly maligned. Perhaps Scappaticci's reputation was more formidable than the reality of what he had done. Even if he had joined the Nutting Squad, maybe he had found a way to avoid being the 'trigger man'. The rumours about Freddie Scappaticci that would later be investigated by Jon Boutcher and his detectives might be no more than that – rumours.

Breaches of the Law

On St Patrick's Day 2002, the IRA launched a raid on a heavily guarded target in Belfast. There was a time in the organisation's history when an operation like this would have involved a team of men in balaclavas armed with automatic rifles and mortars. On this occasion, the volunteers arrived at the headquarters of the Police Service of Northern Ireland disguised as builders. One of them spoke in an English accent. Rather than force their way in, they had a cover story that gave them an excuse to enter the complex. They kept going until they reached the room they were looking for, and left with a bundle of secret files and documents, and a notebook listing the home address of every Special Branch agent in the area.

The IRA had been desperate to see behind the curtain. They wanted to understand, finally, the extent to which their organisation had been infiltrated by the intelligence agencies. Even if they did not come away with all the answers, because the documents they had taken revealed nothing about agents working exclusively for the FRU or MI5, or those who lived outside the Greater Belfast area, what they had gave them a sense of how many people in this part of the region were helping the police.

In the hours after this raid, the authorities waited for an IRA press conference, an announcement, or a spate of killings. Agents whose identities had been compromised were ready to leave at a moment's notice. One of those was Denis Donaldson, who was being run jointly by the police and MI5 and whose address was now in the possession of the IRA.

But nobody came for them, and there was no message from the IRA. Just silence.

As the two IRA volunteers who went through the material discovered, the infiltration was much, much worse than any of them had imagined. In some cases, on discovering the address of a senior republican figure such as Donaldson, their suspicion fell instead on others at the same address, as it was so hard to believe that someone like him could have been working for the British. In time, however, they realised that making all of this public would implicate so many people that the IRA's support, such as it was, would never recover. The same would be true, in a different way, if they had decided to abduct, court martial, and kill every man and woman whose name appeared in that notebook. Instead, the police agents inside Sinn Féin and the IRA were quietly moved out of their positions in the following years.

Every few months, it seemed, another story came out in the media about a British spy inside one paramilitary organisation or another. A new narrative was starting to emerge about why the Troubles ended when it did, but it was still unclear and full of contradictions.

Freddie Scappaticci had been outed as an agent, before going on to deny the whole thing. He was persuasive. Greg Harkin, the journalist who broke the story, had left Scappaticci's house with 'nagging doubts' over whether he had the right man.[1] Some people wondered if 'Stakeknife' referred to Scappaticci's boss in the Nutting Squad, John Joe Magee, the former Royal Marine who had served in the elite 43 Commando before joining the IRA. Even if Magee had a chequered service history and had spent many hours in military prison, his need for money later on in life might have left him open to being recruited.

For every disgruntled former IRA volunteer who came to believe that the organisation was riddled with spies, another would swear that the whole thing was a pack of lies. Senior figures such as Gerry Adams dismissed the allegations against Freddie Scappaticci with contempt, calling them nothing more than 'dirty tricks' from the British. Martin McGuinness also denounced the claims against Scappaticci, making out that they were part of a sinister British plot to discredit an innocent family man.

Amid all this uncertainty, Freddie Scappaticci made a mistake. Soon after being outed in the media, he decided that the government's security minister, Jane Kennedy, needed to state in public that he had never been a British agent. She refused, mainly because it was not true. Unable to let go of this idea, Scappaticci went to his solicitor in Belfast and swore in an affidavit that he was not, and had never been, the agent known as Stakeknife.

In the months leading up to this, Scappaticci had denied the allegations against him to neighbours, friends, and newspaper reporters, and in doing this, he had not broken the law. But this was different. An affidavit is a sworn statement made in the presence of a public notary and has legal weight. Denying that he had ever been Stakeknife in a sworn affidavit was perjury, a criminal offence punishable by up to seven years in jail. This might never have become a problem for him, had it not been for one man's intervention.

Kevin Winters was a lawyer. He was powerfully built, articulate, and sharp, and he had once known Freddie Scappaticci professionally. At the start of his career, just out of law school, Kevin Winters had taken a job working for the lawyer Pat Finucane, who was later murdered by Protestant extremists using intelligence supplied by a British agent. Soon after Finucane's murder, in the early 1990s, Winters was sent to Dublin to see one of the firm's clients – an IRA volunteer then on the run – Freddie Scappaticci.

'He was like any other client,' Kevin Winters said of Scappaticci, or 'Fred', as he knew him. 'What you see is what you get.' It would be many years before he realised the opposite was true.

Scappaticci had fled to Dublin in 1990 after the Sandy Lynch abduction, during which he had tipped off the authorities. One of the people arrested that night was Danny Morrison, Sinn Féin director of publicity, who was later tried for the part he had played in this, and convicted for false imprisonment and conspiracy to murder. More than a decade later, when the stories about Freddie Scappaticci came out, Kevin Winters had Danny Morrison as one of his clients. He realised that if the allegations about Scappaticci were true, then Morrison's sentence could be overturned. Winters and his team decided to make a challenge in the Court of Appeal, and in 2008 the Lord Chief Justice, Sir Brian Kerr, ruled that Morrison's original conviction had been 'unsafe'.

Winters and most of the others involved in the case went out to celebrate, as lawyers do after a win like this. But one of the barristers, Sean Devine, stayed behind to go through the judge's ruling in more detail. He noticed something unusual, and later shared this with Winters. There was a line in the text that seemed out of place. The judge had written that as a result of what he had seen while looking into this case – the one involving the abduction of Sandy Lynch – he felt that there should now be an investigation into whether there had been 'breaches of the law of Northern Ireland'.

'I have never come across a phrase like that,' Kevin Winters recalled. The judge did not say which laws had been breached or who had breached them, only that there should be an investigation. 'I started writing and agitating. I started quoting that judgement, going to the chief constable of the PSNI, to the Police Ombudsman's Office, and to the Director of Public Prosecutions. I was running from pillar to post, trying to find out who should be investigating this. But the more I poked at it, the more I got the response of, "Yeah, yeah, yeah, we'll get round to it".'

Winters then went to a panel discussion on the European Convention of Human Rights (ECHR), the landmark international human-rights treaty drawn up after the Second World War. It contains eighteen articles, the most famous of which is Article 2 concerning the right to life. Under Article 2 of the ECHR, no sovereign government should be responsible for taking an individual's life, and they must intervene if they become aware of a threat to someone's life. Equally, if a government agent is alleged to have carried out a murder, then the state must conduct an independent investigation.

As a signatory to the ECHR, the British government had a duty to investigate any murder that one of its secret agents might have carried out. Everyone at the panel discussion that day knew about the allegations against Stakeknife, and that there had been no investigation into them.

One of the panellists was Al Hutchinson, the police ombudsman, who was asked why his department appeared to be doing nothing to address this.

'It will take me fifty years, to investigate all these cases,' Kevin Winters remembered him saying.

Why fifty years?

He did not have enough money, he said.

Winters was annoyed by this. 'I looked at his body language, and it really suggested he couldn't give a shit. And I remember thinking, Right, I'm going to take a legal challenge against that stance.'

Elsewhere in Belfast, at around the same time, Martin McGuinness was photographed sitting next to Ian Paisley, with both men in hysterics. They were in the Parliament buildings at Stormont, and Paisley was being sworn in as first minister of Northern Ireland's first power-sharing government. McGuinness was the new deputy first minister. The two former enemies had found a way to move beyond their differences, and were starting to enjoy each other's company.

One of the people attending that ceremony, seated just behind Tony Blair, was Peggy McGuinness, Martin's mother. Thirty-seven years earlier, she had found a black beret in her house and realised that her son had joined the IRA, a discovery that had 'traumatised her'.[2] She knew that her son's life would never be the same, and must have prepared herself for the news that he had been killed or was going to jail. It is unlikely that she ever imagined a day like this.

Martin McGuinness appeared to be relishing his new life as a senior government minister and had become more comfortable in the political spotlight. He presented himself in public as a thoughtful family man, a senior statesman, and a doting grandfather who liked nothing more than walking his grandchildren into school. McGuinness was an occasional poet, it was reported, and had a passion for photography. If he saw an interesting flower by the side of the road while he was being driven around on official business, he might stop the car and jump out to take a picture. He loved fly-fishing, walks along the beach, and cookery, and had perfected his signature dish – a Delia Smith recipe for meatballs (although his children thought he overdid it on the garlic).

Perhaps the first real test of Martin McGuinness's reinvention as a senior government minister came in 2009, two years after he had entered office. Members of a breakaway IRA faction had killed two British soldiers and a policeman. McGuinness could have been equivocal in his response, leaning into phrases about why people might resort to violence and some of the historical injustices motivating the killers. Instead, he described those responsible as 'traitors to Ireland'.[3]

Two years later, McGuinness surprised everyone again. After a trip to Hollywood to meet film producers and financiers, he announced, in 2011, that he was running to be the next president of the Republic of Ireland. If the story of his life had been a film, this was the kind of plot twist that would have been cut from the script at an early stage, because it was so improbable. Martin McGuinness running to be Irish president was, according to one newspaper, the 'republican movement's most audacious act since IRA prisoner Bobby Sands stood as an MP'.⁴ This former IRA commander had put himself forward to be Irish head of state and supreme commander of the Irish Defence Forces. It sounded bizarre. But McGuinness was confident that he could win.

Soon Martin McGuinness was travelling around Ireland and campaigning for the presidency. Many of the people he spoke to wished him well and said they would vote for him. On the few occasions that he was asked about his IRA past, he waved the question away as if it was a comment in poor taste. He 'would not be interrogated' on air, he told one radio host who ventured onto the subject.⁵ 'People see me very much as a peacemaker,' he went on, in his statesmanlike way, 'a peacemaker who can be trusted.'⁶

An early poll had Martin McGuinness as the frontrunner to become the next Irish president. One of the country's best-known bookmakers offered odds of 2–1 on a Martin McGuinness victory.⁷ Many people across Ireland were bemused, intrigued, or buoyed up by what they were seeing.

Others had a more limbic reaction. For Frank Hegarty's sisters and brothers, the sight of Martin McGuinness shaking hands with Irish voters and trying to win them over had a triggering effect. He was wooing these people in the way that he had once wooed their mother, promising her that Frank would be safe shortly before his corpse was found by the side of a road. McGuinness had earned their mother's trust, purely, it seemed, to take away from her the thing she cared about most in her life.

Rose Hegarty died five years before Martin McGuinness announced that he was running to be the next president of the

Republic of Ireland. Frank's siblings could either watch his presidential campaign in silence, or they could act.

A month before the Irish people went to the polls, Frank's siblings contacted the journalist Suzanne Breen, and spoke to her for a piece that appeared in the *Daily Mail* under the headline 'A Path Paved With Blood'.[8] Next to it was a picture of Frank's corpse and the lane where he had been found. They had not been put up to this, Frank's sisters were quoted as saying. Nor were they trying to score a political point. They only wanted people to understand the other side to Martin McGuinness. 'We hope and pray the people of Ireland will see through the façade.' They described the Sinn Féin man kneeling at their mother's feet, promising her that Frank would be safe. 'We are still haunted by thoughts of Frank's last hours, of him being interrogated and tortured.' Rose never got over her son's murder, they said. She had once spoken out to *The Cook Report*. 'We're now speaking out, too, as three sisters who dearly loved their brother and still miss him so much.'

The nature of the presidential campaign changed almost at once. Other families of IRA victims came forward to condemn McGuinness. The father of Patrick Kelly, an Irish soldier who was killed by the IRA in 1983, confronted the presidential hopeful in front of the cameras, asking him who had killed his son. Several days later, in a televised RTE debate, the moderator, Miriam O'Callaghan, asked Martin McGuinness if it would be humiliating for him to be confronted by relatives of IRA victims as president of Ireland. She then asked the other candidates in the debate if they thought he was even fit to run for office, before moving on to religious belief. Turning to McGuinness, she asked: 'How do you square, Martin McGuinness, with your God, the fact that you were involved in the murder of so many people?'[9]

Martin McGuinness was taken aback. He had been hoping to set out why he should be the next Irish president. Instead, he spent the last few weeks of his campaign firefighting stories about his IRA past. He denied having had any involvement in Frank Hegarty's death. According to one report, he 'said obliquely that he does not want to divulge any information for the sake of the Hegarty family'.[10] But the damage had been done. Martin McGuinness's presidential campaign fell away over the next two weeks, and having once been the frontrunner, he finished in third place. He had tried to put Frank's murder behind him but was unable to escape the truth of what had happened. Even if he had not heard the four shots in the night that had ended Frank's life, they continued to echo around him.

Gerry Adams blamed the 'southern media' for his friend's defeat, adding that 'Martin was a wee bit shocked' by the tone of the questions from Irish journalists.[11] His Sinn Féin colleague, Mary Lou McDonald, felt that McGuinness was just too much of an outsider for the southern political establishment. 'In part, it's to do with class,' she said. 'The hungry streets of Derry meeting the comfortable affluence of Dublin 4.'[12] But pretty much everyone else drew a straight line between McGuinness's defeat and his IRA past. The *Daily Mail* article about Frank's death had changed the narrative around the McGuinness campaign, and Middle Ireland cooled on the idea of having a former paramilitary as president.

It was a rare defeat for Martin McGuinness, and not one that he found easy to shake off. Something about this experience had an effect on him, and began to change the way he thought about his past. The following year, he agreed to meet the Queen, having previously refused to do so. The moment in which these two shook hands became an iconic one. It spoke to the future and suggested a capacity within both to reach for forgiveness and reconciliation.

Very soon after, Martin McGuinness gave a speech that seemed to mark a break with his life until then. 'I genuinely regret every single life that was lost during that conflict,' he said – words that some people had thought he would never find it in himself to say. 'I want every family who lost a loved one to know that your pain is not being ignored,' McGuinness went on, adding that he was 'willing to work with others to find a way to deal with our past so that we can complete our journey to true reconciliation'.[13]

He did not say how. Perhaps he did not know. But something inside him appeared to have changed. The weather of his mind had cleared. 'Regrettably, the past cannot be changed or undone,' he said the following year. 'It would be hypocritical for me to seek to distance myself from the consequences of the armed struggle or the IRA's role in it,' he admitted, before adding, 'I was once in the IRA. I am now a peace builder. I don't expect anyone to take me at my word. I expect them to take me by my deeds.'[14]

Martin McGuinness was moving towards a larger understanding of who he was and what he had done. It was a defining shift – one that suggested a new self-awareness. The two paths in his life had at last begun to converge. To go forward, he understood that he also needed to go back. The same was true for many people in Northern Ireland.

Kevin Winters had pushed and pushed. He had been told there was no money for an investigation into Stakeknife and it would take too long. But he kept going. Winters was also being approached by families who had heard about his work, and who believed their loved one might have been killed by Freddie Scappaticci. He heard as well from individuals who said that they themselves had been interrogated by him. Winters's firm was soon representing twenty-five victims and victims' families. One of these was the family of Frank Hegarty.

The breakthrough came in 2015, seven years after Kevin Winters began to push for an investigation into Stakeknife. The police ombudsman produced a confidential report on cases that might have involved this former army agent. It was passed to the Director of Public Prosecutions, who said it made for 'chilling reading', and issued a referral under Section 35 (5) of the Justice (Northern Ireland) Act. This required the police to start an investigation. Several months later, he issued another referral. This was the result of Freddie Scappaticci's sworn affidavit that he was not Stakeknife, in which he appeared to have perjured himself.

There was no way back now. A police investigation into Scappaticci was going to happen. The chief constable of the Police Service of Northern Ireland, George Hamilton, felt that it should be handled by an independent team. He spoke to Jon Boutcher, at Bedfordshire Police, and asked if he would consider leading this new investigation, codenamed Operation Kenova. Boutcher spoke to various people about whether to take on the job, most of whom said it was a waste of his time, as Stakeknife was never going to appear in court and he would not be able to arrest him. But Jon Boutcher liked a challenge.

In the Dock

One day in January 2018, a team of police officers gathered outside a detached suburban house on a quiet street in Surrey. They had come to arrest the man inside. The building looked similar to any other on that street, except the privet hedge in the front garden was unusually tall. Neighbours would joke with the owner, Frank, saying that he must have something to hide.

'Frank' was Freddie Scappaticci, and he had a lot to hide. His house contained a hidden network of cameras, alarms, and panic buttons that were monitored around the clock by specialists from MI5.

Scappaticci's life during the fifteen years since he had been outed as Stakeknife was mostly quiet, sedentary, and unremarkable. At first, he had tried to ride out the storm of media interest. But once he realised that it was not safe for him to remain in Belfast, he left his family and went into witness protection. For a short time, he lived in Scotland. He was occasionally in London. He spent a lot of time in the Manchester area and would go as often as possible to the Etihad Stadium to see his beloved Manchester City play football. But he spent most of his exile from Northern Ireland in an ordinary-looking house on the outskirts of Guildford.

Freddie Scappaticci may have led a simple life, but he was not short of money. He drove a silver Mercedes and owned at least one property in London, which he purchased in 2010 for roughly £400,000. He would take his wife, Sheila, still living in Belfast, on holiday to the Canary Islands. During his time as an army agent, Scappaticci had received regular payments, and most of these were invested on his behalf. Recently, his savings had been bolstered by a large payout from the *News of the World* after it emerged, during a police investigation, that they had paid a private investigator to hack Scappaticci's phone, probably in the hope of locating him and running a story about his secret life. As well as the payout, this led to an injunction preventing anyone from disclosing his whereabouts or publishing an up-to-date photograph of him.

Freddie Scappaticci was safe. He had money. His location was a carefully guarded secret. He did not wake up each morning worrying that he might not survive the day. He had a chocolate-coloured cocker spaniel, which he took for walks on a nearby heath. After joining a dog-walking group, he briefly fell in love with a local woman, and would take her out to the local Pizza Express before they went back to his car 'for a fumble'.[1] At one point, Scappaticci told her that he had once been a spy in the IRA. She thought he was making it up.

The relationship did not last, however, and Freddie Scappaticci became increasingly lonely. He would spend long hours at home on his Lenovo laptop, looking at websites devoted to cars, porn, maps, combat, politics, football, or the British Army.[2] After 2016, he would also visit the website of Operation Kenova, the police investigation into him and his activities. He knew that one day they might come for him. He also imagined that the people protecting him would tip him off first. But they did not. That was because Boutcher's team had kept MI5 entirely in the dark about what was about to happen.

On that day in January 2018, there was a knock at Freddie Scappaticci's door. He opened it and saw a team of police officers. They explained that they were part of Operation Kenova and had come to arrest him on the suspicion of murder, torture, and kidnap. Scappaticci did not resist arrest. He was taken to a secure location and began to be questioned by two detectives.[3]

Jon Boutcher had made his first move. He had arrested a man who many people thought to be above the law. For some police officers, the arrest is inevitably the most satisfying part of an investigation. It brings a feeling of complete control, a sense of mission accomplished that only fades away as lawyers, judges, and juries become involved.

But any gratification that Boutcher might have felt in the moments after Scappaticci's arrest was tempered by the knowledge that the man he now had in custody was unlikely to speak to his detectives. Scappaticci was, after all, someone who understood better than most people the dynamics of interrogation. One man who had been questioned by Scappaticci, and survived, remembered the way his inquisitor switched 'from reasonable to homicidal in a flash'. 'Nothing could prepare you for it. I felt utterly disorientated. I felt vulnerable. I felt that, if this went on much longer, I would let something slip.'[4] Scappaticci was said to have studied interrogation techniques, and knew how to stonewall during an interview. Questioned by detectives working for John Stevens, back in 2004, he remained silent throughout the formal part of the interview, only speaking once the recording device had been turned off.

'Look boys,' he had said. 'I'm not the monster people think I am.'[5]

That was it.

Fourteen years later, Scappaticci was interviewed under caution again, but this time by two of Jon Boutcher's detectives. The same thing happened. He said nothing, and the detectives came away empty-handed. Scappatacci was released. But Boutcher had other reasons for making this arrest.

'There are many who see now as the right time to speak and help us get to the truth,' Boutcher told one journalist, in the hours after

Scappaticci went into custody. 'I ask that anyone, from whatever organisation or community, who might be able to contribute to that truth come forward to speak either to me directly or the team.'⁶

Arresting Scappaticci was Boutcher's way of showing the world that this man was not untouchable. It was also a way to assert himself over MI5. Although he had a good working relationship with the police in Northern Ireland and the Army, and a small team of his detectives was embedded within each organisation, his dealings so far with MI5 continued to play out in a different key. He had found them to be consistently less helpful.

This was, in part, a reflection of the service's history. Even if senior MI5 officers had accepted their archives would sometimes need to be accessed by criminal investigations, and had taken on more lawyers to prepare for this, for most of MI5's existence, it had only really been accountable to itself. The main worry within MI5 was that they might by mistake hand over documents endangering individuals who had provided information in the past. The other reason for this caginess was MI5's own relationship with Scappaticci. They had benefitted from his intelligence over the years, and now they were responsible for looking after him.

That was not all. Boutcher was building a case against Scappaticci as well as former IRA personnel, police officers, soldiers, and, crucially, a number of men and women who had worked as MI5 officers. Some of the frostiness towards Boutcher and his investigation probably came from a desire to protect their own.

Jon Boutcher had suspected for some time that MI5 may not have handed over everything they had on Scappaticci, and later that year he was proved right. In December 2018, detectives working for Operation Kenova discovered a new cache of historical Stakeknife material in MI5's central London headquarters. Most of the documents were held on microfiche. They were, according to one source, 'very telling about the role that our man' – Scappaticci – 'played in certain things. They are documents that the service had kept that they probably should have got rid of.'[7]

Relations between Operation Kenova and MI5 became even worse. 'Boutcher has', *The Times* reported, 'upset quite a few people at the service.' When a member of the Kenova team was asked for a comment on this, he replied crabbily, 'MI5 are simply bad people'.[8] It was unusual to hear a police officer say something like this in public, and a sign of just how bad relations had become.

Some intelligence officers wondered if this had become personal for Jon Boutcher, and whether he had some kind of vendetta against the service.[9] Senior police officers were sometimes envious of MI5 and resented being told what to do by them. He insisted, however, that this was not the case. 'It is not a witch-hunt,' he told one reporter. 'It is not a rewriting of history, but it is an authentic search for the truth. It is an investigation that will pull no punches, taking place for the families who have never had an investigation.'[10]

MI5 soon agreed to give members of Boutcher's team more access to their archives. Each morning, detectives from Operation Kenova arrived at MI5 headquarters overlooking the River Thames and would spend the day trawling through classified material for evidence that they could use against Freddie Scappaticci and those who ran him. 'Every couple of weeks,' it was reported, 'they find a new document that they haven't seen before.'[11] Boutcher asked the MI5 director general to provide a written statement setting out everything he knew about Stakeknife. Each of the four retired heads of MI5 – including Stella Rimington, then aged eighty-three, and Stephen Lander, who had once run Joint Section in Belfast – was told to do the same.

Boutcher then arrested Freddie Scappaticci for a second time. His detectives had found on his laptop several hundred sexual images, including some which involved animals. Looking at his search history, they saw thirteen entries for extreme pornography.

Freddie Scappaticci was charged with two counts of possession of extreme pornographic images, and he appeared in Westminster Magistrates' Court less than an hour after Boutcher's team announced the charges. He sat in the dock wearing green tracksuit bottoms and a scruffy blue fleece. Scap looked haggard and old. He had been suffering from depression, he told the magistrate, and had attempted suicide. He had no sexual interest in animals, he assured her, and was more interested in 'women with big breasts'.[12]

As Freddie Scappaticci explained his Internet search history to the magistrate, Boutcher watched from the back of the court. This was a version of the moment he must have imagined to himself countless times. Perhaps it had figured in his dreams. Stakeknife was at last in court, answering charges put together by his team. He was in the dock, and was being forced to defend himself.

The trouble was, it was a magistrates' court, and these charges had nothing to do with his time in the IRA. A man alleged to have carried out multiple murders had been charged instead with possession of pornography. The magistrate hardly knew what to make of it. She noted that he had not appeared in court for fifty years. (His last court appearance was in Belfast at the start of the Troubles.) 'That's good character in my book,' she said. He was sentenced to three months in custody, suspended for twelve months – the judicial equivalent of a rap on the knuckles.[13]

One lawyer familiar with this episode described it as 'bonkers'.[14] Bringing Stakeknife before a magistrate like this seemed to be less about criminal justice than optics. Clearly, Boutcher wanted to demonstrate that Freddie Scappaticci was not 'too big to jail', as some people believed. Perhaps it also reflected a deeper change within the man leading this investigation.

There was a time earlier in his career when Jon Boutcher came across as the kind of police officer who would never go up against MI5 in public. But something had shifted. He was starting to feel that this investigation was about more than justice. It was also about, in a wider sense, Britain's response to historic episodes of this kind. 'It's what sets us apart as a democracy', he said, 'that having been unable to deal with these cases properly at the time, due to the danger that existed for everyone, we should now do whatever we can to give families information.'[15]

Boutcher's motivation might have changed, but by the summer of 2019, three years after the start of Operation Kenova, it was still unclear whether he was going to find a way to get Scappaticci behind bars. Boutcher had a team of more than seventy detectives working for him by this stage. They had gathered over 10,000 documents and taken roughly a thousand statements. There had never before been a murder investigation in Britain on this scale. Boutcher's team had also uncovered new forensic evidence using technology that was not available to earlier police investigations. More recently, Boutcher had hired one of the country's leading criminal barristers, Jonathan Laidlaw QC, who had previously prosecuted Al-Qaeda operatives and the IRA team accused of planting the 1996 Canary Wharf bomb. Laidlaw was there to bring his investigation to a conclusion.

In some ways, the problem Boutcher faced was about knowing when to stop. Similar to writing a work of non-fiction, it is possible for anyone leading an investigation like this to become trapped in a mindset where they never have enough material, and there is always another scrap of evidence to chase down, one more person to interview, a final lead to follow up . . . The hardest part of an investigation like Operation Kenova was knowing when to let go.

Jon Boutcher decided, at last, that he had enough evidence. On a busy day in 2019, he submitted twelve case files to the Director of Public Prosecutions in Northern Ireland. In these, he recommended that Freddie Scappaticci and more than twenty other individuals – among them IRA volunteers and former members of the armed forces and MI5 – be prosecuted for a series of crimes, including kidnap, perverting the course of justice, grievous bodily harm, and murder.[16] Nine of the files related to murder offences. More would follow in the months ahead until there were thirty-three case files under consideration that covered more than twenty murders.

'Kenova is one hundred per cent confident', one of Boutcher's detectives said, that these submissions were 'way over the threshold for the evidential test.'[17] If the Director of Public Prosecutions agreed, then the next step was for the attorney general to decide whether criminal prosecution was in the public interest. After that, Scappaticci and others could appear in court.

The case files being read by the Director of Public Prosecutions were full of eye-opening detail, but they did not read like historical accounts of what had happened. They concerned a series of charging decisions. The Director of Public Prosecutions had to decide whether there was enough evidence for the individuals listed in the files to be charged with specific crimes, and the only people who could be charged were those who were still alive.

Boutcher had played his hand. Now he had to wait for everyone else to play theirs.

39

Óglach

Two years earlier, in 2017, Martin McGuinness died at the age of sixty-six, following a brief illness. Operation Kenova was at the time still a long way off putting together case files, and his death meant that he would never be charged by Boutcher's team.

On the day of McGuinness's funeral, large parts of Derry came to a standstill and many schools and shops were closed. Although some people chose to stay away, thousands of mourners came out to line the streets as his coffin moved through the city. Many held up their phones to record the moment. The air was filled with the drone of bagpipes and smatterings of applause that sounded like birds breaking cover.

Even if McGuinness had not been given a state funeral, at times it felt like one. The service in St Columba's Church was attended by political dignitaries, including Bill Clinton, the former US president, who told the congregation that he had come 'to treasure every minute I spent with Martin McGuinness'.[1] One of the mourners listening to Clinton speak was Arlene Foster, leader of the Democratic Unionist Party, whose father had almost been killed by the IRA. She had been weighing up whether to attend right up to the night before, and her arrival in the church that morning was met with an ovation.

In the following days, Martin McGuinness's widow, Bernie,

received hundreds of messages of condolence from her husband's friends and neighbours, his colleagues, and many others, including the US President Barack Obama. She also received a personal message of condolence from the Queen.

Martin McGuinness was laid to rest after the funeral in Derry City Cemetery, in the Republican Plot reserved for IRA volunteers. The atmosphere out here, as his coffin was lowered into the ground, felt different, and in the speeches by his grave there were more references to his other life – the one he had before entering government. When his headstone went up several weeks later, a part of the inscription read 'MP MLA Minister' – a nod to his career as a politician; but above this were the words 'Óglach Martin McGuinness', *óglach* being the Irish word used by the IRA to refer to its volunteers, followed by 'Óglaigh na hÉireann', which is how the IRA describes itself. In death, it seemed that McGuinness had found a way to reconcile the different parts of himself.

In the months after his funeral, one question about Martin McGuinness began to be asked more openly on the streets of Derry, and elsewhere across the region. Given everything that had come out about all the spies inside the IRA, was it possible that McGuinness could have been one of them? If someone as senior as Scappaticci was an agent, then why not McGuinness?

It was the kind of question that no self-respecting republican would have dared to ask during the Troubles. But times had changed, and for those disillusioned republicans who felt let down by the Good Friday Agreement the answer was obvious: of course he was. If you didn't believe that, you weren't thinking about it hard enough. The idea that Martin McGuinness had been a British agent all along seemed to explain everything for them – not just how he had been able to stay out of jail for many years, but the way he remained at such a senior level of the IRA for so long.

But all the evidence suggests that Martin McGuinness was never taken on as an agent. He was more important than that. Instead, he was singled out as early as 1981, along with Gerry Adams, as someone with the ability and desire to steer the IRA towards a political settlement. Once this had become clear to the British, the case for taking on either man as an agent fell apart. From a practical, legal, and moral point of view, it made more sense to protect them both rather than recruit either one. This explains why attempts to kill each man came to nothing, and why the police were instructed, in 1993, not to charge Martin McGuinness in relation to Frank Hegarty's murder.

Gerry Adams was one of those leading the procession on the day of Martin McGuinness's funeral. He was there both as a friend and in his capacity as president of Sinn Féin. Two years later, the party that he and McGuinness had done so much to revive won 23 per cent of the vote in Northern Ireland at the British general election. Very soon after that, they won 25 per cent of the vote south of the border in the Irish general election. And several years later, in 2023, Sinn Féin exceeded even its own expectations by winning more local council seats than any other party in Northern Ireland.

These were astonishing results. The political experiment that Adams and McGuinness had started almost four decades earlier when they agreed to put up candidates for election on both sides of the border looked as if it might be about to come good. A party committed to Irish unification, which had once been infiltrated and assisted by agents working for MI5, had become almost the largest political force on the island of Ireland. Perhaps one day this would be seen as a part of McGuinness's legacy, alongside everything else.

40

Licence to Kill

In 2020, less than a year after Jon Boutcher submitted the first of his Stakeknife case files to the Director of Public Prosecutions, while he was still waiting to hear the decision, he learned about a controversial bill set to go before Parliament. One of the biggest problems his team had faced when building their case against Freddie Scappaticci was the lack of legislation setting out what a British agent could be authorised to do by their handler, and whether there were situations in which they might be allowed to commit a serious crime. This new law that had been proposed by the government would, for the first time, give agent handlers from MI5, SIS, the police, and a surprisingly long list of other agencies, the power to authorise their agents to participate in criminal activity.

Critics of this bill called for an upper limit on what government agents were permitted to do. For example, no agent should ever take part in a sexual crime or murder. But the argument against this was that having a list of proscribed activities, according to the intelligence agencies, would allow any terrorist group to rid itself of spies simply by asking its members to carry out a task that was on the list. For this reason, the new legislation would not set an upper limit on how far a British spy could go. If, at any point in the future, an agent like Freddie Scappaticci found himself in the equivalent of the

IRA's Nutting Squad, then under the provisions of the bill that was about to go before Parliament, he could be authorised to take part in killing a suspected informer. The title of the proposed legislation was the Covert Human Intelligence Sources (Criminal Conduct) Bill, but this was hard to remember, so the media began to refer to it as the 'licence to kill' bill.

A Rubicon had been crossed. For decades, the question of whether British government agents should have essentially a licence to kill was too sensitive to go before Parliament and was 'best played long' – if it was ever played at all.[1] Now that had changed. Part of the reason for this shift was a recent ruling by the Investigatory Powers Tribunal, an independent oversight body that handled complaints against Britain's intelligence agencies. It had shown that the law surrounding agent criminality was seriously inadequate and needed to change.

The other reason for this controversial bill going before Parliament was the investigation into Freddie Scappaticci. Boutcher had shown that it was possible to build a watertight criminal case against a British agent. He had demonstrated that the country's intelligence agencies were more vulnerable than they had realised.

The atmosphere in the House of Commons as the bill began to be debated was subdued and sober. As one Conservative politician put it, 'those of us who like the red meat of law enforcement and law and order' were being asked 'to look inside the abattoir, and of course we do not like what we see'.[2] Perhaps this was a reflection of a deeper contradiction. The attitude that so many of us have towards our spies and what they should be allowed to do is surprisingly personal. It shows us as we are when we think nobody is looking. As John le Carré wrote, the secret world is 'the collective couch where the subconscious of each nation is confessed'. Listening to the debate in the House of Commons was like eavesdropping on a conversation that was meant to be held in private. Nobody was used to having the inner workings of espionage set out in the open like this.

One of the politicians who spoke that day in Parliament was Labour's shadow security minister, Conor McGinn, the son of a Sinn Féin councillor and someone who had grown up in Northern Ireland during the Troubles. 'I do not need to be convinced about the consequences of the state exceeding its power in this arena,' he told the house. 'I do not need to hear it in a meeting because I and the community in which I grew up live with the consequences of it, which is why we need to get this right.' But he would not oppose the bill. McGinn and his party wanted amendments, but he believed it was better to have something on statute about what spies like Freddie Scappaticci could do than nothing. The lesson from the past was that the greatest danger occurred when Crown servants were forced to operate in areas that were not covered by the law.

The bill was passed. British agents could now be authorised by their handlers or case officers to take part in criminal activity within the United Kingdom. It was a landmark in the history of British intelligence. The 'necessary hypocrisy' that the journalist and author Janet Malcolm once described appeared to have been written into law. The price that is sometimes paid for peace was no longer a secret. The world of intelligence had become more accountable, in a way that was hard to imagine forty years earlier.

Jon Boutcher followed all this with interest, and must have been relieved to see that this new law could not be applied retrospectively. Freddie Scappaticci and the others named in his case files were still liable to be charged. Stakeknife remained on course to appear in court. All Boutcher had to do was keep waiting for a decision from the Director of Public Prosecutions. He knew that the evidence he had put together was extremely strong. He was confident about the quality of the submissions, and it was hard to imagine what could get in the way of this going to court.

*

Not long after, on a bright autumn day in 2021, Dennis Hutchings joined a protest in Parliament Square. He was an eighty-year-old suffering from an incurable kidney disease, and had once served in the British Army. Hutchings was surrounded by army veterans and their supporters. There were only a few hundred of them, but they were well organised, and clear about what they wanted.

The protesters had come to voice their concern about former British soldiers being tried for incidents that had taken place during the Troubles. One of these was Dennis Hutchings, who was due to stand trial later that year on the charge of attempted murder. This was in relation to the 1974 killing, in County Tyrone, of John Pat Cunningham, a man with a learning difficulty who was shot in the back as he ran away from an army patrol.[3] Hutchings was one of the soldiers who had opened fire. But he did not believe that Cunningham had been killed by a bullet from his gun. Several months later, Hutchings attended court in Belfast. This was the last journey he ever made. After three days on trial, Hutchings caught Covid-19; the court was adjourned, and he died later that day.

Shortly after the protest in Parliament Square, the Queen processed into the House of Lords and sat down on the Sovereign's Throne, a gilded Victorian affair, and read out the government's agenda for the next parliamentary session. She described no fewer than thirty-one different bills, including one that was greeted by the protesters with relief.

The Northern Ireland Troubles (Legacy and Reconciliation) Bill sounded at first like the government making good on its earlier pledge to protect army veterans such as Dennis Hutchings. But the text went much further than many people expected. This bill proposed an amnesty, in all but name, for every crime which had taken place during the Troubles in Northern Ireland. It would prevent former soldiers from being prosecuted, as well as paramilitaries, policemen and women, and civilians. It also offered immunity to agents such as Freddie Scappaticci. In other words, this new bill would kill off Operation Kenova. Boutcher had already played his hand. Now someone had put down a royal flush.

Where had this legislation come from? Those close to the process would tell you right away that it had not originated with the prime minister, Boris Johnson. Yes, he had agreed to it. But he was not the source. Nor did this bill sound like something dreamed up inside the Northern Ireland Office, the government department which had its name on the bill.

One of the journalists covering this story was Sean O'Neill, chief reporter at *The Times*. He recognised that this new law would end the criminal investigation into the man he called 'Britain's most important double agent inside the IRA' – Freddie Scappaticci. O'Neill was also curious about where it had come from. 'I cannot help but wonder if', he wrote, 'the real energy behind this bill is the desire of the shadowy guardians of "national security" to ensure that the Stakeknife story is never aired in a court of law.[4]

From the moment Freddie Scappaticci was outed as Stakeknife, back in 2003, one question that began to be asked was how far the people looking after him would go to keep him out of court. Here, it seemed, was an answer. But this was about more than Scappaticci. Jon Boutcher's investigation was set to incriminate him as well as a number of former intelligence officers. This new law would keep them all out of court.

The fact that Scappaticci might never take the stand was also significant given what he had begun to say to those looking after him. By this point in his life, Scap had no hobbies, few interests, and even fewer friends. He had recently had a stroke. The last time he was ill, Sheila, his wife, came over from Belfast to look after him. But she had died in 2019, shortly after Boutcher's files were submitted. Scappaticci had nobody left. What had once been a life was starting to look more like a bare existence. His world was beginning to be presided over by his own paranoia, and he found it hard to trust the people looking after him. He was also furious at the thought of defending himself in court as a result of Jon Boutcher's investigation.

The way Freddie Scappaticci saw it, he had performed a valuable service for the British state. He had done the right thing by them, and now they were coming after him. It felt wrong, and made him increasingly angry. If he were to end up in court, he said, he was not going to maintain a dignified silence. He would name names and give up everything he knew. If he was going down, everyone else was coming with him. The new bill going through Parliament would ensure that this could never happen.

Boutcher was left staring at what one commentator called a 'legislative guillotine'.[5] If the bill was passed, his investigation was effectively over. His team of seventy-two detectives had spent the last five years investigating Stakeknife, at a cost of more than £31 million.[6] Boutcher himself had been working up to ten hours a day, sometimes seven days a week. The job had taken over his life. He had even brought forward his retirement as chief constable of Bedfordshire Police to devote more time to Operation Kenova, and had worked hard to gain access to files held by MI5, the Ministry of Defence, and the police, and to keep his investigation compliant with Article 2 of the ECHR. His team had overcome an array of challenges, whether MI5's reluctance to share material or attempts by the modern-day incarnation of the IRA to intimidate some of the individuals they wanted to interview.

Now the whole thing looked like it was about to go up in smoke. Frank Hegarty's family would be denied criminal justice, and the same was true for most families who had lost a loved one during the Troubles. There were thought to be more than a thousand unsolved murders dating back to this period.

But there was still hope. Boutcher might yet see Freddie Scappaticci charged with murder. The Director of Public Prosecutions could reach a decision *before* this bill became law, and its passage through Parliament looked as if it might take longer than the government had expected – certainly if the initial reaction to it was anything to go by.

Politicians across Northern Ireland, as well as lawyers, academics, and the relatives of those killed during the Troubles seemed to be united in their condemnation of the new government bill. The commissioner for human rights at the Council of Europe, Dunja Mijatovic, went on the record to express her grave concern about 'unilaterally shutting down options that many victims and families value greatly'.[7] A group of US Congress members denounced the government's proposed legislation as a 'massive cover-up' that would take Northern Ireland backwards, with one representative saying it sounded more extreme than the 1978 amnesty introduced by the Chilean dictator Augusto Pinochet.[8]

Amid the uproar, one part of this proposal was often overlooked. Alongside what was effectively a legal amnesty, the government planned to set up a new body called the Independent Commission for Reconciliation and Information Recovery (ICRIR). This would 'deliver as much information as possible, to as many people as possible, as quickly as possible'.[9] In most Troubles cases, the chances of a successful criminal prosecution were vanishingly small and justice was all but out of reach. The new law would give perpetrators immunity from prosecution if they cooperated with this truth-recovery body. Anyone who refused could still end up in court. The government hoped that this would give families a better chance of finding out the truth about what had happened to their loved one, even if, as a consequence, it removed the small possibility of criminal justice. Perhaps they were right. Maybe this would release some people from the grip of the past.

Jon Boutcher had every right to be furious about the new bill, but if he was, he gave no sign of it. Long before the legislation was announced, he had begun to hint at a different ending to the story of Operation Kenova. 'Outcomes should not be judged by criminal justice processes alone,' he had said, adding that in many cases, victims' families were not clamouring to see Scappaticci in court.[10] 'Most relatives have told me they want the truth of what happened, in particular the "how" and "why" of their loved ones' deaths, rather than a criminal prosecution.'[11]

When Boutcher first appeared before the media, back in 2016, his priority was to see Stakeknife appear in the dock. There was no doubt about that. It was how he had always worked: He would gather the evidence, build the case, and have the suspect charged. But things had changed since then. Boutcher had shaped Kenova, and at the same time it had moved something inside him. The resistance he had come up against when trying to access MI5 material seemed to have ignited in him a desire to reveal more about what had happened in the shadows during the Troubles than a criminal case might disclose. If he had come into Operation Kenova wanting justice, he, like the families for whom he was fighting, was beginning to have more of an interest in sharing the truth. The people of Northern Ireland deserved a better understanding of what had happened. The past could not be hidden away. It needed a proper burial.

Perhaps the only thing holding Boutcher back was that he had not yet finished his career in the police. In May 2022, while still waiting for a decision from the Director of Public Prosecutions, Boutcher put his name forward to be the next commissioner of the Metropolitan Police, the top job in British policing. He hoped to replace Cressida Dick, the woman who had been his superior in the operations room on the day that the Brazilian Jean Charles de Menezes was killed.

Boutcher made it to the final three in the selection process before being eliminated. He was close to retirement age now. Kenova was probably going to be his last job in policing. He owed nothing to anyone. His future was his own. It would not be long before he found out if Scappaticci was going to end up in court.

Escape

One night, in April 2023, US President Joe Biden arrived at Belfast International Airport in an oversized Boeing airliner known as Air Force One. Once the aircraft had come to a standstill, he made his way carefully down the steps to the tarmac below. Biden grinned through the cold and the wind, shook hands with the new British prime minister, Rishi Sunak, and was soon in his car – a bulletproof, armour-plated monster called The Beast. Light gusts of snow buffeted the runway. The photographers hurried back inside. Biden's motorcade slipped out of the airport and began to make its way towards the city centre.

President Biden was in the region to mark the twenty-fifth anniversary of the Good Friday Agreement. He had been one of the US senators to accompany Bill Clinton on his trip to Northern Ireland in 1998 to build support for these accords. Although Biden would soon be south of the border to visit his ancestral homeland, the emphasis that day was on Northern Ireland, twenty-five years of hard-won peace, and the prospect of a better and more prosperous future. On almost any other day, the president's arrival would have been the main story in Northern Ireland, but today was different.

Fewer than five hours before President Biden's arrival, as he began to cross the Atlantic Ocean, it was reported that Freddie Scappaticci had died. The story dominated the news. Obituaries appeared in the *Daily Telegraph*, *The Times*, and the *Financial Times*. Scappaticci was described as a 'top IRA enforcer', an 'icy IRA inquisitor', and 'the man said to be the British Army's top undercover agent within the Provisional IRA'.[1]

Jon Boutcher's seven-year-long pursuit of Scappaticci was over. The Director of Public Prosecutions was no longer required to consider possible charges against this individual now that he was dead. The man Boutcher had chased for so long had, in death, made the ultimate escape.

'The very nature of historical investigations', Boutcher said soon after the news was announced, shortly before Biden touched down, 'will mean a higher likelihood that old age may catch up with those affected, be they perpetrators, witnesses, victims, family members, or those who simply lived through those times'. But this was not the end, he stressed. 'We remain committed to providing families with the truth of what happened to their loved ones.' If Boutcher could not deliver criminal justice, he would, as he had become increasingly committed to doing, try everything he could to give them the truth.

Several weeks earlier, Boutcher had gone to see Frank Mulhern, whose son, Joe, was thought to have been killed in 1993 by Freddie Scappaticci. Frank Mulhern had campaigned hard to find out what happened to his son, but it seemed that he would never know, having been told by his doctors that he had just weeks to live.

Jon Boutcher had been unable to give Frank Mulhern his day in court, but he knew that instead he could offer him a final chapter in the story that had taken over his life. Soon after he heard that Frank Mulhern was dying, Boutcher went to see him in hospital. He sat with him, and told him everything he knew about his son's death. Boutcher gave him the truth. He did so quietly, and without committing anything to paper. He provided the dying man with a different kind of ending.

Frank Mulhern died several days later. 'Frank may not have got justice,' someone close to him said, 'but he closed his eyes knowing the exact truth.'[2]

Boutcher would speak to other families in the months ahead. One of those on his list was Frank Hegarty's. The conversations Boutcher had with the victims' families were private, and we will never know exactly what was said. But it is possible to imagine what he might have said to the Hegartys.

We know that Frank Hegarty was interrogated in May 1986 by three senior IRA men and that one of them was Martin McGuinness. We also know that they came away from this convinced that Frank was a British agent, and within the IRA the punishment for that was death. But the sentence had to be approved by at least one member of the IRA Army Council. All three of Frank's interrogators belonged to the council, but the one with the strongest connection to this case and the most to gain from Frank's death in terms of his reputation among the hardliners was McGuinness. It is extremely hard to imagine anyone other than Martin McGuinness giving the order to have Frank Hegarty killed.

Who pulled the trigger? One of the most compelling pieces of evidence that Boutcher's team found in their investigation was the recording of Freddie Scappaticci speaking to the team behind *The Cook Report*. His account of Frank's murder was unexpectedly detailed, and, as we know, included facts which could only have been known by someone present when Frank died. Scappaticci suggested that there were four shots in the night, as indeed there were. He also went to considerable lengths to play down the importance of the man, or men, who pulled the trigger. Everything he said was consistent with the idea that he, Freddie Scappaticci, was instructed by Martin McGuinness to carry out this murder, and that he went through with it because he could see no way to get out of it.

Jon Boutcher's team also heard a plausible explanation for the masking tape found over Frank's eyes. Shortly before his murder, the IRA was said to have killed another suspected informer using a new and more powerful weapon, which had the horrific effect of dislodging the victim's eyeballs. The family was convinced that their loved one must have had his eyes gouged out during the interrogation.[3] To spare the Hegarty family a similar kind of anguish, and to give them the possibility of an open casket at the wake, someone involved in Frank's murder had made sure to cover his eyes with masking tape before he was killed. This detail underlines the savage intimacy of this slaughter. The killers were thinking about the pain they were about to inflict on Frank's family even before they committed the murder.

One of the people who carried the heaviest burden of grief in the years after Frank Hegarty's murder was his mother, Rose. She died some years before Jon Boutcher could sit down with her relatives and tell them what he knew about Frank's death. Shortly before her own death, Rose gave instructions for where she would like to be buried. She asked to be interred in the same grave as Frank, so that, in death, they could be together again.

Derry City Cemetery is open at most times of day, and it is not hard to find the grave of Rose and Frank Hegarty. The headstone is a short distance up the hill from the Republican Plot and on higher ground than McGuinness's grave. It also faces the other way to his, so that when you stand to read the inscription, you can see in the background a generous sweep of the city.

This is where Rose and Frank's journeys came to an end – one in a time of peace, the other in a time of conflict. The love between mother and son was such that both struggled in their own ways to live apart. Even though he tried, Frank was unable to start a new life overseas in some ways because it would mean being away from his mother. Rose could never reconcile herself to the betrayal by

McGuinness which had led to her beloved son's death. Some people might have withdrawn into themselves in the face of this, but Rose decided to fight for the truth about Frank's murder to come out, and her family did the same after her death.

Without all this, Freddie Scappaticci would never have spoken to the television producers, and the story of Frank's murder would not have remained in the public imagination in the way that it did. In all likelihood, Ian Hurst would not have come forward to lift the lid on the Stakeknife story. Martin McGuinness might have become the Irish president. At the very least, Rose ensured that more was known about the underground world in which her son had operated. The truth will not always lead to peace or reconciliation, but it is hard to heal without it.

Beyond the grave shared by Frank and Rose, you can make out the local greyhound track, as well as Derry's city walls, clumps of terraced houses, and fields in the distance that reach away from the city to the valley beyond. Birds gust overhead. The smell of grass fills the air. The traffic in the distance makes a light shuddering sound that reaches up to this part of the cemetery. There are moments when it feels as if everything in this vast panorama is held together by something that is just out of sight; that the shapeless presence of the past is here – a ghost longing for release – and will not leave until it has been seen.

Through the middle of this vista is the slow, seductive presence of the River Foyle. Like time itself, it creeps through the centre of the city with a head-down kind of seriousness. Overhead, clouds start to make way. The sun shimmers on the surface of the water. The river slides on past what was once the army barracks, beneath the bridges, and on, until it leaves the buildings behind, and somewhere out of sight it opens up to embrace the sea. In this silent meeting, a moment of closure and hope, one story draws to a close so that another one can begin.

Acknowledgements

Usually when I'm researching a book what I'll do is spend a year or so reading around the subject before starting to write. This tends to involve nothing more dramatic than visiting an archive or a nearby library. This book has been different, mainly because it's involved a long list of interviews with individuals who were connected to the story in some way. The interesting thing about these conversations was how little they had in common with each other. Some took more than a year to arrange. Others came about on the spur of the moment. One of them lasted less than a minute, and another was still going four hours after it had started. In almost all of them, I was in the position of interviewer, except for the time when I realised, on walking into the venue where we had agreed to meet, that I was the one to be interrogated. Most of these interviews were in the flesh, but the most revealing one was over the phone. What was also surprising, for me, was how hard I found it to predict, as we began to talk, what kind of conversation was about to unfold and where it would lead.

But if there is one thing that these interviews do share, it is that most of them were off-the-record. The majority of people I spoke to about this book have asked to remain anonymous. Rather than list here the interviewees who agreed to be named, I want to thank everyone who agreed to talk. I am enormously grateful for the time you gave, and, most of all, for the trust you placed in me. It would not have been possible for me to bring this story to light without your help.

One person I can name with more confidence is Jonathan Conway, my literary agent in the UK, to whom this book is dedicated. He was the first to hear about the idea for this story, and was instrumental in shaping the narrative and adding finesse. It's not often that you find someone whose literary instinct you trust just as much as you enjoy spending time with them. I'm extremely lucky to be represented by him.

I'd also like to thank George Lucas, at Inkwell Management, for his shrewd and timely insights into the text. Luke Speed, at Speed Literary and Talent Management, has done a fantastic job of helping to bring this story to the screen and I'm hugely grateful for all of his hard work. Thanks also to Anne Newman for her copy-edit, which was sensationally good – imaginative and wise, and at the same time sensitive to the spirit of what I was trying to do. It has made a huge difference to the text.

At Quercus, Ben Brock was the one to launch this ship and Richard Milner has steered it home. I am absolutely indebted to both of them, as well as Freya Alsop, and to Elizabeth Masters and Ana McLaughlin for all the effort and creativity they have put into promoting the book. It's been wonderful working with them again.

At PublicAffairs, Ben Adams and Clive Priddle have both played a critical part in shaping the manuscript, and, as usual, have asked all sorts of important and pertinent questions. I am forever grateful for their insight and the faith they've shown in this project from the start.

Closer to home, I want to thank Mattie and Sam for their love, their questions and their curiosity. And finally, my special thanks to Helena for, well, for everything. You are the ultimate playmate, office colleague (sort of), and partner-in-crime. I am in awe of the way you tell stories, your sense of adventure and the brilliant energy with which you come at the world. I can't thank you enough for all your help.

Notes

Prologue

1   Defence secretary to prime minister, 'Northern Ireland: Agent Resettlement', 2 May 1986, UK National Archives, PREM 19/1814.
2   'Coroner's Inquest relating to the death of Francis Gerald Hegarty who died 25 May 1986', 9 September 1989, Public Records Office of Northern Ireland, TYR/6/1/1/36/13.

Note to Reader

1   The Northern Ireland Veteran's Health and Wellbeing Study quoted in Larisa Brown, 'Veterans in Northern Ireland are traumatized from never leaving the battlefield', *The Times*, 22 April 2021.
2   K. C. Koenen, A. Ratanatharathorn et al., 'Posttraumatic stress disorder in the World Mental Health Surveys', *Psychological Medicine*, 2017, Volume 47, Number 13, pp. 2260–74.
3   Janet Malcolm, *The Journalist and the Murderer* (London: Granta, 2018), p. 153.
4   E. Alex Jung, 'Michaela Coal Isn't Going to Tweet This', *New York Magazine*, 1 February 2019.

PART ONE

Chapter 1

1   Darran Anderson, *Inventory* (London: Chatto & Windus, 2020), p. 236.

Chapter 2

1   Eamonn McCann quoted in Jude Collins, *Martin McGuinness* (Cork: Mercier Press, 2018), p. 114.

2   Kenneth Branagh quoted in Jonathan Dean, 'Kenneth Branagh on his boyhood flight from the Troubles and new film Belfast', *The Times*, 3 October 2021.

3   Brendan O'Leary, 'Mission Accomplished?', *Field Day Review*, researchgate.net, January 2005.

4   Tony Geraghty, *The Irish War* (London: HarperCollins, 1998), p. xvii.

5   'Brian' quoted in Peter Taylor, *Brits* (London: Bloomsbury, 2014), p. 25.

6   Bill Taylor quoted in Ken Wharton, *A Long, Long War* (London: Helion, 2008), p. 48.

7   'Officer from a Welsh Regiment' quoted in Ken Wharton, *A Long, Long War* (London: Helion, 2008), p. 54.

8   Confidential interview with ex-army officer quoted in M. Frampton, 'Agents and Ambushes: Britain's "Dirty War" in Northern Ireland', *Democracies at War Against Terrorism*, ed. Samy Cohen, (London: Palgrave Macmillan, 2008), pp. 77–100.

9   General Sir Ian Freeland quoted in David A. Charters, "Have A Go': British Army/MI5 Agent-running Operations in Northern Ireland, 1970–72', *Intelligence and National Security*, 2013, Volume 28, Issue 2, pp. 202–29.

Chapter 3

1   Gerry Doherty quoted in Eamonn Houston, 'Volunteer's Youth Taken by Involvement in War', *Daily Ireland*, 29 July 2005.

2   'Newssheet', Northern Ireland Office, quotation from *Daily Mirror*, cain.ulster.ac.uk.

3   'Tabulations (Tables) of Basic Variables', cain.ulster.ac.uk.

4   Major Mick Sullivan quoted in Ken Wharton, *A Long, Long War* (London: Helion, 2008), p. 123.

5   John Wilsey, *The Ulster Tales* (Barnsley: Pen and Sword, 2011), p. 50.

Chapter 4

1   Merlyn Rees and Frank King quoted in Thomas Leahy, *The Intelligence War against the IRA* (Cambridge: Cambridge University Press, 2020), p. 122.

2   Quoted in Dominic Sandbrook, *Who Dares Wins* (London: Penguin, 2020), p. 558.

3   Ian Cobain, *Anatomy of a Killing* (London: Granta, 2021), p. 47.

4   Peter Hennessy, *The New Protective State* (London: Bloomsbury, 2008), p. 17.

5   Jimmy Glover quoted in Peter Taylor, *The Provos* (London: Bloomsbury, 1998), p. 216.

6   Robert Armstrong to Margaret Thatcher, re. OD (79) 12, 13, 14, 15, 9 July 1979, UK National Archives, PREM 19/80.

7   Jimmy Glover quoted in 'The Long War', *Panorama*, BBC, first broadcast on 29 February 1988.

8   Planning Staff, 'South Armagh Area Review', March 1980, UK National Archives, CJ 4/3072.

9   Michael Asher quoted in John Newsinger, 'The truth, the whole truth . . .', *The Northern Ireland Troubles in Britain*, eds Graham Dawson, Jo Dover, and Stephen Hopkins, (Manchester: Manchester University Press, 2017), pp. 26–7.

10   Peter Taylor, *The Provos* (London: Bloomsbury, 1998), p. 228.

11   'Statement by I. R. A.', *New York Times*, 31 August 1979, p. 6.

12   Dominic Sandbrook, *Who Dares Wins* (London: Penguin, 2020), p. 561.

13   Brigadier David Thorne quoted in Charles Moore, *Margaret Thatcher: Volume 1* (London: Penguin, 2014), p. 482.

14   Margaret Thatcher, Note, 31 August 1979, UK National Archives, PREM 19/81.

15   UK National Archives, PREM 19/82.

16   Kenneth Stowe to Clive Whitmore, 2 July 1980, UK National Archives, PREM 19/281.

17   R. Harrington, Minutes of PM's Meeting on Security, 2 January 1980, UK National Archives, CJ 4/3116.

Chapter 5

1   Sean O'Callaghan, *The Informer* (London: Corgi, 1999), p. 93.

2   Dolours Price quoted in Patrick Radden Keefe, *Say Nothing* (London: William Collins, 2018), p. 348.

3   Thomas Blenerhasset, *A Direction for the Plantation in Ulster* (London), 1610, C4v.

4   Clare Jackson, *Devil-land* (London: Allen Lane, 2021), p. 1.

5   Tony Geraghty, *The Irish War* (London: HarperCollins, 1998), p. 266.

6   Andrew Boyd, *The Informers* (Cork: Mercier, 1984), pp. 15–16.

7   'Loose Talk Can Be Fatal', *An Phoblacht*, 25 January 1974, p. 4.

8   Kevin Toolis, *Rebel Hearts* (London: Picador, 2000), p. 294.

Chapter 6

1   John Hume quoted in Liam Clarke & Kathryn Johnston, *Martin McGuinness* (Edinburgh: Mainstream, 2001), p. 74.

2   Liam Clarke & Kathryn Johnston, *Martin McGuinness* (Edinburgh: Mainstream, 2001), p. 42.

3   Willie Carlin quoted in Aaron Edwards, *Agents of Influence* (Newbridge: Merrion, 2021), pp. 152–3.

4   Pat McArt quoted in Jude Collins, *Martin McGuinness* (Cork: Mercier Press, 2018), p. 324

5   Private information.

6   Mary Lou McDonald quoted in Jude Collins, *Martin McGuinness* (Cork: Mercier Press, 2018) p. 296.

7   Ed Moloney, *A Secret History of the IRA* (London: Penguin, 2007), p. 383.

8   Chistopher Andrew, *Defence of the Realm* (London: Penguin, 2012), p. 652.

9   'The Long War', *Panorama*, BBC, first broadcast on 29 February 1988.

10   Willie Carlin, *Thatcher's Spy* (Newbridge: Merrion Press, 2019), p. 152.

11   'Peter Taylor: Ireland After Partition', BBC2, first broadcast on 14 June 2021.

12   Frank Steele quoted in Peter Taylor, *The Provos* (London: Bloomsbury, 1998), pp. 138–9.

13   Martin McGuinness quoted in David McKittrick & David McVea, *Making Sense of the Troubles* (London: Viking, 2012), pp. 97–8.

14   Quoted in Freddie Cowper-Coles, '"Anxious for peace": the Provisional IRA in dialogue with the British government, 1972–5', *Irish Studies Review*, 2012, Volume 20, Issue 3, pp. 223–42.

Chapter 7

1   Willie Carlin quoted in Aaron Edwards, *Agents of Influence* (Newbridge: Merrion, 2021), p. 80.

2   Rob Lewis, *Fishers of Men* (London: John Blake, 2017), p. 222.

3   Rob Lewis, *Fishers of Men* (London: John Blake, 2017), p. 222.

PART TWO

Chapter 8

1   David Young, 'British police chief opens Stakeknife inquiry', *The Times*, 11 June 2016.

2   *Ibid.*

3   *Ibid.*

4   Jon Boutcher quoted in James Harkin, 'Unmasking Stakeknife', *GQ*, 1 November 2016.

5   Cliodhna Russell, '"No stone to be left unturned" in investigation of west Belfast British spy 'Stakeknife', thejournal.ie, 10 June 2016.

6   Jonny Bell, 'Stakeknife probe to be led by officers from outside Northern Ireland, reveals police chief Hamilton', *Belfast Telgraph*, 10 June 2016.

7   Alan Simpson, *Duplicity and Deception* (Dublin: Brandon, 2010), p. 47.

8   Ian Cobain, *The History Thieves* (London: Portobello Books, 2016), p. 171.

9   John Ware, 'Exposed: The murky world of spying during the Troubles', *Irish Times*, 11 April 2017.

10   Jon Boutcher quoted in James Harkin, 'Unmasking Stakeknife', *GQ*, 1 November 2016.

11   'McGuinness: Queen's comment brought "considerable amusement"', Amanpour, edition.cnn.com, 29 June 2016.

Chapter 9

1   'Miriam meets ... Gerry Adams and Martin McGuinness', RTE, Radio 1, first broadcast on 21 March 2017.

2   Gerry Adams quoted in Jude Collins, *Martin McGuinness* (Cork: Mercier Press, 2018) p. 338.

3   Gerry Adams quoted in Jude Collins, *Martin McGuinness* (Cork: Mercier Press, 2018) p. 337.

4   Ed Moloney, *Voices from the Grave* (London: Faber, 2011), p. 209.

5   Liam Clarke & Kathryn Johnston, *Martin McGuinness* (Edinburgh: Mainstream, 2001), p. 115.

6   'Martin McGuinness', theconversation.com, 21 March 2017.

7   *Record of the Rebellion in Ireland 1920–21, and the Part Played by the Army in Dealing With It*, 1922, Volume 2, p. 18, UK National Archives, WO 141/94.

8   Ed Moloney, *A Secret History of the IRA* (London: Penguin, 2007), p. 156.

9   Kieran Conway, *Southside Provisional* (Blackrock: Orpen Press, 2014), p. 68.

10   'Spy in the IRA' *Spotlight*, BBC, first broadcast on 20 September 2016.

11   'The Long War', *Panorama*, BBC, first broadcast on 29 February 1988.

Chapter 10

1   'The Spy in the IRA', *Panorama*, BBC, first broadcast on 4 November 2017.

2   'Kevin Myers On The Meaning of Freddie Scappaticci, The IRA Spy Hunter Turned Spy', thebrokenelbow.com, 24 January 2020.

3   Martin Ingram, '"I discovered that Scap really WAS Stakeknife . . . the source at the very top of the PIRA"', *Sunday People*, 21 March 2004.

4   Peter Fulton, *Unsung Hero*, (London: John Blake, 2008), p. 18.

5   Stephen Gordon, 'Robert Nairac', *Belfast Telegraph*, 13 May 2007.

6   Peter Jones quoted in John Wilsey, *The Ulster Tales* (Barnsley: Pen & Sword, 2011), p. 60

7   Stephen Grey, *The New Spymasters* (London: Viking, 2015), p. 74.

8   'Kevin Myers On The Meaning of Freddie Scappaticci, The IRA Spy Hunter Turned Spy', thebrokenelbow.com, 24 January 2020.

9   Stephen Grey, *The New Spymasters* (London: Viking, 2015), p. 64–5.

10   John Wilsey, *The Ulster Tales* (Barnsley: Pen and Sword, 2011), p. 58.

11   Frederick the Great, 'Military Instructions' retrieved from https://
        www.pattonhq.com/militaryworks/frederick.html on 20 July 2023.

12   *Record of the Rebellion in Ireland 1920–21, and the Part Played by the
        Army in Dealing With It*, 1922, Volume 2, p. 28, UK National Archives,
        WO 141/94.

Chapter 11

1   John Le Carré, 'In Ronnie's Court', *New Yorker*, 10 February 2002.

2   Stella Rimington, *Open Secret* (London: Arrow, 2002), p. 104.

3   Chistopher Andrew, *Defence of the Realm* (London: Penguin, 2012),
        p. 618.

4   'Londonderry Area Review', May 1980, UK National Archives, CJ
        4/3474.

5   Stella Rimington, *Open Secret* (London: Arrow, 2002), p. 106.

6   Chistopher Andrew, *Defence of the Realm* (London: Penguin, 2012),
        p. 696.

7   Martin Dillon, *The Dirty War* (London: Arrow, 1991), p. 367.

8   'Security Service, submission to the Review' quoted in Desmond de
        Silva, *The Report of the Patrick Finucane Review*, December 2012,
        p. 224.

9   Michael Dewar, *The British Army in Northern Ireland* (London: W&N,
        1997), p. 164.

10   William Matchett, *Secret Victory* (Lisburn: Hiskey, 2016), p. 173.

Chapter 12

1   Bobby Sands, 'Prison Diary', 1 March 1981, bobbysandstrust.com.

2   D. J. Wyatt, 1 April 1981, UK National Archives, CJ 4/3327.

3   Margaret Thatcher quoted in Sally Hayden, 'Hunger for Knowledge',
        The University Observer, 17 January 2012, p. 11.

4   'Gadafy urged end to hunger strike', *Irish Times*, 30 December 2011.

5   Michael Dewar, *The British Army in Northern Ireland* (London: W&N, 1997), p. 166.

6   Peter Taylor, *Operation Chiffon* (London: Bloomsbury, 2023), Kindle location 1828 of 7257.

7   Charles Moore, *Margaret Thatcher: Volume 1* (London: Penguin, 2014), p. 612.

8   Anthony McIntyre, *Good Friday* (New York: Ausubo, 2008), p. 95.

9   Michael Oatley quoted in Peter Taylor, *Operation Chiffon* (London: Bloomsbury, 2023), Kindle location 1091 of 7257.

10   Brendan Duddy quoted in Peter Taylor, *Operation Chiffon* (London: Bloomsbury, 2023), Kindle location 999 of 7257.

11   Brendan Duddy and Michael Oatley, Call No. 3, 1045–1125, 5 July 1981, UK National Archives, PREM 19/506.

12   David Ranson, 'The Provisionals – Political Activity', 16 June 1981, UK National Archives, PREM 19/505.

Chapter 13

1   Gerry Bradley, *Insider* (Dublin: O'Brien Press, 2009), p. 163.

2   Richard English, *Armed Struggle* (London: Picador, 2008), p. 227.

3   Peter Taylor, *The Provos* (London: Bloomsbury, 1998), p. 282.

4   David Sharrock & Mark Devenport, *Man of War, Man of Peace?* (London: Macmillan, 1997), pp. 191–2.

5   David Sharrock & Mark Devenport, *Man of War, Man of Peace?* (London: Macmillan, 1997), p. 166.

6   Patrick Pearse, 'Why We Want Recruits', *The Political Writings and Speeches of Pádraig Pearse*, cartlann.org.

7   Private information.

8   Pat McArt quoted in Jude Collins, *Martin McGuinness* (Cork: Mercier Press, 2018) p. 326.

9   Danny Morrison quoted in Jude Collins, *Martin McGuinness* (Cork: Mercier Press, 2018) p. 121.

10   Eamonn McCann quoted in Jude Collins, *Martin McGuinness* (Cork: Mercier Press, 2018) p. 111.

Chapter 14

1   'IRA Supergrass Gilmour: I Know Woman Who Provided Gun For
     Census Worker Murder', belfastdaily.co.uk, 22 September 2014.

2   'Myself Alone', *Spotlight*, BBC, first broadcast on 14 November 2000.

3   'Vote stealing: Now no one is laughing at a sick Irish joke', *Belfast
     Telegraph*, 30 June 1983.

4   Willie Carlin quoted in Aaron Edwards, *Agents of Influence*
     (Newbridge: Merrion, 2021), p. 118.

5   Willie Carlin, *Thatcher's Spy* (Newbridge: Merrion Press, 2019), p. 78.

6   Willie Carlin quoted in Aaron Edwards, *Agents of Influence*
     (Newbridge: Merrion, 2021), p. 118.

7   Willie Carlin, *Thatcher's Spy* (Newbridge: Merrion Press, 2019), p. 54.

8   Willie Carlin, *Thatcher's Spy* (Newbridge: Merrion Press, 2019), p. 78.

9   Brendan Hughes quoted in Ed Moloney, *Voices from the Grave*
     (London: Faber, 2011), p. 274.

10   'Report of the Study Group on Personation and the Abuse of Postal
     Voting', Northern Ireland Office, 26 January 1983, UK National
     Archives, CJ 4/4751.

11   'Donaldson was La Mon bomber, Hotel Massacre Revelation', *Sunday
     Mirror*, 19 February 2012.

12   'Donaldson's statement', *Belfast Telegraph*, 18 December 2005.

Chapter 15

1   Martin Dillon, *The Dirty War* (London: Arrow, 1991), p. 380.

2   Private information.

3   Suzanne Breen, 'British spy handler says Hegarty was sacrificed to
     save "agent McGuinness"', *Irish Mail on Sunday*, 2 October 2011.

Chapter 16

1   William of Malmesbury, 'Chapter VI: Of Athelstan, The Son Of Edward', *Chronicle of the Kings of England, Book II* retrieved from https://www.gutenberg.org/files/50778/50778-h/50778-h.htm on 20 July 2023.

2   Private information.

3   'IRA statement' quoted in Raymond Murray, *The SAS in Ireland* (Cork: Mercier, 2004), p. 375.

4   Desmond de Silva, *The Report of the Patrick Finucane Review*, December 2012, p. 89.

5   'Note of interdepartmental meeting on Agent Handling Guidelines', 22 January 1993, quoted in Desmond de Silva, *The Report of the Patrick Finucane Review*, December 2012, p. 74.

6   'Geoff' quoted in Peter Taylor, *Brits* (London: Bloomsbury, 2014), p. 293.

7   Private information.

8   Aaron Edwards, *Agents of Influence* (Newbridge: Merrion, 2021), p. 128.

9   Private information.

10 Gerry Bradley, *Insider* (Dublin: O'Brien Press, 2009), p. 235.

Chapter 17

1   '"Martin has to OK everything"', *Sunday People*, 20 July 2003.

2   Gerry Adams quoted in Jude Collins, *Martin McGuinness* (Cork: Mercier Press, 2018), p. 350.

3   Danny Morrison quoted in Jude Collins, *Martin McGuinness* (Cork: Mercier Press, 2018), p. 123.

4   Private information.

5   Author interview with Anthony McIntyre, 10 March 2022.

6   Sean O'Callaghan, *The Informer* (London: Corgi, 1999), p. 144.

7   Tony Geraghty, *The Irish War* (London: HarperCollins, 1998), p. 143.

8   'Officer A' quoted in *Report of the Bloody Sunday Inquiry, Volume
      VIII* (London: The Stationery Office, 2010), p. 95.
9   Liam Clarke, 'The British Spy at Heart of IRA', *Sunday Times*, 8
      August 1999.
10   John Wilsey, *The Ulster Tales* (Barnsley: Pen and Sword, 2011), p. 58.
11   Stephen Grey, *The New Spymasters* (London: Viking, 2015), p. 63.
12   Aaron Edwards, *Agents of Influence* (Newbridge: Merrion, 2021),
      p. 106.
13   Martin Dillon, *The Dirty War* (London: Arrow, 1991), p. 416.

Chapter 18

1   Ed Moloney, *Voices from the Grave* (London: Faber, 2011), p. 281.
2   Henry McDonald, 'Stakeknife's world of doublespeak', *Guardian*, 18
      May 2003.
3   Liam Clarke & Kathryn Johnston, *Martin McGuinness* (Edinburgh:
      Mainstream, 2001), p. 145.

PART THREE

Chapter 19

1   Jon Boutcher, 'Addressing the Legacy of Northern Ireland's Past',
      Northern Ireland Affairs Committee, 2 September 2020, committees.
      parliament.uk.
2   Ciaran O'Neill, 'Stakeknife spy case', *Irish Independent*, 30 October
      2022.
3   Raymond White, 'Addressing the Legacy of Northern Ireland's past',
      Northern Ireland Affairs Committee, 15 July 2020, committees.
      parliament.uk.
4   Ciaran O'Neill, 'Stakeknife team pulls DNA evidence from victims'
      last letters to families', *Belfast Telegraph*, 30 October 2022.

5   Jon Boutcher, 'Addressing the Legacy of Northern Ireland's Past', Northern Ireland Affairs Committee, 2 September 2020, committees. parliament.uk.

6   Charles Pottins, 'I don't think anything went wrong', opendemocracy. net, 4 October 2008.

7   Private information.

Chapter 20

1   Martin Dillon, *The Dirty War* (London: Arrow, 1991), p. 382.

2   Willie Carlin quoted in Aaron Edwards, *Agents of Influence* (Newbridge: Merrion, 2021), p. 148.

3   Liam Clarke & Kathryn Johnston, *Martin McGuinness* (Edinburgh: Mainstream, 2001), p. 151.

4   Brian Feeney, *Sinn Féin* (Dublin: O'Brien Press, 2002), p. 327.

5   Sean O'Callaghan, *The Informer* (London: Corgi, 1999), p. 192.

6   Liam Clarke & Kathryn Johnston, *Martin McGuinness* (Edinburgh: Mainstream, 2001), p. 160.

7   Mark Urban, *Big Boys Rules* (London: Faber, 1992), p. 104.

Chapter 21

1   Ed Moloney, *A Secret History of the IRA* (London: Penguin, 2007), p. 24.

2   Rob Lewis, *Fishers of Men* (London: John Blake, 2017), p. 217.

3   'Libya and Irish Terrorism – FCO Background Brief', June 1984, UK National Archives, FO 973/368.

4   Ed Moloney, *A Secret History of the IRA* (London: Penguin, 2007), p. 15.

Chapter 22

1   Peter Taylor, *Brits* (London: Bloomsbury, 2014), p. 268.

2   Nicholas Watt, 'Thatcher suggested "Cromwell solution" for Northern Ireland', *Guardian*, 16 June 2001.

3   'Thatcher proposed sending Northern Ireland Catholics to the Republic', *Belfast Telegraph*, 15 April 2013.

4   Nicholas Watt, 'Thatcher suggested "Cromwell solution" for Northern Ireland', *Guardian*, 16 June 2001.

5   Mr Davenport, Note, 27 November 1979, UK National Archives, CJ 4/3116.

6   P. W. J. Buxton, 'Meeting with the Monday Club', 12 March 1981, UK National Archives, CJ 4/3335.

7   David Sharrock & Mark Devenport, *Man of War, Man of Peace?* (London: Macmillan, 1997), p. 310.

8   Charles Moore, *Margaret Thatcher: Volume 1* (London: Penguin, 2014), Kindle location 711 of 1084.

9   Peter Taylor, *The Provos* (London: Bloomsbury, 1998), p. 294.

10 Peter Taylor, *The Provos* (London: Bloomsbury, 1998), p. 294–5.

11 Mark Urban, *UK Eyes Alpha* (London: Faber, 2013), p. 57.

12 Mark Urban, *UK Eyes Alpha* (London: Faber, 2013), p. 58.

13 Willie Carlin, *Thatcher's Spy* (Newbridge: Merrion Press, 2019), p. 78, p. 33.

Chapter 23

1   David Goodall, *The Making of the Anglo-Irish Agreement of 1985* (Dublin: National University of Ireland, 2021), p. 4.

2   David Goodall, *The Making of the Anglo-Irish Agreement of 1985* (Dublin: National University of Ireland, 2021), p. 11.

3   Charles Moore, *Margaret Thatcher: Volume 2* (London: Penguin, 2015), Kindle location, 387 of 1042.

4   Charles Moore, *Margaret Thatcher: Volume 2* (London: Penguin, 2015), Kindle location 347 of 1042.

5   Charles Moore, *Margaret Thatcher: Volume 2* (London: Penguin, 2015), Kindle location, 388 of 1042.

6   Charles Moore, *Margaret Thatcher: Volume 2* (London: Penguin, 2015), Kindle location 386 of 1042.

7   Peter Taylor, *Brits* (London: Bloomsbury, 2014), p. 268.

8   Defence secretary to prime minister, 'Northern Ireland Minute', 10 January 1986, UK National Archives, PREM 19/1810.

9   'Margaret Thatcher press conference with American reporters', UK National Archives, CJ 4/6746.

10   Simon Hoggart, 'Ian Paisley', *Guardian*, 12 September 2014.

11   Margaret Thatcher, *The Downing Street Years* (London: HarperPress, 2012), p. 410.

12   Robert Armstrong, 'Cabinet 9 January: Northern Ireland', 8 January 1986, UK National Archives, PREM 19/1810.

13   Geoffrey Howe, 'Prime Minister Minute', 15 January 1986, UK National Archives, PM/86/002.

Chapter 24

1   Paul Theroux, *Kingdom by the Sea* (London: Penguin, 1985), p. 231.

2   Shane O'Doherty, *The Volunteer* (Durham: Strategic Book Publishing, 2011), p. 45.

3   'Guns Used in Killings', *Derry Journal*, 14 January 1986.

4   'Detention Absolutely Scandalous – McGuinness', *Derry Journal*, 7 January 1986.

5   'United Ireland in my lifetime – GLC chief', *Londonderry Sentinel*, 29 January 1986, p. 31.

6   Liam Clarke & Kathryn Johnston, *Martin McGuinness* (Edinburgh: Mainstream, 2001), p. 161.

7   Dorothy Robb quoted in 'The Long War', *Panorama*, BBC, first broadcast on 29 February 1988.

8   'Statement from Battery Commander, 5 Heavy Regiment, Royal Artillery', 11 February 1976, UK National Archives, CJ 4/3715.

Chapter 25

1   'Free to Kill', *The Cook Report*, Series 8, Episode 6, ITV, first broad-
    cast on 24 August 1993.
2   Bill Clinton quoted in Jude Collins, *Martin McGuinness* (Cork: Mercier
    Press), 2018, p. 333.
3   Mary Lou McDonald quoted in Jude Collins, *Martin McGuinness*
    (Cork: Mercier Press), 2018, p. 302.
4   Jonathan Powell quoted in Jude Collins, *Martin McGuinness* (Cork:
    Mercier Press), 2018, p. 144.
5   William Scholes, 'Informer "murdered on orders of SF man"', *Irish
    News*, 15 July 2003
6   Stephen Grey, *The New Spymasters* (London: Viking, 2015), p. 77.

Chapter 26

1   Defence secretary to prime minister, 'Northern Ireland: Compromise
    of an Army Agent', 5 February 1986, UK National Archives, PREM
    19/1814.
2   Defence secretary to prime minister, 'Northern Ireland: Compromise
    of an Army Agent', 2 May 1986, UK National Archives, PREM 19/1814.

Chapter 27

1   Liam Clarke & Kathryn Johnston, *Martin McGuinness* (Edinburgh:
    Mainstream, 2001), p. 152.
2   Ed Moloney, *A Secret History of the IRA* (London: Penguin, 2007),
    p. 246.
3   Thomas Leahy, *The Intelligence War against the IRA* (Cambridge:
    Cambridge University Press, 2020), p. 134.
4   'Telegram from MI5's Agents Running Section to London HQ', 21 May
    1987, quoted in Desmond de Silva, *The Report of the Patrick Finucane
    Review*, December 2012, pp. 170–1.

5   David Sharrock & Mark Devenport, *Man of War, Man of Peace?* (London: Macmillan, 1997), p. 222.

6   Tony Geraghty, *The Irish War* (London: HarperCollins, 1998), p. 239.

7   'McGuinness did work for British: Faul', *Irish Independent*, 25 June 2006.

8   Henry McDonald, *Martin McGuinness* (Newtownards: Blackstaff Press, 2017), p. 117.

Chapter 28

1   'Free to Kill', *The Cook Report*, Series 8, Episode 6, ITV, first broadcast on 24 August 1993.

2   'Coroner's Inquest relating to the death of Francis Gerald Hegarty who died 25 May 1986', 9 September 1989, Public Records Office of Northern Ireland, TYR/6/1/1/36/13.

3   'Punishment Beating', *Derry Journal*, 29 April 1986.

4   Liam Clarke & Kathryn Johnston, *Martin McGuinness* (Edinburgh: Mainstream, 2001), p. 162.

5   Peter Murtagh, 'McGuinness's link to IRA "execution" merits attention', *Irish Times*, 29 September 2011.

6   Suzanne Breen, 'A path paved with blood', *Daily Mail*, 25 September 2011.

Chapter 29

1   Toby Harnden, *Bandit Country* (London: Hodder, 2000), p. 199.

2   Truman Capote, *In Cold Blood* (London: Penguin, 2017), p. 95.

3   Martin Cowley, 'IRA "excuse" for killing is rejected at Derry funeral', *Irish Times*, 28 May 1986.

4   'Tempers Flare in Council Chamber', *Derry Journal*, 30 May 1986.

5   Martin Cowley, 'IRA "excuse" for killing is rejected at Derry funeral', *Irish Times*, 28 May 1986.

6   John Hume, 'Speech by John Hume MP MEP to the SDLP's 18th Annual Conference 25-27 November 1988', cain.ulster.ac.uk.

7   Martin Cowley, 'IRA "excuse" for killing is rejected at Derry funeral', *Irish Times*, 28 May 1986.

8   Peter Murtagh, 'McGuinness's link to IRA "execution" merits attention', *Irish Times*, 29 September 2011.

9   Willie Carlin, *Thatcher's Spy* (Newbridge: Merrion Press, 2019), p. 210.

10 Harry McCallion, *Undercover War* (London: John Blake, 2020), p. 83.

11 Martin Ingram & Greg Harkin, *Stakeknife* (Dublin: O'Brien Press, 2004), p. 121, p. 117.

PART FOUR

Chapter 30

1   Ed Moloney, *A Secret History of the IRA* (London: Penguin, 2007), p. 576.

2   Henry McDonald, *Gunsmoke and Mirrors* (Dublin: Gill & Macmillan, 2008), p. 33.

3   Stephen Grey, *The New Spymasters* (London: Viking, 2015), p. 74.

4   Aaron Edwards, *Agents of Influence* (Newbridge: Merrion, 2021), p. 225.

5   Eamon Collins, *Killing Rage* (London: Granta, 1997), p. 234.

6   'Freddie Scappaticci Stakeknife Secret Recordings', youtube.com, uploaded on 8 February 2012.

7   'The Spy in the IRA', *Panorama*, BBC, first broadcast on 4 November 2017.

8   Peter Fulton, *Unsung Hero* (London: John Blake, 2008), p. 189.

9   'Home Office Briefing note on Agent-Handling' quoted in Desmond de Silva, *The Report of the Patrick Finucane Review*, December 2012, p. 87.

10 Desmond de Silva, *The Report of the Patrick Finucane Review*, December 2012, p. 90.

11 Secretary of State for Defence to Attorney General, 19 March 1991,

quoted in Desmond de Silva, *The Report of the Patrick Finucane Review*, December 2012, p. 75.

12 Author interview with Raymond White, 23 September 2020.

13 Janet Malcolm, *The Journalist and the Murderer* (London: Granta, 2018), p. 55.

14 Peter Hennessy, *Whitehall* (New York: The Free Press, 1989), p. 347.

15 Michael McHugh, 'Stakeknife investigation "is not a witch-hunt", *The Times*, 19 December 2018.

Chapter 31

1 'The Secret Peacemaker', BBC, first broadcast on 26 March 2008.

2 'The Secret Peacemaker', BBC, first broadcast on 26 March 2008.

3 'The Secret Peacemaker', BBC, first broadcast on 26 March 2008.

4 Niall Dochartaigh, *Deniable Contact* (Oxford: Oxford University Press, 2021), p. 235.

5 Ed Moloney, *A Secret History of the IRA* (London: Penguin, 2007), p. 527.

6 Gerry Bradley, *Insider* (Dublin: O'Brien Press, 2009), p. 220.

7 Brendan Hughes quoted in Peter Taylor, *Brits* (London: Bloomsbury, 2014), p. 302.

8 John Major, House of Commons, 1 November 1993, hansard.parliament.uk.

Chapter 32

1 'Free to Kill', *The Cook Report*, Series 8, Episode 6, ITV, first broadcast on 24 August 1993.

2 Private information.

3 David McKittrick, 'McGuinness denies he is IRA boss', *Independent*, 25 August 1993.

4 Liam Clarke & Kathryn Johnston, *Martin McGuinness* (Edinburgh: Mainstream, 2001), pp. 205–6.

Chapter 33

1   'Freddie Scappaticci Stakeknife Secret Recordings', youtube.com, uploaded on 8 February 2012.
2   Ed Moloney, 'The Day The IRA Sacked Freddie Scappaticci ...', 26 July 2022, thebrokenelbow.com.
3   '"Martin has to OK everything"', *Sunday People*, 20 July 2003.
4   '"Martin has to OK everything"', *Sunday People*, 20 July 2003.
5   '"Martin has to OK everything"', *Sunday People*, 20 July 2003.
6   Liam Clarke & Kathryn Johnston, *Martin McGuinness* (Edinburgh: Mainstream, 2001), pp. 205–6.
7   'Loose Talk, the Scappaticci Case', *Insight*, UTV, first broadcast on 15 March 2004.
8   'Joint Declaration on Peace', 15 December 1993, cain.ulster.ac.uk.

Chapter 34

1   Tony Blair, *A Journey* (London: Arrow, 2011), Kindle location 3562 of 15038.
2   Tony Blair, *A Journey* (London: Arrow, 2011), Kindle location 3725 of 15038.
3   Tony Blair, *A Journey* (London: Arrow, 2011), Kindle location 3846 of 15038.
4   Ed Moloney, 'An Observation On That Thesis About IRA Informers & The Peace Process', 18 March 2020, thebrokenelbow.com.
5   'Spy in the IRA', *Spotlight*, BBC, first broadcast 20 September 2016.
6   'Spy in the IRA', *Spotlight*, BBC, first broadcast 20 September 2016.
7   Stephen Lander quoted in Chistopher Andrew, *Defence of the Realm* (London: Penguin, 2012), p. 783.
8   Peter Taylor, *Operation Chiffon* (London: Bloomsbury, 2023), Kindle location 3461 of 7257.
9   'Operation Banner: An Analysis of Military Operations in Northern Ireland', Ministry of Defence, 2006, Chapter 8, p. 5 retrieved from vilaweb.cat on 20 July 2023.

10   'Spotlight on the Troubles', Episode 4, BBC, first broadcast on 1
      October 2019.
11   Richard Kerbaj, *The Secret History of the Five Eyes* (London: Blink,
      2022), p. 187.

Chapter 35

1   John McCallister quoted in Jude Collins, *Martin McGuinness* (Cork:
      Mercier Press, 2018) p. 158.
2   Ian Paisley, House of Commons, 4 February 1998, api.parliament.uk.
3   Ryan Hegarty interview, BBC Radio Foyle, first broadcast on 25
      November 2015.

Chapter 36

1   Liam Clarke, 'The British Spy at the Heart of IRA', *Sunday Times*, 8
      August 1999.
2   Martin Ingram & Greg Harkin, *Stakeknife* (Dublin: O'Brien Press,
      2004), p. 241.
3   Dan Keenan, '"Jesus, what are my family going to think when they
      see this?"', *Irish Times*, 20 May 2003.
4   John Ware, 'How, and why, did Scappaticci survive the IRA's wrath?'
      Irish Times, 15 April 2017.
5   'The Spy in the IRA', *Panorama*, BBC, first broadcast on 4 November
      2017.
6   Dan Keenan, '"Jesus, what are my family going to think when they
      see this?"', *Irish Times*, 20 May 2003.
7   *Ibid.*
8   *Ibid.*
9   David Gordon, 'Freddie Scappaticci: I'm not a killer', *Belfast Telegraph*,
      19 May 2003.

Chapter 37

1   Martin Ingram & Greg Harkin, *Stakeknife* (Dublin: O'Brien Press, 2004), p. 244.

2   Maurice Fitzmaurice, 'Martin McGuinness' mum traumatized after finding out he was in IRA', *Irish Mirror*, 26 September 2014.

3   Danny Morrison quoted in Jude Collins, *Martin McGuinness* (Cork: Mercier Press, 2018) p. 127.

4   'Martin McGuinness to run for President', *Irish Examiner*, 16 September 2011.

5   'Sinn Féin's McGuinness "won't be interrogated" about IRA past', CNN.com, 19 September 2011.

6   'Sinn Féin's McGuinness "won't be interrogated" about IRA past', CNN.com, 19 September 2011.

7   Henry McDonald, 'Martin McGuinness slumps in the polls as IRA past threatens bid for presidency', *Guardian*, 23 October 2011.

8   Suzanne Breen, 'A path paved with blood', *Daily Mail*, 25 September 2011.

9   'RTE gets over 100 complaints about Miriam O'Callaghan's Prime Time debate', *Irish Independent*, 14 October 2011.

10 Jim Cusack, 'SF "attack dog" mauls journalist over story on McGuinness meet', *Irish Independent*, 2 October 2011.

11 Gerry Adams in Jude Collins, *Martin McGuinness* (Cork: Mercier Press, 2018) p. 345.

12 Mary Lou McDonald in Jude Collins, *Martin McGuinness* (Cork: Mercier Press, 2018) p. 300.

13 'McGuinness: "I genuinely regret every single life that was lost during that conflict"', leftfootforward.org, 29 June 2012.

14 Mark Hennessy, 'McGuinness says he regrets the past cannot be changed', *Irish Times*, 19 September 2013.

Chapter 38

1   Ian Gallagher, 'The IRA scoured the world hunting for Stakeknife',
    Daily Mail, 17 June 2023.

2   David Brown, '"Stakeknife" case: Freddie Scappaticci sentence for
    possessing extreme pornography', *The Times*, 5 December 2018.

3   James Harkin, 'Unmasking Stakeknife', *GQ*, 1 November 2016.

4   Peter Fulton, *Unsung Hero* (London: John Blake, 2008), p. 227.

5   John Ware, 'How, and Why, Did Scappaticci Survive the IRA's Wrath?'
    Irish Times, 15 April 2017, p. 6.

6   Michael McHugh, '"Stakeknife" suspect Freddie Scappaticci is
    released on police bail', *The Times*, 3 February 2018.

7   Richard Kerbaj and Tom Harper, 'MI5 chief to be questioned over IRA
    double agent Stakeknife's 17 murders', *The Times*, 16 December 2018.

8   James Harkin, 'Unmasking Stakeknife', *GQ*, 1 November 2016.

9   Sean O'Neill, 'MI5 chiefs to be challenged over IRA double agent
    Stakeknife's role', *The Times*, 18 December 2018.

10 Michael McHugh, 'Stakeknife investigation "is not a witch-hunt", *The
    Times*, 19 December 2018.

11 Richard Kerbaj and Tom Harper, 'MI5 chief to be questioned over IRA
    double agent Stakeknife's "17 murders"', *The Times*, 16 December 2018.

12 James Harkin, 'Unmasking Stakeknife', *GQ*, 1 November 2016.

13 David Brown, '"Stakeknife" case: Freddie Scappaticci sentence for
    possessing extreme pornography', *The Times*, 5 December 2018.

14 James Harkin, 'Unmasking Stakeknife', *GQ*, 1 November 2016.

15 Jon Boutcher, 'Addressing the Legacy of Northern Ireland's Past',
    Northern Ireland Affairs Committee, 2 September 2020, committees.
    parliament.uk.

16 Owen Bowcott, 'MI5 policy "gives agents legal immunity to commit
    serious crimes"', *Guardian*, 5 November 2019.

17 Richard Kerbaj and Tom Harper, 'MI5 chief to be questioned over IRA
    double agent Stakeknife's "17 murders"', *The Times*, 16 December 2018.

Chapter 39

1   'The funeral of Martin McGuinness was one of a kind', *Irish News*, 23 March 2017.

Chapter 40

1   'Home Office Briefing note on Agent-Handling' quoted in Desmond de Silva, *The Report of the Patrick Finucane Review*, December 2012, p. 87.

2   Steve Baker, House of Commons, 5 October 2020, hansard.parliament. uk.

3   'Dennis Hutchings: Ex-soldier's challenge over Troubles killing fails', BBC News, bbc.co.uk, 3 June 2020.

4   Sean O'Neill, 'Truth of the Troubles now trumps justice', *The Times*, 4 January 2023.

5   Deidre Young, 'Jon Boutcher, the head of Operation Kenova has entered choppy waters', coverthistory.ie, 22 December 2022.

6   'Operation Kenova', FOI disclosure log, psni.police.uk, 30 September 2022.

7   Commissioner for Human Rights, 'United Kingdom: backsliding on human rights must be prevented', coe.int, 4 July 2022.

8   Mark Hilliard, 'UK "changing position" on North prosecution amnesty, ex-officer says', *Irish Times*, 15 February 2022.

9   Northern Ireland Secretary, 'Addressing the Legacy of Northern Ireland's Past', Command Paper, assets.publishing.service.gov.uk, July 2021.

10 Jon Boutcher, 'Addressing the Legacy of Northern Ireland's Past', Northern Ireland Affairs Committee, 2 September 2020, committees. parliament.uk.

11 Jon Boutcher, 'Written evidence submitted by Jon Boutcher', Northern Ireland Affairs Committee, 23 June 2020, committees.parliament.uk.

Chapter 41

1   'Freddie Scappaticci, suspected IRA informer "Stakeknife", dead at 77', *The Times*, 12 April 2023; 'Freddie Scappaticci, top IRA enforcer suspected of being a British Army mole codenamed "Stakeknife" – obituary', *Daily Telegraph*, 12 April 2023; Jude Webber, 'Freddie Scappaticci, suspected IRA informer, circa 1946–2023), *Financial Times*, 14 April 2023.

2   Sharon O'Neill, 'Freddie Scappaticci: Dying dad of murder victim hears truth about his son on his deathbed', *Belfast Telegraph*, 16 April 2023.

3   Jim Cusack, 'SF "attack dog" mauls journalist over story on McGuinness meet', *Irish Independent*, 2 October 2011.

Index